The White R

In this book Joe R. Feagin extends the systemic racism framework in previous Routledge books by developing an innovative new concept, *the white racial frame*. Now four centuries-old, this white racial frame encompasses not only the stereotyping, bigotry, and racist ideology accented in other theories of "race," but also the visual images, array of emotions, sounds of language, interlinking interpretations, and inclinations to discriminate that are still central to the frame's everyday operation. Deeply imbedded in American minds and institutions, this white racial frame has for centuries functioned as a broad worldview, one essential to the routine legitimation, scripting, and maintenance of systemic racism in the United States. Here Feagin examines how and why this white racial frame emerged in North America, how and why it has evolved socially over time, which racial groups are framed within it, how it has operated in the past and in the present for both white Americans and Americans of color, and how the latter have long responded with strategies of resistance that include enduring counter-frames.

Joe R. Feagin is Ella C. McFadden Professor at Texas A & M University. Feagin has done research on racism and sexism issues for forty-five years and has served as the Scholar-in-Residence at the U.S. Commission on Civil Rights. He has written 54 scholarly books and nearly 200 scholarly articles in his research areas, and one of his books (*Ghetto Revolts*) was nominated for a Pulitzer Prize. His recent books include *Systemic Racism* (Routledge 2006) and *Two Faced Racism: Whites in the Backstage and Frontstage* (Routledge 2007). He is the 2006 recipient of a Harvard Alumni Association lifetime achievement award and was the 1999–2000 president of the American Sociological Association.

The White Racial Frame

Centuries of Racial Framing and Counter-Framing

WILLOW INTERNATIONAL LIBRARY

Joe R. Feagin

Routledge
Taylor & Francis Group

NEW YORK AND LONDON

First published 2010
by Routledge
270 Madison Ave, New York, NY 10016

Simultaneously published in the UK
by Routledge
2 Park Square, Milton Park, Abingdon, Oxon OX14 4RN

Routledge is an imprint of the Taylor & Francis Group, an informa business

Typeset in Minion by RefineCatch Limited, Bungay, Suffolk
Printed and bound in the United States of America on acid-free paper by
Edwards Brothers, Inc.

Library of Congress Cataloging in Publication Data
Feagin, Joe R.
  The white racial frame : centuries of racial framing and counter-framing /
  Joe R. Feagin.
    p. cm.
  Includes bibliographical references.
  1. United States—Race relations. 2. Race discrimination—United States.
  3. African-Americans—United States—Social conditions. 4. African-
  Americans—United States—Public opinion. 5. Whites—United States—
  Attitudes. I. Title.
  E184.A1F395 208
  305.800973—dc22   2009004855

ISBN10: 0–415–99438–1 (hbk)
ISBN10: 0–415–99439–X (pbk)
ISBN10: 0–203–89064–7 (ebk)

ISBN13: 978–0–415–99438–5 (hbk)
ISBN13: 978–0–415–99439–2 (pbk)
ISBN13: 978–0–203–89064–6 (ebk)

Contents

Preface

In November 2008, more than two centuries after this country's founding, Senator Barack Obama became the first American of color ever to win the U.S. presidency. He won nearly 53 percent of the total national vote, compared to about 46 percent for his white opponent, Senator John McCain. Since Obama's election, the increase in emphasis on the United States being *post-racial* has been dramatic, especially among whites and in the mainstream media. From this perspective the United States is now a society where racism is in great decline, a society that is indeed colorblind.

Like many media outlets, the national business newspaper, *The Wall Street Journal*, framed Barack Obama's election as a great tribute to how democratic and non-racist the United States now is:

> A man of mixed race has now reached the pinnacle of U.S. power only two generations since the end of Jim Crow. This is a tribute to American opportunity, and it is something that has never happened in another Western democracy—notwithstanding European condescension about "racist" America.[1]

After this assertion of moral superiority over Europe, this white-framed editorial added: "One promise of his victory is that perhaps we can put to rest the myth of racism as a barrier to achievement in this splendid country. Mr. Obama has a special obligation to help do so."[2] Writing from a common white viewpoint, this editorial writer further called on President-elect Obama himself to lead the effort to kill the supposed "myth of racism."

But did this election really signal a major decline in racism in the

United States? Even the election itself was revealing on this score. While it was not as close as the two previous presidential elections, it was close enough that a shift of just 4 percent or so of the total voters from Obama to McCain would have given McCain a national victory. Moreover, if it had only been up to white voters, Senator McCain would have become the 44th U.S. president, for he won an estimated *55 percent* of the white vote nationally, and a substantial majority of white voters in 32 of the 50 states. In contrast, more than two thirds of voters of color voted for Senator Obama.[3]

In some ways, the United States came out of the 2008 presidential election more polarized and segregated than it was a generation or so ago. Researchers have shown that about *half* of all the presidential votes cast were in counties where Senator Obama or Senator McCain won by at least 20 percent of the total vote. The percentage of voters residing in these very polarized "landslide" counties has grown substantially, from 27 percent in 1976 to 48 percent in 2008. Even more striking is the racial polarization of these counties. Those where candidate McCain won with a landslide margin of 20 percent or more were overwhelmingly white, with the black and Latino voting age population averaging only a sixth of those counties' populations. Where Obama won a county, in contrast, the black and Latino population averaged about 43 percent of the voting age population. Paralleling this voter polarization, moreover, is the continuing and extensive residential and public school segregation that is revealed in research on U.S. towns and cities.[4] Without a doubt, even with the election of an African American president, the harsh reality of institutional racism in major sectors of U.S. society is still quite evident.

Today, those who do this significant research and analysis of U.S. racial patterns frequently make use of a disease metaphor, such as the idea that racism is a "cancer" in the "body" of society. In a recent search for phrases like "racism is a cancer" or the "cancer of racism" in published research papers and popular articles, including on the Internet, I found thousands of uses of this strong metaphor. The commonplace idea here is that racism is an unhealthy social condition, one stemming from pathogenic conditions in an otherwise healthy societal body. Yet, this view is both misleading and inadequate. Our society was built from the beginning with racial oppression as a *central part* of its societal structure. There never was a "healthy" societal body which the cancer of racism could invade.

In this book I argue that a much better societal metaphor is that of racism as an important part of the structural "foundation" of the U.S. "house." Racial oppression was not added later on in the development of this society, but was the foundation of the original colonial and U.S. social systems, and it remains as a foundation to the present day. This structural-foundation metaphor relates much better to the historical and contemporary reality of this country, and it is the one I prefer in this book. I recently searched hundreds of relevant academic research papers and many important Internet websites for phrases like "racial foundation of the United States," the "country's racial foundation," and the "nation's racial foundation," and not one such phrase appeared. In light of the historical and contemporary data assessed throughout this book, this structural-foundation metaphor captures the actual realities of colonial and U.S. racism much better than a disease metaphor. From its first decades, as I demonstrate in the next chapters, racial oppression has been indeed part of this nation's *undergirding foundation.*

This political-economic reality is significantly different from that of any other major industrialized country in the West. European countries like Great Britain and France were central to centuries of European colonialism, including the Atlantic slave trade and slave plantations in the Americas, but their early and later growth specifically as nations was not built directly on an *internal* labor force of enslaved African Americans or on the land stolen by recent conquests of millions of indigenous people. Given these strikingly different historical realities, then, one would expect that the long term consequences of these histories for systemic racism to be significantly different.

Knowing North American racial history is very important for making sense out of the current realities of this society. For many years, I have been researching this history in an attempt to analyze accurately the major impacts on U.S. culture and institutions of this country's foundation in systemic racism—in slavery, Jim Crow segregation, and contemporary discrimination. In this book we will examine the many lasting legacies of past oppression in contemporary racism. We will explore evidence of systemic racism in the colonial and U.S. economic, legal, and political systems, up to the present day. As in the past, systemic racism today includes the complex array of exploitative and discriminatory white practices targeting Americans of color, the institutionalized economic and other resource inequalities along racial lines, and the dominant racial frame that was generated to rationalize white privilege and dominance. *Systemic* here means that the oppressive racist realities have from the early decades been institutionalized and thus manifested in all of this society's major parts. Break a three-dimensional hologram into its separate parts and shine a laser through any one, and you can project the whole three-dimensional image again from that part. Much like this hologram, major parts of this society, such as the economy, politics, education, religion, the family, reflect in numerous ways the fundamental reality of systemic racism.

In this book I focus mainly on systemic racism's reality as it operates in and through what I term the *white racial frame*, the broad, persisting, and dominant racial frame that has rationalized racial oppression and inequality and thus impacted all U.S. institutions. I explain in detail what I mean by this white racial frame in the next chapter, but for now let me note that the white racial frame is a centuries-old worldview and has constantly involved a *racial construction of reality* by white and other Americans, an emotion-laden construction process that shapes everyday relationships and institutions in fundamental and racialized ways. For the period of North American development from the early 1600s to the present day, I track closely the societal persistence and evolution of this well-developed racial framing of society.

In particular, I accent the holistic and gestalt character of this overarching white racial frame. As I show, this omnipresent white frame encompasses much more than verbal-cognitive elements, such as racist stereotyping and ideology, concepts emphasized by most scholars of racial matters. It includes many other important elements, such as deep emotions and visceral images, even language accents and sounds, that have long been essential to the creation and maintenance of a system of racial oppression. Today, as in the past, this dominant racial frame is taught in thousands of different ways—at home, in schools, on public playgrounds, in the mass media, in workplace settings, in courts, and in politician's speeches and corporate decisions. As a result, in its turn this dominant racial frame both rationalizes and structures the racial interactions, inequalities, and other racial patterns in most societal settings.

In my view the best social science is both interpretive, searching for complex webs of meanings connecting particular individuals and their everyday groups, and thoroughly empirical, bringing relevant data to bear on important societal questions. In this book I use a broad interpretive approach that examines the complexities of interpersonal and intergroup meanings and relationships in this still highly racialized society and that brings much empirical data, historical and contemporary, to bear on critical questions about how this society works in its everyday racial framing and related social operations.

Acknowledgments

I am greatly indebted to hundreds of colleagues and students who over several decades have helped me sort out the general and specific research issues raised in this book. I cannot name them all, but among them are Jessie Daniels, Pat Bell, Yanick St. Jean, Sean Elias, Reuben May, Clarence Munford, Ruth Thompson-Miller, Ben Carrington, Glenn Bracey, Jennifer Mueller, Chris Chambers, Kristen Lavelle, Shari Valentine, Rosalind Chou, and Dan Rigney. I am especially indebted to Wendy Moore, Adia Harvey Wingfield, Bernice M. Barnett, Brittany Slatton, Louwanda Evans, Nestor Rodriguez, Terrence Fitzgerald, Hernán Vera, and Sean Chaplin for extensive discussions, suggestions, or comments on specific issues in this book, often over some years now.

CHAPTER 1

The White Racial Frame

Why a New Concept?

The better we know our racial past, the better we know our racial present. The United States is a young country, just over 400 years old if we date its beginning from Jamestown's settlement. For much of this history, extreme racial oppression in the form of slavery and legal segregation was our foundational reality. The first successful English colony was founded at Jamestown in 1607, and a few years later in 1619 the first Africans were purchased by English colonists from a Dutch-flagged slave ship. It was exactly 350 years from 1619 to 1969, the year the last major civil rights law went into effect officially ending legal segregation. Few people realize that for *more than 85 percent* of our history we were a country grounded in, and greatly shaped by, extensive slavery and comprehensive legal segregation.

In terms of time and space, we are today not far from our famous "founding fathers." There have been just three long human lifetimes since the 1776 Declaration of Independence was proclaimed, a document principally authored by the prominent slaveholder Thomas Jefferson. We are just two long human lifetimes from the 13th amendment that ended two-plus centuries of slavery. And we are only one human lifetime from the era when viciously segregationist mobs brutally lynched African Americans and other Americans of color, and when many whites, including Supreme Court justices and U.S. Senators, were members of the Ku Klux Klan, the world's oldest violence-oriented, white supremacist group. For just four decades now, we have been an officially "free" country without massive legal discrimination. Certainly, that is not enough time for this country to eradicate the great and deep impacts of three and a half centuries of extreme racial oppression that preceded the current era. Much social science analysis of major aspects of this society today, as I show throughout this book, reveals the *continuing* impact and great significance of the systemic racism created by these long centuries of extreme racial oppression.

Let us consider briefly some contemporary spatial impacts. In its geographical patterns the twenty-first century United States clearly demonstrates the impact of this oppressive past. Even a brief study of the U.S. demographic map reveals that a substantial majority of African Americans today still live in just fifteen of the fifty U.S. states—and very disproportionately in southern and border states. In these states, as elsewhere, the majority of these truly "old stock" Americans reside in racially segregated areas of towns and cities. In many cities there are still the infamous railroad tracks, as well as major highways, that clearly divide them into communities of mostly whites and communities of mostly people of color. Why is this highly segregated residential pattern still the reality in this "advanced democracy"? The answer lies in the centuries of slavery, legal segregation, and contemporary racial discrimination that have set firmly in place and maintained this country's important geographical contours. For the most part, these racially segregated areas and geographical dividing lines are not recent creations, but have been shaped by white decisionmakers' actions over centuries. Consider too that these distinctive area patterns signal much more than information about our geographical realities, for they have many serious consequences for much that goes on in this society. We can see this clearly, to take just one example, in the racially polarized voting patterns for the landmark 2008 election noted in the preface.

Well into this twenty-first century, racial segregation and separation along the color line is also very much a major part of our psychic geography. Racial separation affects the ways in which white Americans view our society, especially on racial matters. The evidence of white denial and ignorance of the reality of U.S. racism is substantial. For example, one recent national survey of 779 whites found that 61 percent viewed the average black person as having health care access at least equal to that of the average white person. Yet, the field data show whites are far more likely to have good health insurance and to get adequate medical care than black Americans. About half the white respondents felt that black Americans had a level of education similar to or better than that of whites. Half the white respondents felt that, on average, whites and blacks are about as well off in the jobs they hold. Once again, the research data show that neither view is true. When the results of several such questions were combined, 70 percent of whites were found to hold one or more erroneous beliefs about important white-black differentials in life conditions. Moreover, only one in five whites evaluated the current societal situation accurately on a question about how much racial discrimination African Americans faced. The majority of whites are willfully ignorant or very misinformed when it comes to understanding the difficult life conditions that African Americans and other Americans of color face today. Interestingly, in another survey white respondents were asked if they "often have sympathy for blacks" and again if they "often feel admiration for blacks." Only *five percent* of whites said yes to both questions.[1]

One goal of this book is to examine why so many white Americans believe what is in fact not true about our important racial realities. In insisting on these apparently sincere fictions about black life conditions, the majority of whites exhibit serious collective denial in believing what is demonstrably untrue. The principal reason for these strong white views is what I term the *white racial frame*. This racial frame is an overarching worldview, one that encompasses important racial ideas, terms, images, emotions, and interpretations. For centuries now, it has been a basic and foundational frame from which a substantial majority of white Americans—as well as others seeking to conform to white norms—view our highly racialized society.

Mainstream Social Science: The Need for A New Paradigm

Traditional social science and other mainstream academic analysis has mostly portrayed U.S. racism as mainly a matter of racial bigotry, prejudice, and stereotyping—of racial attitudes directed at outgroups that indicate an ethnocentric view of the world and that incline individuals to take part in bigotry-generated discrimination. These concepts, though useful, are far from sufficient to explain the systemic racism of the United States. We need more powerful concepts that enable us to move beyond the limitations of conventional social science approaches. The traditional approaches do not capture or explain the deep structural reality of this society's racial oppression in the past or the present.

The dominant paradigm of an established science makes it hard for scientists to move in a major new direction in thinking or research. Almost all scientists stay mostly inside the dominant paradigmatic "box" because of fear for their own careers, as well as out of concern for accepted scientific constraints. One important barrier to developing new social science paradigms is that new views of society are regularly screened for conformity to preferences of elite decisionmakers in academia and in society generally. This vetting and validation process is implemented by research-granting public agencies, faculty advisors in academic programs, promotion reviews in educational institutions, and public criticism of scholars who deviate.[2]

Today, most mainstream social science analysis of racial matters is undertaken and accepted because it more or less conforms to the preferences of most elite decisionmakers. For this reason many of the racial realities of U.S. society have rarely or never been intensively researched by social scientists. Ironically, U.S. social scientists who research societies overseas often accent the importance of uncovering the hidden empirical realities and concealing myths of other societies, yet are frequently reluctant to do similar in-depth research on their home society.[3]

Since the full emergence of the social sciences in the United States in the late nineteenth and early twentieth centuries, mainstream social scientists have periodically developed influential theories and concepts designed to interpret "racial and ethnic relations" in this society. These mostly white mainstream analysts have historically included such prominent scholars as Robert E. Park, Gunnar Myrdal, and Milton Gordon. These influential scholars and their associates have usually had difficulty in viewing U.S. society from any but a white, albeit often liberal, racial framing. Moreover, over more recent decades the broad analytical perspectives and much conceptual terminology of mainstream researchers like Park, Myrdal, and Gordon, though periodically elaborated and revised, have continued to significantly influence the way that a majority of social scientists and other researchers have viewed and researched important U.S. racial issues.[4]

Certainly, the mainstream "race relations" theories and concepts have provided handy interpretive tools for understanding numerous aspects of racial oppression in this society, but they also have significant limitations and carry hidden assumptions that frequently trap analysts into a limited understanding of racial inequalities and related racial patterns. Included among these are traditional concepts such as bigotry, prejudice, stereotype, race, ethnicity, assimilation, and bigot-generated discrimination. These concepts have been widely used, and are often valuable, but they do not provide the essential array of conceptual tools necessary to make sense out of a highly racialized society like the United States.

These conventional concepts tend to be used in decontextualized and non-systemic ways. Even a quick look at today's social science journals and textbooks reveals the frequency and limitations of these concepts. Those analysts who use them tend to view racial inequality as just one of the U.S. "social problems." Numerous social problems textbooks dealing with racial issues have a section or chapter on something like the U.S. "race problem," as do numerous other textbooks such as those used in law school courses dealing with the U.S. Constitution and racial issues. This "problem" view is similar to the cancer view of racism mentioned in the preface, in that the problem is considered to be just an abnormality in an otherwise healthy system.[5] This approach typically views the race problem as not foundational to society, but rather as temporary and gradually disappearing as a result of our advanced modernity. Thus, one common approach in these conventional analyses is to view historical or contemporary acts of discrimination as determined by individual prejudice or by a concern for the prejudices of a few others. This bigot-causes-discrimination view is, like numerous other mainstream views, generally oriented to individual or small-group processes and does not examine the deep structural foundation in which acts of discrimination are always imbedded.[6]

Classical Social Scientists: Trapped in a White Racist Context

The habit of not thinking realistically and deeply about a country's undergirding racial structure extends well beyond U.S. social scientists, past or present, to the most prominent figures in the long tradition of Western social science. Consider the still influential, towering intellectual giants of the Western tradition such as Max Weber, Karl Marx, Emile Durkheim, and Sigmund Freud. They loom large in much contemporary U.S. and Western social science, yet *not one* of these intellectual giants gave serious research or analytical attention to the systems of racial oppression that operated conspicuously within Western countries' imperial spheres during their lifetimes. They did not assess in any significant way the racialized oppression that played out in front of them as a central aspect of European imperialism and colonialism. Not even Karl Marx, the vigorous critic of class oppression who knew Western history well and wrote articles for a New York newspaper about U.S. issues, paid any sustained attention to the highly racialized character of the colonizing adventures overseas by Western governments and corporate enterprises. It is a truism to note that a social science analyst's societal context often limits his or her research and analysis. But, even so, the widespread omission of a serious and sustained analysis of Western racial expansion and oppression, and the consequent structures, is particularly striking given how fundamental these processes and structures have been to the global dominance and prosperity of Western countries.

Historically, of course, almost all influential social science theorists and analysts have been white, and almost all of these have been male. These influential analysts have characteristically viewed Western racial matters from a usually educated version of the dominant white racial frame, which I explain fully in the next section of this chapter. For the most part, these white theorists and analysts have been handicapped by their privileged position in European and U.S. racial hierarchies, and by the fact that they typically think out of the broad racial framing that most whites at all social levels have used for centuries. Take the example of Max Weber, who died in the early twentieth century but has had a great impact on U.S. and other Western social science ever since. Like other social scientists of his era, he held to the tenets of blatant biological racism, a view that infected his historical and geopolitical arguments, yet one that almost never gets critically discussed in the social science textbooks and empirical analyses that to this day use his important concepts. Weber wrote openly and unreflectively of the "hereditary hysteria" of Asian-Indians, of Africans as genetically incapable of factory work, and of the Chinese as slow in intelligence and docile, with these latter traits viewed as significantly shaped by biology. As with most scientists of his day, central to Weber's work was the idea of "Western rationality," which he viewed as having some hereditary grounding. Western capitalism had evolved through the process of "modernization," which Weber and his educated peers regularly contrasted to the "traditionalism" of "Oriental" civilizations. Weber held to the white Eurocentric view that contemporary European capitalism was the endpoint in a successful evolutionary process—an "intellectual progression, an ascent of human 'rationality,' meaning intellect and ethics" from ancient society to modern society.[7] Beyond Europe, other countries were viewed as "traditional" and thus to some degree backward and irrational. The contemporary scholar, Edward Said, has described this as an ideology of "Orientalism," an old Western-centered framing unable to see beyond its Eurocentrism.[8] Since the time of Max Weber, indeed, Western social scientists assessing European industrialization and capitalism have continued to accent, explicitly or implicitly, some type of European rationality and superiority in modernity.

To take a more recent example, we can note the leading U.S. social theorist and analyst, Harvard professor Talcott Parsons. Parsons viewed U.S. racism as an anachronism representative of a premodernist mode of thinking and one likely to be dissolved with yet more U.S. industrialization, urbanization, and modernization. Even a scholar who probed deeply into the major values of Western civilization, as Parsons did, was unable to see the racialized "water" in which he metaphorically swam, the water of a sophisticated white racial framing of Western societies.[9] That frame and the system of material racial oppression it aggressively rationalizes have always been much more than a "premodern survival" attached to an otherwise advanced society. Both the system of racism and its rationalizing frame have long been part of the foundational realities of U.S. society, yet not one of the major mainstream theorists in the U.S. social science canon has substantially analyzed and understood that foundation.

Consider too that the idea of Western civilization's modernity, which includes a superior "rationality," has long been important in U.S. and other Western analysis, from Max Weber's time to the present day. The term "modernity" has functioned as social science shorthand for industrial and technological civilization, for societies shaped by the views that human beings should actively transform physical environments, that market economies are best, and that bureaucratized nation-states are necessary for societal well-being.[10] Yet this idea of modernity emerged about the same time as the white framing that, since at least the 1600s, has rationalized racial oppression in North America and elsewhere. The concept of "advanced Western civilization" grew out of the extensive European and European American history of imperialistic subordination of peoples of color and, thus, often within the social crucibles of slavery and genocide. Modern "civilized" societies were first conceptualized over against "traditional and inferior" societies, such as those of the "Orient" or those of indigenous peoples in the Americas and Africa.

According to contemporary analysts of Western history, modern Western societies supposedly have proceeded well beyond the premodern impulses of group irrationality, primitive superstition, and primitive violence. Yet the European enslavement of Africans in North America and the European-generated genocides targeting indigenous peoples across the globe, which operated openly until a century or so ago, did *not* result from premodern violent impulses somehow breaking through modernity, but rather these actions did and do constitute the economic and cultural foundations of Western modernity—with its advanced sciences and technologies, international markets, developed nation-states, and overseas military adventures. Racial oppression and its rationalizing and structuring frame have long been central to modern and imperialistic Western societies, indeed to the present day.

The White-Centered Perspective of Contemporary Social Scientists

Today, one observes the continuing reality of a white-centered framing in many contemporary social science analyses and in numerous other scholarly and popular analyses of U.S. society. As with canonical scholars like Max Weber, the language chosen to describe a society demographically or sociologically often reveals white perspective. For many scholarly and popular analysts in the United States (and across the globe) the English word "Americans" is routinely, if unconsciously, used to mean "white Americans." Terms like "American dream" and "American culture" are typically used to refer primarily to the values, ideals, or preferences of whites. In addition, language deflection strategies are often used to play down or circumnavigate racial matters. For example, a great many social science and popular analysts of this society phrase their analytical sentences about U.S. racial issues in the passive tense (such as, "prejudice has been a problem over the years for African Americans"), or they put vague or general nouns in the subject position of important sentences about racial issues ("society discriminates against Latinos"). By these and similar artifices, the important white actors who did or do specific acts of racial oppression are not positioned as active agents and named as such in the key sentences of a serious book's text. Of course, all authors need a diversity of sentences in order to maintain readers' interest, and using such passive or general phrasing might be in order to maintain that interest. However, in too many cases such sentences are not there for diversity of presentation, but rather to avoid directly asserting that whites, in general or in particular, are the critical actors in the long U.S. drama of racial oppression. Whites are, as it is sometimes said in defense of such writing strategies, just "implied."[11]

In addition, in many social scientists' writings a good scholarly discussion of the white role in U.S. racial issues, such as in slavery or legal segregation, is somehow balanced with some positive statements about whites because these authors apparently feel a great need to say something good about whites in the same era. An example is paralleling a written section on "bad slaveholders" with another section on supposedly "good slaveholders," an oxymoronic phrase indeed. Take the case of George Washington. Numerous white historians have portrayed him as a superior "moral" leader and "good" slavemaster in spite of his bloody involvement in extending the slavery system. The same George Washington periodically asserted his harshly negative stereotyping of African Americans, had enslaved runaways chased down, participated in the callous raffling off enslaved workers, had enslaved workers whipped, and even had teeth taken from the mouths of those he enslaved for his own mouth. One otherwise critical historian insists Washington was "not a racist" and that "his unique eminence arises from his sterling personal qualities . . . and from the eerie sense that, in him, some fragment of divine Providence did indeed touch this ground."[12] Similarly, otherwise critical white social scientists seem to be unable to name accurately the gendered brutality often directed at black women during the slavery and legal segregation eras as "rape" or "coerced sex." Thus, pioneering historian Winthrop Jordan noted that "white men of every social rank slept with Negro women" and that "miscegenation was extensive" in English colonies, but he did not use the words "rape" or "sexual coercion" in his analyses of this bloody, often violent white male behavior.[13]

Today remarkable numbers of white scholars and policy analysts seem surprised or puzzled about the constant recurrence of blatantly racist incidents, events, and commentaries in this society. They have often accepted a contemporary racial framing that views U.S. society as truly "colorblind" or "post-racial" and considers racism to be dead or in significant decline (see Chapter 5). Even scholars of a liberal inclination regularly tiptoe around or underestimate the depth and extensiveness of racial hostility and discrimination today. For example, the liberal political writer and influential neuroscientist, Drew Westen, has recently remarked on contemporary whites in this fashion: "It's not that most people *want* to be racist anymore." Similarly, liberal economist and *New York Times* columnist Paul Krugman has argued that U.S. whites are becoming much less racist, so much so that this has made possible a presidential victory like that of Senator Barack Obama in 2008.[14] The serious errors in these uninformed commentaries will become clear in later chapters. Suffice it to say here that just because there seem to be fewer overtly racist actions and performances by whites today in public—at least performances that are viewed as racist by whites—does not mean that whites' racist thought and action in this society has sharply decreased to a low level. A great many contemporary U.S. scholars and popular analysts of all political backgrounds seem unable to step outside a white-centered perspective on racial matters in their research and analytical writings to see our racialized world as it really is.

The White Racial Frame: Dimensions and Impact

Today, we are in the early stages of developing a major new conceptual paradigm on U.S. racial matters, with a new array of conceptual and interpretive tools and a growing number of social scientists, legal scholars, and others starting to realize the old "racial relations" paradigm's limits.[15] Those working in this contemporary paradigm are attempting to develop a better theory of racial oppression, one that shows racial oppression's deep structures, assesses its dimensions and reproductive processes, and demonstrates how both inertial forces and change forces have shaped it over time. For this we need innovative, better, and agreed-upon analytical and interpretive concepts, including resurrected concepts from the counter-mainstream tradition of scholars of color such as W. E. B. Du Bois and Oliver C. Cox (see Chapter 7). Inspired by this long tradition, I make much use in this book of strong concepts like the white racial frame, the black counter-frame, and institutional and systemic racism. These concepts link well to critical insights that help us build a better social science paradigm that fosters research into the racial foundation of this society. The empirical world of racial experiences is diverse, complex, and saturated with meaning, and these always structured experiences often have no adequate analytical categories in traditional social science.

The central concept of the white racial frame that I suggest and develop in this book is one that helps greatly in digging deeply into the operation of racial oppression in this society. What do I mean by "frame"? Several contemporary sciences, especially the cognitive, neurological, and social sciences, have made use of the idea of a perspectival frame that gets imbedded in individual minds (brains), as well as in collective memories and histories, and helps people make sense out of everyday situations. People have numerous frames for understanding and interpretation in their minds.

Cognitive and neurological scientists have used the concept of frame to examine human minds at work, with significant recent attention to how mostly unconscious frames shape individuals' socio-political inclinations and actions. Some social scientists, in contrast, have in recent years used the concept of frame to examine the relatively conscious frames of people in particular social movements. Their concern is with how framed messages aid in getting a particular social movement's members to protest. Other social scientists, especially media researchers, have accented how mass media framing of stories is typically quite conscious. Specific media frames select out limited aspects of an issue in order to make it salient for mass communication, a selectivity usually promoting a narrow reading of that issue. In all these disciplines a frame is form-giving and makes meaningful what otherwise might seem meaningless to the people involved. A particular frame structures the thinking process and shapes what people see, or do not see, in important societal settings.[16]

In examining racial oppression in the United States, I build on and extend these conceptions of societal framing and emphasize the central importance of a broad and long-dominant white racial frame. As I show in later chapters, much historical research demonstrates that there is in North America and elsewhere a dominant, white-created racial frame that provides an overarching and generally destructive worldview, one extending across white social divisions of class, gender, and age. Since its early development in the seventeenth century, this powerful frame has provided the vantage point from which white Americans have constantly viewed North American society. Its centrality in white minds is what makes it a dominant frame throughout the country and, indeed, much of the Western world. Over time, this powerful frame has been elaborated by, and/or imposed on, the minds of most Americans, becoming thereby the country's dominant "frame of mind" and "frame of reference" in regard to racial matters.

In this broad racial framing of society, white Americans have combined at least these important features:

1. racial stereotypes (a beliefs aspect);
2. racial narratives and interpretations (integrating cognitive aspects);

3. racial images (a visual aspect) and language accents (an auditory aspect);
4. racialized emotions (a "feelings" aspect); and
5. inclinations to discriminatory action.

Over its centuries of operation this strong racial framing has encompassed both a positive orientation to whites and whiteness and a negative orientation to those racial "others" who are exploited and oppressed. The dominant racial frame is negative and ethnocentric toward the racial others, yet it is much more than this. In the next chapter I show that early in this country's history this overarching racist framing assertively accented a very positive view of white superiority, virtue, and moral goodness. For centuries the white racial framing of ingroup superiority and outgroup inferiority has been, to use Antonio Gramsci's term, *hegemonic* in this society—that is, it has been part of a distinctive way of life that dominates all aspects of this society. For most whites, thus, the white racial frame is more than just one significant frame among many; it is one that has routinely defined a way of being, a broad perspective on life, and one that provides the language and interpretations that help structure, normalize, and make sense out of society.

Let us consider a recent racial event that illustrates several of these important dimensions of the white racial frame. In a journal kept for a college course, Trevor, a white student at a midwestern college, reported on an evening party with five other white male students:

> When any two of us are together, no racial comments or jokes are ever made. However, with the full group membership present, anti-Semitic jokes abound, as do racial slurs and vastly derogatory statements. . . . Various jokes concerning stereotypes . . . were also swapped around the gaming table, everything from "How many Hebes fit in a VW beetle?" to "Why did the Jews wander the desert for forty years?" In each case, the punch lines were offensive, even though I'm not Jewish. The answers were "One million (in the ashtray) and four (in the seats)" and "because someone dropped a quarter," respectively. These jokes degraded into a rendition of the song "Yellow," which was re-done to represent the Hiroshima and Nagasaki bombings. It contained lines about the shadows of the people being flash burned into the walls ("and it was all yellow" as the chorus goes in the song).

There is nothing subtle or ambiguous about these performances that frame and target specific groups. Trevor recorded yet more racist performances in this long evening event:

A member of the group also decided that he has the perfect idea for a Hallmark card. On the cover it would have a few kittens in a basket with ribbons and lace. On the inside it would simply say "You're a nigger." I found that incredibly offensive. Supposedly, when questioned about it, the idea of the card was to make it as offensive as humanly possible in order to make the maximal juxtaposition between warm- and ice- hearted. After a brief conversation about the cards which dealt with just how wrong they were, a small kitten was drawn on a piece of paper and handed to me with a simple, three-word message on the back. . . . Of course, no group is particularly safe from the group's scathing wit, and the people of Mexico were next to bear the brunt of the jokes. A comment was made about Mexicans driving low-riding cars so they can drive and pick lettuce at the same time. Comments were made about the influx of illegal aliens from Mexico and how fast they produce offspring.[17]

These white men are well-educated and having great "fun" as part of an extended social gathering, one they reportedly often engage in. Even in this relatively brief journal account we observe that the white racial frame involves a relatively broad framing of society, one that encompasses multiple dimensions. We observe an array of racial stereotypes and images, both explicitly and implicit, that mock, and signal the inferiority of, several groups of color. Even Jewish Americans are included, apparently as people who are not authentically white. Note too that there is more here than just cognitive stereotypes. The visual images are vivid, as is the song playing off the "yellow" metaphor. The performances are barbed, emotion-laden, and generally set in a joking format. We observe too that the white racial frame prizes whiteness, which is the obvious stance of superiority taken by these young whites doing the racialized performances. Old racially-framed notions and emotions that they have learned from previous generations have become the basis for extensive racist performances at times when these white friends gather to socialize.

Note too that the white racial frame structures events and performances, which in turn feed and add to the frame. Several different roles are played by the whites in this one racialized evening. There are the protagonists centrally acting out numerous racialized notions from important subframes within the white racial frame, here for an all-white audience. Others who are present agree with the racial performances and seem to act as cheerleading assistants. The recording student apparently acted either as a passive bystander or mild dissenter showing awareness of the moral issues here. No one, however, aggressively dissents and remonstrates strongly with the active protagonists.

In situations like this we see that the socially inherited racial frame is a comprehensive orienting structure, a "tool kit" that whites and others have long used to understand, interpret, and act in social settings. The important aspects of the frame listed above become taken-for-granted "common sense" for those who hold to them, and most holders use these tools in automatic or half-conscious ways.[18] From the beginning of this country, this white frame has been deeply held and strongly resistant to displacement, and it includes many important "bits"—that is, frame elements such as the stereotyped racial knowledge, racial images and emotions, and racial interpretations in this diary account. These elements are important pieces of cultural information passed along from one person and group to the next. They include elementary elements such as the word-concepts "white," "black," "race," and white-created racist epithets like "nigger"— key words that in daily life regularly activate other elements of the frame. Frame elements are generally grouped into several key subframes within a broad overarching frame, and this broader frame operates as a gestalt, a unified whole that is in significant ways more than the sum of its parts.

At its highest level, this gestalt framing imbeds racist items that are relatively constant, while at lower levels it has changing connections to the ebb and flow of the data of everyday experience. This dominant frame does not exist apart from everyday experience, and racist practices flowing from it are essential parts of the larger system of racial oppression. Such practices are made meaningful to perpetrators by the dominant frame, and these practices show well the intersections of people's material, social, and mental lives.

Central to the dominant racial frame in the United States are several "big picture" narratives that connect frame elements into historically oriented stories with morals that are especially important to white Americans. These emotion-laden scenarios include stories about white conquest, superiority, hard work, and achievement. They make powerful use of stereotypes, images, and other elements from the overarching frame. They include numerous rags-to-riches narratives such as that for the early Pilgrims. According to this mythological narrative, these English "settlers" came with little, but drawing on a deep religious faith and much hard work they "settled" and made a nearly "vacant" land prosper, against the "savage" Indians. This heroic narrative was later extended as whites moved westward and concocted a "winning the West," manifest destiny myth. In that story white "settlers" again fought battles against "savage" Indians, with the heroes being rewarded with land and villainous Indians being killed off or isolated and punished on reservations. (The facts, such as the reality that the indigenous peoples were the successful and established settlers of these lands, are suppressed in these narratives.) Interestingly, these fictional white narratives are still very much with us. Today, in their homes and in schools and the media a great many whites tell themselves and others false and fabricated narratives of how this country was created and founded. Perhaps most importantly, many try to live by the emotion-laden values and fiction-laden interpretations that they claim as meaningful from these common mythological narratives.[19]

It is clear from such narratives, as well as from the student diary account, that the old white racial framing of society is about much more than words. In addition to its many racial stereotypes and other such belief elements, this powerful racial frame includes deep emotions, visual images, language, and the everyday sounds of spoken language such as accents. Powerful emotions, deep negative feelings, about Americans of color frequently shape how most whites behave and interact, and in spite of the liberty-and-justice language they may periodically assert. Seen best when it structures behavior, the emotions of the conventional white frame have included racial hatred, racial arrogance, and a sense of racial superiority; greed and other emotions of gratification; and a desire for dominance over others. The emotions of white racism also include the fears and anxieties, conscious and unconscious, that whites have long held in regard to Americans of color because of the latter's resistance to white-imposed oppression. Moreover, for some whites guilt and shame have become central emotions, especially as the venality and immorality of racism have become more obvious to them. Significantly, those whites who do move to a substantial anti-racist framing of society and into significant anti-racist action often feel and accent the positive emotions of empathy, compassion, and hope for the future.

Operating Out of the White Frame

Although they live in several regions and often have different occupations and educations, most whites have revealed in numerous research studies that they hold broadly similar positive stereotypes, images, and understandings about whites and broadly similar negative stereotypes, images, and understandings of Americans of color.[20] Nonetheless, as I see it, the concept of the white racial frame is an "ideal type," a composite whole with a large array of elements that in everyday practice are drawn on *selectively* by white individuals acting to impose or maintain racial identity, privilege, and dominance vis-à-vis people of color in everyday interactions. People use what they need from the overarching frame's major elements to deal with specific situations. Individual whites and others mostly do not make use of the bits of this dominant frame in exactly the same way. For most people there seems to be an internal hierarchy of racist ideas, images, and emotions, such that a given person may be more comfortable with some of these elements, especially once they become conscious to the individual, than of other known frame elements. Indeed, racially liberal whites may reject certain elements of the traditional racist frame while unconsciously accepting or highlighting yet others. Moreover, over time some people may rework, challenge, or transform the version of the white frame they inherited.

The use of critical frame elements often varies by age, gender, class, and other major social variables. The strength and use of white power and privilege is variable across these subgroups, so the utilization of the framing to rationalize and act in societal situations also varies. In addition, the dominant racial frame regularly overlaps with, and is connected to, other collective frames that are important in viewing and interpreting recurring social worlds. Once a frame is utilized by a person, it often activates related frames or subframes. Indeed, quite frequently, the dominant racial frame activates and relates to class-oriented and patriarchal ways of looking at society. Indeed from the first century of European colonization, as we will see in the next chapters, the class and patriarchal (gender) frames of oppression have been linked to the white racial frame or even nested within it.

By constantly using selected bits of the dominant frame to understand and interpret society, by integrating new items into it, and by applying its stereotypes, images, and interpretations in their exploitative and discriminatory actions, whites have for centuries incorporated this interpretive frame in their minds as well as, to varying degrees, the minds of many people of color. Contemporary neurological research shows that strongly held views, such as those of the white frame, are deeply imbedded in the neuronal structure of human brains. Repetition is critical in this process. The dominant racial frame becomes implanted in the neural linkages of a typical brain by the process of constant repetition of its elements—which are heard, observed, or acted upon repeatedly by individuals over years and decades.[21]

Once inculcated in the mind and brain, this frame tends to be lasting and resistant to change. Activation of it tends to suppress alternative or countering frames. For most whites the dominant frame has become so fundamental that few are able to see it or think about it critically. When important but inconvenient facts are presented that do not fit this frame, whites tend to ignore or reject those facts. For example, for several centuries whites have held to very negative views of black Americans as not nearly as hard-working as white Americans, in spite of great historical evidence to the contrary. Frames as entrenched as the dominant white frame are hard to counter or uproot. In fact, the white racial frame has become part of most whites' *character structure*, a character structure habitually operated out of, with individual variations, in everyday life.

Moreover, from the beginning the white racial frame has not only rationalized the exploitative structure of racial oppression, but also played a central role in *actually structuring* this society on a daily basis by providing important understandings, images, narratives, emotions, and operational norms that determine a great array of individual and group actions within all major societal sectors. The dominant white frame is active and directing; it is learned at parent's knee, in school, and from the media; and, once learned, it both guides and rationalizes discriminatory behavior. Whether it is a white child abusing a black child in the schoolyard, or a white adult discriminating against a Latino adult in a job situation, the frame is both activating and activated, and thus is central in creating the social texture of everyday life.

Frame interpretations do *not* somehow stand outside daily life just in the minds of individuals but directly shape the scripts that whites and others act on, such as in acts of discrimination in important social settings—thereby re-creating, maintaining, and reinforcing the racially stratified patterns and structures of society. For centuries, the white racial frame has directly protected and shaped this society's inegalitarian structure of resources and hierarchy of power. This dominant frame has persisted now over centuries only because it is constantly validating, and thus validated by, the inegalitarian accumulation of social, economic, and political resources.[22]

Collective Memories and Collective Forgetting

Very important to the persistence of the white racial frame are friendship and kinship groups, for in such social networks the racial elements of that frame become common cultural currency. Sociologist Maurice Halbwachs suggested that our personal understandings about society are not in some nook of our minds to which we alone have access. Instead, our social understandings, and thus our important frames, are regularly recalled to us externally, and the social groups of which we are part give us the "means to reconstruct them" if we "adopt, at least for the moment, their way of thinking." An individual's understandings, images, knowledge, and framing hang together because they are part of the "totality of thoughts common to a group."[23] Over time our groups, small and large, become major repositories of congealed group memories and associated social frames. We human beings gain most of our racial frame's understandings, images, and emotions from imbibing and testing those of parents and peers, the media, and written accounts handed down over generations. We do this learning mostly within significant networks of relatives, peers, and friends—as we saw in the example of white college students engaging in racist performances earlier in the chapter. Constant repetition and performance of the frame's racialized information and other bits—together with relevant intonation and style, nonverbal gestures, and facial expressions—are essential to the successful reproduction of that frame across social networks, geography, and time.[24]

Collective memory is central to these networks. How we interpret and experience our racialized present depends substantially on our knowledge of and interpretations of our racialized past. The collective memory of that racist past not only shapes, but legitimates, the established racial structure of today's society. Moreover, if major groups in society hold significantly different collective memories of that racist past, they will as a rule have difficulty in sharing understandings of racial experiences in the present. Most groups have important collective memories, but those with the greatest power, principally white Americans in the U.S. case, have the greatest control over society-wide institutional memories, including those recorded by the media and in most history books, organizational histories, laws, textbooks, films, and public monuments.[25]

What the dominant racial framing ignores or suppresses is critical to the continuation of oppression. Collective *forgetting* is as important as collective remembering, especially in regard to the prevailing narratives of this country's developmental history. Historical events may stay in the collective records of memory, or they may be allowed to deteriorate, slowly or rapidly, through the overt choices of the powerful. The latter usually seek to suppress or weaken collective memories of societal oppression, and to construct positive and often fictional memories. White Americans and their acolytes in other groups have long tried to sanitize this country's collective memories and to downplay or eliminate accurate understandings of our racist history. Over nearly four centuries, as I detail in later chapters, a critical part of the dominant framing of whites' unjust enrichment at the expense of Americans of color—for example, killing off Native American populations and enslaving millions of Africans—has included much collective forgetting and mythmaking in regard to these bloody historical realities. Significant portions of North American histories of centuries of oppression have been allowed to disappear from public consciousness, or to be downplayed and mythologized in scattered societal portrayals.

This historical mythmaking has been absorbed even by those Americans who are not white, but who have incorporated in their minds significant elements of the dominant white framing. For example, Fareed Zakaria—an immigrant journalist who studied at Harvard with the influential nativistic scholar, Samuel Huntington, and works for a major U.S. newsmagazine—has written recently about the historical rise and power of the West, yet with no significant references to the role of European-generated slavery and genocide in that process. He writes like many contemporary white historians: "Contact with the rest of the world stimulated

Europe. . . . Everywhere Europeans went they found goods, markets, and opportunities. By the seventeenth century, Western nations were increasing their influence over every region and culture with which they came in contact." Indeed, most areas of the world became "marked for use by Europeans."[26] In a substantial discussion of these historical issues Zakaria makes only one fleeting reference to the enslavement of Africans and has no explicit reference to the genocide directed at indigenous peoples. For him, as for most historians of the United States and the West, modernization is about industrialization, urbanization, education, and wealth, and not centrally about genocide, slavery, and the unjust enrichment of European colonists and countries.

When such a momentous and bloody past is suppressed, downplayed, or mythologized by elites and historians, ordinary Americans, especially whites, understandably have difficulty in seeing or assessing accurately the present-day realities of unjust enrichment and impoverishment along racial lines. Moreover, misunderstandings and myths of our highly oppressive past are frequently passed along from one generation to the next, and from one person to the next, by means of recurring and ritualized performances. Commemorative ceremonies on holidays, such as July 4th or Columbus day, honoring our history celebrate and sanitize a horrific past, thereby shaping contemporary communal memories by accenting the continuity of the present racial status quo with a positively portrayed racial past. Sharing elements of the white racial frame in such ceremonies generally promotes solidarity in the dominant group, and often with other racial groups that accept white dominance.[27]

The Importance of Counter-Frames

While the central concern of this book is developing the concept of the white racial frame and showing how it has developed and operated across the centuries, we also need to realize and accent the point that this is not the only important collective frame directed at racial matters. Most people carry several perspectival frames applicable to particular situations in their heads at the same time. We might call such people "multiconceptuals" or, even better, "multiframers." In examining the significant and sometimes contested history of the dominant white racial frame, I will deal to some degree with three other important categories of frames in everyday operation: (1) a white-crafted liberty-and-justice frame; (2) the anti-oppression counter-frames of Americans of color; and (3) the home-culture frames that Americans of color have drawn on in developing their counter-frames.

One of the great ironies of this country's early history is that white

Americans' conceptions of their freedom and of social justice were honed within a slavery system. By the mid- to late eighteenth century, the white colonists had developed what I call the white "liberty-and-justice frame," one that they loudly proclaimed against British officials who were suppressing their liberties. This liberty-and-justice frame is important because most white Americans have in the past and in the present articulated some version of this framing. We see the importance of this framing in the founding documents of the United States, including the "establish justice" and "secure the blessings of liberty" language of the preamble to the U.S. Constitution.

Since the American revolution most whites have held in their minds some version of a liberty-and-justice frame, one that is real to them, but one that is usually treated as rhetorical or hypothetical when it comes to serious threats to the perpetuation of the U.S. system of racism. The liberty-and-justice frame has been routinely trumped by the white racial frame, and has too often been reserved just for rhetorical speeches and sermons. Still, over the centuries of this country's existence, modest numbers of whites have taken the liberty-and-justice frame very seriously in regard to the racially oppressed situations of Americans of color. We see this in the white abolitionists who, with black abolitionists, protested and fought to bring down the slavery system. Later on, in the 1950s and 1960s we again see a small group of whites actively allying themselves with black civil rights protestors, whose efforts played a major role in bringing down legal segregation.

In addition to the dominant white racial frame and the white version of the liberty-and-justice frame, there are two groups of perspectival frames that are highly relevant to understanding resistance to systemic racial oppression in North America over the centuries: (1) the anti-oppression counter-frames of Americans of color, and (2) the home-culture frames that Americans of color have drawn on to develop effective anti-oppression counter-frames. In opposing the dominant racial frame, Americans of color have frequently developed a significant counter-frame, an important frame that has helped them to better understand and resist oppression. Freedom-oriented resistance frames appear in the earliest period of racial oppression. The early counter-frames of Americans of color, primarily those of Native Americans and African Americans, were initially developed for survival purposes, and over time they have added critical elements that have strengthened the understandings of racism and the strategies of everyday resistance.

The resistance frames have often drawn heavily on material from the cultural backgrounds of those oppressed. For example, since the first century of their enslavement, African Americans have maintained a home-culture that is a hybrid, with cultural features stemming in part from the African cultural background and in part from their experiences in North America. Confronted daily by extreme oppression and white attempts to eradicate their African cultures, the many African groups among those enslaved became a single African American people with a home-culture that drew substantially on family, spiritual, and moral elements from their African backgrounds. With strong African roots, these new Americans shaped their religion, art, music, and strategies against oppression and for social justice.

The resistance counter-frames of Americans of color have also drawn on the ideals or terminology from whites' own liberty-and-justice frame. Indeed, since the early decades of slavery and genocide whites have greatly feared that African Americans and Native Americans would operate out of a liberty-and-justice counter-frame of their own. Thus, whites feared its influence and use in African Americans' revolts against slavery, and such fears even accelerated with the end of slavery—fears that played some role in the emergence and structure of the near-slavery of Jim Crow segregation. Today, as we will see in later chapters, white Americans still fear, and attack, the stronger counter-frames as they are used by many Americans of color. One example of such white fear can be seen in the widespread, fierce, and irrational white reactions during the November 2008 election to the strong anti-racist perspective articulated by Dr. Jeremiah Wright, who at the time had been President Barack Obama's pastor for several decades.

In Chapter 7, thus, I examine Dr. Wright's critical perspective on U.S. history as an example of a contemporary counter-frame arising out of the black tradition and black communities. I will also explore briefly other important counter-frames, including those of Native Americans, Latinos, and Asian Americans. Historically and in the present, these counter-frames have regularly provided valuable tool kits for oppressed Americans, offering both individual and collective tools for countering widespread white hostility and discrimination.

Conclusion

In this chapter I have defined and detailed the concept of the white racial frame and suggested its utility and importance in making sense out of racial oppression, mainly in North America. In the next few chapters I examine several questions about how this dominant racial frame and its important elements arose over the centuries, and why they did so. I also ask, how has this frame shaped the past and present structure of this society? In these chapters I seek to answer these and related questions, and thus to make the often hidden racist realities of this country more obvious—to take them "out of the closet" so that they can be openly analyzed and, hopefully, redressed or removed.

For centuries, to the present day, the dominant racial frame has sharply defined inferior and superior racial groups and authoritatively rationalized and structured the great racial inequalities of this society. In a white-washing process, and most especially today, this dominant framing has shoved aside, ignored, or treated as incidental numerous racial issues, including the realities of persisting racial discrimination and racial inequality. By critically analyzing this dominant racial frame's elements and its numerous structuring impacts, we can discern more clearly how this country is put together racially—and perhaps how it might be able to change in the direction of the liberty-and-justice society long proclaimed in this country's still-dominant political rhetoric.

CHAPTER 2

Building the Racist Foundation

Colonialism, Genocide, and Slavery

Why is the white racial frame so deep and so foundational in the United States? The central reason is that this country is built on 350 years of extreme racial oppression. Over its first centuries of operation, this oppression aggressively targeted indigenous peoples for extermination or expulsion, and targeted African Americans with a bloody slavery system. From the 1840s to the 1960s, powerful white capitalists and politicians gradually brought into this preexisting system of racism yet more people of color such as the Chinese and Mexicans in the 1840s and 1850s—frequently to secure low-wage labor for whites' wealth-generating economic enterprises. Given this extensive and racialized oppression, whites have long tried to rationalize, and hide or disguise, the extensive and lasting patterns of oppression they have created and maintained. Over centuries a large majority have become fervent partisans and defenders of white power and privilege, especially by means of the white racial frame. Playwright Eugene O'Neill once wrote that "There is no present or future, only the past, happening over and over again, now." The better we understand this past of bloody racial oppression, the better we can understand our present racial situation, with its dominant racial hierarchy and rationalizing racial frame.

European Colonialism: Bloody Exploitation

Today, many scholars and popular analysts continue to describe contemporary Western societies with terms like "modern" and "modernity." They emphasize as positive certain characteristics of these modern societies: industrialization and technology, market economies, national governments, and complex bureaucratization. Significantly, however, numerous supposedly positive features of this distinctive modernity have played a major and negative role in the genocide, land theft, and labor theft that accompanied the global expansion and colonialism of European countries beginning in the late 1400s. Strikingly, colonialism, capitalism, modernity, and global exploitation all have a *common* genealogy. European colonialism and capitalism were in their early stages of development when they generated the cross-Atlantic slavery system. European colonialism took on its exploitative wealth-generating form in concert with the enslavement of Africans and other indigenous peoples across the growing north and south Atlantic economies. The bloody European theft of land and super-exploitation of enslaved labor were presided over by ever-growing and bureaucratized nation-states, the latter usually described by Western social scientists as signs of the modernization process. From its beginnings, European colonialism relied heavily not only on a growing entrepreneurial bourgeoisie but also on these nation-states, most especially upon their well-equipped military organizations.[1]

The social scientist and political theorist, Karl Marx, once captured the world-shattering significance of this European colonialism and imperialism in a brief statement in a major book on Western capitalism:

> The discovery of gold and silver in America, the extirpation, enslavement and entombment in mines of the aboriginal population, the beginning of the conquest and looting of the East Indies, the turning of Africa into a warren for the commercial hunting of black-skins, signaled the rosy dawn of the era of capitalist production. These idyllic proceedings are the chief moments of primitive accumulation. . . . [C]apital comes dripping from head to foot from every pore with blood and dirt.[2]

The rise of Western capitalism is rooted in the global seizing of the land, resources, and labor of people of color by violent means. Note too that coercing of the labor of Africans and indigenous Americans by European colonizers meant not only the extraction of "surplus value" from the productive work of these coerced workers, but even the extraction of the "subsistence value" of their work, so much so that many coerced laborers (men, women, and children) died from not having enough food, clothing, or shelter under European colonialism. This global theft of Native American and African labor by state-sanctioned capitalistic enterprises did not end after the first century of European wealth generation, but lasted for centuries—in some important ways to the present day.

Significant here is that, for the first time in world history, militaristic colonialism and imperialism were becoming *global* in scope and thus encompassed several continents. From the sixteenth to the nineteenth centuries the European colonial invasions forced a political-economic and demographic reorganization of a large part of the globe at the expense of many indigenous peoples. The Spanish nation state was the first to colonize and plunder on a large scale various indigenous societies in the Americas for their land, mineral, and labor resources, but its growing wealth and military apparatus were soon countered by the imperial expansion of competing English, Dutch, and French nation-states and private companies also seeking to gain wealth from overseas exploitation. Numerous European nation-states and associated private companies, such as English firms operating in the Caribbean and North America, discovered that there were huge profits to be made from overseas agricultural plantations using enslaved African labor on seized indigenous Americans' lands. Indeed, researchers have shown that by the end of the eighteenth century the lion's share of profits coming into British coffers came from overseas slave plantations producing important agricultural products.[3]

Well-organized nation-state and private bureaucracies in Europe and the emerging colonies were critical to this aggressive colonization. In North America the English colonies were often state enterprises created under auspices of the king or state-fostered enterprises developed by entrepreneurs, plantation owners, and merchants. The first English joint-stock companies were formed by merchants under the auspices of James I of England. Employees of the Southern Company settled Jamestown, Virginia, the English colony that brought in the first African laborers. A principal objective of this colonization was to secure land and raw materials and to develop markets. Once land was taken from indigenous societies, the Europeans' search for labor led to the extensive use of the African slave trade, which became critical to exploitation of land and other resources of the Americas. At an early point in time, the private-sector and the state-sector collaborated in global exploitation and enslavement, which were soon rationalized in a Eurocentric racial framing. Some recent social science theorizing, such as that of racial formation theorists Michael Omi and Howard Winant, has greatly expanded our understanding of government actors' role in regularly creating racialized organizations and institutions. Yet, their historical analyses do not go far enough in analyzing how at an early point in time the principal European nation-state actors collaborated with elite economic actors to generate the imperialism, genocide, and slavery that created the racial underpinning of Western countries like the United States.[4]

Celebrated social scientist Max Weber wrote famously of the "Protestant ethic and the spirit of capitalism" in assessing the fostering conditions before and around modern capitalism. However, in this European economic expansion one sees what might more accurately be termed the "predatory ethic" of Western capitalism. Central to European colonialism and capitalism was a predatory ethic that asserted the right of Europeans to take the land and labor of others by violence for their own individual and collective gain. As we will see in Chapter 7, this highly materialistic and greedy approach to encounters with new environments and peoples baffled Native Americans at the time, and still does today. It has been described by indigenous Americans as a "despiritualized" worldview, and in their view a despiritualized approach to environments and other beings resulted in their dehumanization and exploitation. The expansionist European invaders showed little concern for the lives and livelihoods of indigenous peoples during the bloody process of colonial wealth generation. Indeed, by the nineteenth century, in the United States, this predatory ethic was given an explicit rationalizing name, "manifest destiny," which asserted the right and duty of whites to expand wherever they needed to increase their prosperity, no matter the cost to those killed, displaced, and exploited in the process. Significant too is the fact that this predatory ethic was from the first dressed up in religious language, indeed as something that was God-ordained.

We should underscore another key dimension of this European colonialism, one that even critical white analysts have seldom emphasized: the highly racialized reality of this European colonization. Since Marx's time, Marxist analysts and other critical analysts have usually ignored or downplayed the racist architecture of centuries of Western colonialism. Even for these analysts, the dominant racial frame seems to be a difficult set of blinders to get beyond. Most major groups that were central to early and later European accumulation of wealth in this global colonizing system were non-European, and each of these groups was soon denigrated (the word literally means "blackened") in an increasingly developed Eurocentric framing of colonialism and the colonial societies thereby created. European entrepreneurs and colonists carried with them, or soon developed, not only the often noted realities of Western modernity such as so-called private enterprise and advanced technology, but also social developments ignored or neglected by most historical analysts—that is, systemic racial oppression and a rationalizing racist frame. The concurrent emergence of European capitalism, colonialism, and racial oppression marked the creation of a global racial order with European-origin people at the top, one that has ever since regularly shaped not only individual societies but also world patterns of trade, finance, politics, and communications.

White Prosperity: Native American Lands and African American Labor

As most schoolchildren know, the first task the European colonists undertook in North America was to "settle the land." This is the euphemistic phrase European Americans have long used for the theft of Native American land—which often required bloody wars, often genocidal wars, because Native Americans usually had resources to resist and did not comply. Once the land had been stolen, the need for labor to work the land soon exceeded the supply of white agricultural workers. Enslaved African Americans became a group that was internally central, as essential labor, to the prospering of the North American colonies. By the eighteenth century, the slavery-centered society directly involved a large proportion of white Americans in all major social classes. These included economically successful slaveholders in southern and northern states, the owners of slave-trading enterprises (often in the North), associated bankers and insurance brokers (often in the North), and leading southern and northern politicians who supported slave plantations and the Atlantic slave trade.

A very large number of ordinary whites in all colonies, northern and southern, worked in occupations linked directly or indirectly to the slavery system. These included white-collar clerks and other white employees working for various slave-related enterprises, overseers on slave farms and plantations, sailors on slave ships, slave-catchers who chased enslaved runaways, small farmers who grew agricultural products needed on slave plantations, lumber workers who cut timber for slave ships, fishers who traded fish meal to U.S. and Caribbean plantations, local and federal government workers policing enslaved runaways or processing the slave-produced products destined for export, and small farmers and urban entrepreneurs who rented their enslaved workers for temporary profit to other whites.[5] Most benefited economically in one way or another from what I term as the *slavery-centered economic complex*—which encompassed the slave trade, commercial trade with slave farms and plantations, international trade in slave-produced products, and the great array of slavery-supporting occupations across the country and, indeed, across the Atlantic. Over the next century, most whites gained significant material or symbolic benefits from this country's racialized system of African American slavery, as well as continuing anti-Indian oppression.

The word "exploit," in the sense of taking advantage of another for personal gain, first appears in the English language in the 1840s during the peak period of African American enslavement. For more than two centuries, as pioneering historians like Edmund Morgan have long made clear, this African American enslavement was a major foundation for this country—for its economy, politics, and other important institutions. If there had been no African American enslavement, there probably would not have been the huge North American wealth generation—and possibly no modern wealth-generating British and America capitalism on the massive scale that developed over the centuries. Enslaved workers cultivating tobacco, rice, sugar, cotton, and other major crops generated very large amounts of economic capital, much of which circulated throughout the European and North American banking and other economic institutions generating much spin-off prosperity, including important industrial breakthroughs. Enslaved black Americans created much of the surplus capital (wealth) of this country for its first two centuries, indeed for half this country's lifetime. They provided the wealth that the white colonists used to fight a successful war against Britain. As Morgan has put it, white Americans "bought their independence with slave labor."[6] Without the early enslavement of African Americans, thus, there would quite probably have been no United States and no U.S. Constitution—at least not when it happened in the seventeenth and eighteenth centuries.

Creating a Racial Hierarchy: Racial Capital and Frame Assumptions

As the colonies expanded over the first decades of the seventeenth century, European American officials, assisted by ordinary colonists, institutionalized a rigid social hierarchy, with group positions arranged in ladder-like levels and with significant socioeconomic benefits associated with the white level at the top, and none attached to the bottom level, which was initially reserved for Africans and Indians. These societal benefits and privileges were a type of *racial capital* reserved for European Americans. From the seventeenth century to the present, whites have gained much racial capital from this country's system of racial oppression.

This important racial capital has encompassed not only *economic and other material capital*, such as greater income and wealth, but also substantial *social status, social networking, and symbolic capital.* Symbolic capital comes from shared assumptions, understandings, and inclinations to interact in certain ways, and much of it is unrecognized and taken for granted. From the beginning symbolic capital has been a central part of whites' racial framing of society, for it operates to link white acquaintances and strangers. Examples of these shared assumptions and understandings can be seen, today or in the past, in the relatively easy ways in which even white strangers relate to each other, as compared to the tensions and other difficulties whites often have in relating to people, strangers or acquaintances, who are not white. Part of this process is what I call *frame assumption*—that is, the assumption that other whites share one's own racialized framing of the everyday social world. Perceiving and accenting white skin privilege in everyday interactions is very important for the operation of the long-dominant racial hierarchy in the United States. Historically, and in the present, most whites have operated as though the racial hierarchy is part of the natural order of things.

This hierarchy has persisted as the heart of systemic racism to the present day. It involves not only recurring racial discrimination and exploitation, but also an alienating racist relationship—at the bottom, the racially oppressed, and at the top, the racial oppressors. These socially separated and alienated groups have significantly different *interests*. The former seeks to overthrow the racial hierarchy, while the latter seeks to maintain it. The interests of the white racial group have included not only a concrete interest in labor and other social exploitation during the slavery and Jim Crow segregation eras, but also a concrete interest later on, in our contemporary era, in maintaining the racial power and privileges inherited from white ancestors. Everyday interactions have thus long involved the calculation of particular racial-group interests. Given the great alienation from one end of the racial hierarchy to the other, and thus the greatly divergent interests of the key groups, it is not surprising that, in dialectical fashion, these great societal contradictions regularly create protests seeking racial change.

Legalizing Oppression: The U.S. Constitution

One reason that the bloody realities of slavery, and later the near-slavery of Jim Crow segregation, have shaped this society so fundamentally is because from the first decades they were firmly imbedded in important private and public bureaucracies, and were firmly legitimated under this country's overtly racist legal system. The early and systematic oppression of Native Americans and African Americans was made possible by the increasing power of bureaucratic organizations, both private companies and the agencies of European nation-states. The norms of these bureaucratized organizations accented written rules, official roles, organizational discipline, and impersonality. Mass killings and attacks on Native Americans would have been possible without military and other bureaucratic organizations, but recurring wars on Indians and a large-scale system of African enslavement were not. Then, as in recent times, extensive oppression requires complex organization and organizational agents carrying out dominant group goals. Elite whites at the helm of colonial organizations collectively presided over numerous lower-level officials and other employees, such as overseers on slave plantations, clerks in government bureaucracies, and police and military agents.

The bureaucratization of oppression was accompanied by a strong accent on written records and laws. Walter Ong has shown how a heavy accent on the written word and literacy is a societal development that represents a different way of viewing society—a viewpoint that typically emphasizes abstraction, distancing of people from one another, and a new kind of dogmatic authority. The written word "distances the writer for a thought from the receiver" of that thought.[7] In contrast, the oral worlds of the invaded indigenous peoples have vivid and accessible collective memories and orientations, which tend to make people much more sensitive to and responsive to those around them. Institutionalization of written rules and records in colonial America, and later the United States, helped to assist the white elite and populace in operating effectively to dominate the new country—by means of a growing number of powerful political, legal, and economic organizations. It reinforced the type of distancing thought that went along with the bureaucracies that organized the systemic exploitation directed at Native and African Americans.

Central to the legitimation and organization of North American slavery was the colonial legal system. As philosopher Charles Mills has pointed out, this society began with a generalized "racial contract" in which people's duties and rights were routinely distributed on a racially discriminatory and unequal basis. From the beginning, the legal system was written, formally institutionalized, and distancing. For centuries now, this extensive institutionalization has involved many white judges and other officials, thereby solidifying well white power and privilege. The principal foundation of this country's legal system is the U.S. Constitution. In 1787, at Philadelphia, fifty-five white men met and created a constitution for what most have viewed as the "first democratic nation." These founders were of European background and mostly well-off. Some 40 percent were or had been slaveowners, and many others profited as merchants, shippers, lawyers, or bankers from economic connections to the slavery system.[8]

In the preamble to the Constitution these white male founders cite "We the People," but this phrase did not include those enslaved, then a fifth of the population. They viewed the world from an aggressive white racial framing of society. At least seven sections of the new Constitution protected the already 160-year-old system of racialized enslavement: (1) Article 1, Section 2 counts an enslaved person as only three fifths of a white person; (2) Article 1, Sections 2 and 9 apportion taxes using the three-fifths formula; (3) Article 1, Section 8 gives Congress authority to suppress slave insurrections; (4) Article 1, Section 9 prevents abolishing the slave trade before 1808; (5) Article 1, Sections 9 and 10 exempt slave-made goods from export duties; (6) Article 4, Section 2 requires the return of fugitive slaves; and (7) Article 4, Section 4 stipulates that the federal government must help states put down domestic violence, a provision that the framers included in part to deal with slave uprisings.[9] As we see in these provisions, enslaved African Americans were frequently on the minds of the white framers, who referred to African American enslavement numerous times at the Constitutional convention and with euphemistic language in the final Constitution. Their constitutional debates revealed that they generally viewed those enslaved as property, as less than fully human. At this point in time, the white racial frame and the slavery system it rationalized were more than a century old and were aggressively enhanced and imbedded in the new and inegalitarian U.S. political institutions.

Numerous provisions of the Constitution besides those listed above also helped to institutionalize the slavery system. One surprising example is the provision for a required federal population census. While some type of local or national census would have been necessary to apportion the new U.S. House, requiring a U.S. census as part of the Constitution was an idea aggressively pressed by southern slaveholders seeking to insure that the South's growing white and black populations would be carefully counted for the purpose of increased *white* representation. In this way southern white elites would soon be able to counter the North's demographic dominance. Leading northern delegates, however, opposed the provisions for a regular national census in the Constitution, in part because the North then dominated in population and would have a majority in the Congress. When the census provision was passed, it guaranteed that a new government bureaucracy, the U.S. State Department (later, the Bureau of the Census), would do official counts. Soon after the U.S. government was created, in 1790, the Secretary of State used federal marshals to do a federal census of the country, which counted 3.9 million inhabitants. About one fifth were African Americans who were *not* citizens and thus had no political representation under the new U.S. Constitution.[10]

These careful federal population counts buttressed the Constitution's infamous three-fifths clause (often termed the "federal ratio"), which counted three-fifths of all enslaved African Americans for the purpose of expanding white political representation in the growing southern slave states. With their large enslaved populations in mind, the representatives of southern slaveholders at the constitutional convention operated out of a strong white master frame and insisted on carefully counting those enslaved and thereby got many extra members in the new Congress—and thus extra votes in the undemocratic electoral college that has chosen the U.S. president ever since.

Thomas Jefferson would not have become the third president of the United States without the extra twelve or so votes that he got in the electoral college because of the white electors who were there only because of the three-fifths counting of enslaved black Americans in southern states. Also, without these extra white members of Congress provided to southern whites by the three-fifths clause, numerous actions of Congress and presidents in the slavery era would have had different results. Slavery would have been banned in the new state of Missouri, the slaveholding President Andrew Jackson would have failed to pass his extreme 1830 Indian Removal Act, and the Kansas-Nebraska bill allowing residents to choose slavery in these midwestern areas would not have become law. The United States, thus, became a quite different country than it might have been because of the seven long decades of substantial slaveholders' control of our early U.S. political institutions.[11]

In addition, operating out of a strong white framing, these elite founders instituted a U.S. Senate, an antidemocratic political institution designed, as the slaveholding architect of the U.S. Constitution James Madison put it, "to protect the people against the transient impressions into which they themselves might be led." As a result, until the early twentieth century U.S. Senators were elected by state legislators, not directly by voters, and they have always served staggered six-year terms so they can serve longer than members of the more democratic U.S. House. This oligarchical U.S. Senate institution was critical to the protection of the racialized interests of slaveholders and white segregationists for most of U.S. history, from the 1790s to the 1970s. Southern senators frequently and openly articulated accentuated versions of the white racist frame for the general public and the polity, and, using antidemocratic Senate rules, were able to block *every* significant piece of anti-slavery legislation before the Civil War and every significant piece of civil rights legislation between the 1870s and the 1964 Civil Rights Act.[12]

Another undemocratic invention of the white framers is the U.S. Supreme Court. Intentionally created as an unelected body with little democratic overview, over time the Court has gained great unsupervised power, much of it legislative: "No other tribunal on earth rivals it. No other government reserves the last word for the judiciary to pronounce."[13] Consider too the racial demography of the Supreme Court over its history. For long periods a majority of Supreme Court justices were southern slaveholders or segregationists. As of 2009, a total of just 110 people, 108 men and 2 women, have ever served as powerful Supreme Court justices. More than *98 percent* have been white, and *96 percent* have been white men. Given this extremely biased demographic reality, the dominance of a strong patriarchal version of the white racial frame in many U.S. court decisions and in much U.S. law, now over more than two centuries, is certainly unsurprising. That dominant frame has long been central in decisions of the high court. Like the U.S. Senate, from the 1790s to the 1930s, the Supreme Court played a central and overt role in the maintenance of racial slavery and Jim Crow segregation for African Americans, as well as in the oppression of other Americans of color. In this long era, the high court usually rejected accounts of oppression and pleas for redress provided by African Americans in regard to slavery, segregation, and other racial oppression. The all-white-male justices in that era periodically made it clear that African Americans did *not* have any legitimate voice in

U.S. social and legal affairs. In the infamous 1856 *Dred Scott v. Sandford* decision the Court's slaveholding majority ruled that black Americans were, in the words of that chief justice, "beings of an inferior order, and altogether unfit to associate with the white race, either in social or political relations; and so far inferior that they had no rights which the white man was bound to respect."[14] A strong racist framing of black inferiority and white superiority was openly articulated by many Supreme Court and other federal judges for the next century, indeed into the 1950s and 1960s.

Another slavery-shaped feature of the U.S. Constitution and of numerous later Congressional actions and judicial decisions is the heavy accent on "state's rights," which emphasis has from the beginning been used to protect racial oppression—first slavery, then legal segregation, and now contemporary racial discrimination. For centuries now, whites in many areas have insisted on strong white-controlled local and state governments, and a relatively weak federal ability to intervene in local government matters. From the beginning, a major reason for this emphasis has been to insure that the federal government cannot interfere forcefully in most matters of white oppression of Americans of color.

The colonial and U.S. slavery system was a direct contradiction of the white liberty-and-justice frame in numerous ways, not the least of which was that major slaveholders would not allow majorities, even of white men, to have substantial power over their economic and political concerns, especially within southern and border states. Once the colonies had banded together in a federal union, these slaveholders, as Robin Einhorn has shown, came to understand that democratic governments at the local level could be a serious threat to slavery. For that reason, the slaveholding elite generally took control over state and local governments in areas where there were numerous enslaved Americans. In the early decades, the areas with little slavery were more likely to have *more democratic* local and state governments (still, usually for whites only) than those with substantial numbers of enslaved Americans. Furthermore, the states' rights and other anti-federal-government rhetoric that has long pervaded this country's legal and political debates is *rooted* in the interests of whites during the slavery and Jim Crow eras—and not just in idealistic conceptions of liberty from the white liberty-and-justice frame.[15] While there are other sources of contemporary anti-government rhetoric, a major early source was the fear of slaveholders and their segregationist descendants in more recent decades that federal agencies might interfere with their "freedom" to oppress and dominate Americans of color.

As noted previously, using the great power given to them by the three-fifths clause and other provisions of the U.S. Constitution, southern slaveholding interests effectively used the federal government to support their interests until 1860. In 1850, in one especially strong victory for slaveholders, Congress passed a Fugitive Slave Law, which slaveholders won only because of the federal ratio. Under this law, with yet more legitimation of slavery, a federal marshal could command any citizen to "aid and assist" in apprehending enslaved runaways. Such a provision for a federal "posse comitatus" was another support for what white southerners framed in their minds as a white slaveholding republic. From 1850 to 1865 such laws were used to *force* all white citizens, however they felt, to support slavery.[16]

The "founding fathers" created a U.S. origins narrative that was (and still is) substantially mythological, a story in which a mostly anti-democratic, often slaveholding, group of elite white men were said to be heroes championing ideals of equality and democracy for a new United States. These elite economic and political leaders created what social scientists call an *imagined community*, that is, a heralded "democratic" society in which all Americans supposedly shared real comradeship. However, contrary to this political mythology, the U.S. Constitution did *not* create a democracy where most people had the right to participate substantially and freely in political institutions. Native Americans and African Americans were completely excluded. As Vincent Harding has put it, the U.S. constitutional convention was "more like a poorly attended dress rehearsal, with most of the rightful and necessary performers and creators *barred from the stage*."[17]

From the beginning, this democratic rhetoric was more about public relations than about creating actual democratic social and political relationships. The new U.S. society was highly inegalitarian, with the extreme inequality across the entrenched color line. The new United States was mostly led by men who were overt white supremacists. It was a society that had *no* sense of shared comradeship among its white, black, and Native American residents. In 1843 no less a figure than former president John Quincy Adams asserted in a congressional speech that the United States had *never been a democracy* because it had long been controlled by a few thousand slaveholders.[18] These white-supremacist U.S. political institutions were openly proslavery and in full operation for the first seven decades of U.S. history, and an overtly white supremacist framing and dominance were regularly asserted by white leaders through these institutions until the end of Jim Crow segregation in the late 1960s.

Local Enforcement of Systemic Racism

Operating under the undemocratic Constitution, and under white-framed congressional and presidential actions flowing from it, white elites in slaveholding states enforced and extended the slavery system using local and state governments and private institutions. The abolitionist, Harriett

Beecher Stowe, famous for her anti-slavery novel *Uncle Tom's Cabin*, put together a nonfiction book with much evidence to support the accounts of brutal enslavement in her novel. In that second book she provides many examples showing the active and assertive role of southern white judges, ministers, and newspaper publishers in routinely protecting and extending that enslavement. As one historian has noted, "Slavery brutalized, made insensitive to the suffering of others not only the masses but judges and magistrates, legislators, professors of religion, preachers of Christianity, persons of property and members of the highest strata."[19] Most whites' capacity for empathy across the imposed color line withered with the rise of North America slavery—an essential condition for the dominance of the white racial frame among white Americans.

In her nonfiction book Stowe reprints many slaveholders' advertisements for enslaved runaways, in which references to scars and disabilities reveal how physically abused they were. These advertisements signal how well-organized and bureaucratized the slave-catching system was across many states. Stowe concludes from extensive research that the "legal power of the master amounts to an absolute despotism over body and soul; and that there is no protection for the slave's life and limb, his family relations, his conscience, nay, more his eternal interests, but the character of the master."[20] North American slavery was a "totalitarian" system, one that actually controlled and shaped all major aspects of the lives of African Americans (and some Native Americans) who were enslaved, as well as of those who were technically "free."

Significantly, Stowe does not spare the New England states in her criticism of racial oppression. The official, and slow, abolition of slavery there did not remove the

> most baneful feature of the system—that which makes American worse than Roman slavery—the prejudice of caste and color. In the New England States the negro [sic] has been treated as belonging to an inferior race of beings;—forced to sit apart by himself in the place of worship; his children excluded from the schools; himself excluded from the railroad car and the omnibus, and the peculiarities of his race made the subject of bitter contempt and ridicule.[21]

Indeed, these New England whites created the first Jim Crow segregation laws and customs that excluded African Americans from schools, juries, and voting. Even most antislavery organizations were internally segregated, with white northerners in top positions and few black northerners in significant positions. Moreover, in numerous northern areas whites tried to drive out local black residents by means of special settlement laws or tax laws, and sometimes by violently destroying their homes and businesses. In northern newspapers, as in southern newspapers, there was a recurring racial framing of black Americans as alien, lazy, or dangerous, stereotyped images that rationalized and facilitated the segregation or enslavement of black Americans in those areas. In northern and western areas, as in the South, most whites also held to the idea of the United States being a "white republic." For example, in the 1850s even the celebrated U.S. "poet of democracy," Walt Whitman, asked this rhetorical question aggressively from the white frame: "Is not America for Whites?"[22] Both racial oppression and the white frame were omnipresent across the relatively new United States.

Conclusion: The Persistence of Racial Oppression

A striking feature of systemic racism in the United States is how long it has persisted with a strikingly inegalitarian racial hierarchy firmly in place. A useful concept here is that of the *social reproduction* of this racial hierarchy. The perpetuation of this hierarchical system has required a constant reproducing of major inegalitarian institutions and their discriminatory arrangements and processes. For systemic racism to persist across many generations, white individuals and small groups have had to participate actively in the ongoing collective and discriminatory reproduction of the family, community, legal, political, economic, educational, and religious institutions that necessarily undergird this system.

Substantial inequality between white Americans and Americans of color has been routinely reproduced over the generations in these areas both by individual actions and by institutional forces. Most white Americans are not aware that a majority of white families today are relatively affluent because of large-scale federal assistance programs and giveaways—such as the 246 million acres of land given away almost exclusively to white families under federal homestead laws from the 1860s to the 1930s. Such *unjust enrichment* for whites has long meant *unjust* impoverishment for Americans of color. Over centuries the social relations of exploitation have created much income, wealth, social status, political power and privilege, and other racial capital for whites, which have in turn provided much racial capital for later generations of whites, indeed to the present day.

The deep structure of racial oppression and inequality has been relatively stable over time because its evolution has gradually ruled out other options as important societal choice points pass by. Still, the development of this deep structure has *not* been inevitable, but has been generated to a substantial degree by elite white choices at key points in time, choice points that have shaped the internal arrangement of its institutional parts and the patterned activities of the actors that constantly reinforce that arrangement. Our racist system exists because of the recurring actions of a great array of human actors, but especially those of powerful white actors. One revealing bias in many mainstream social science and humanities analyses of North American history is that, while they sometimes depict ordinary whites as racially prejudiced, they rarely discuss critically and in detail the actions of *elite* white actors that greatly shaped and maintained this country's system of racial oppression. Moreover, when they do deal with elite figures, most soften their language rather than discuss critically the bloody realities of their actions propping up the racist system.

The constant reinforcing decisions of these elite whites have perpetuated and reinforced the deep structure of U.S. racism through many reciprocal linkages and social feedback loops. The longer a system is in operation, the more ways its actors, especially its controlling actors, develop connecting relationships among themselves within major institutions, share important socioeconomic resources, and become skilled at maintaining our inegalitarian system. Even if obvious political barriers to significant change in our system of racial oppression can be overcome, there will still be the major problem of the interwoven relationships and greatly unequal resources of the powerful white actors—which have for centuries been constantly regenerated as part of the deep U.S. societal structure.[23]

In a society's history early social choice points are often the most important. In the case of systemic racism in North America, to cite a major example, the choice by elite whites to go with African American enslavement to create economic development and white wealth has had large-scale impacts ever since. The elite choice *not* to go with free labor, and the elite and rank-and-file whites' choices to kill off or drive out the indigenous Americans, have had profound longterm consequences for the racial structure of this society. Moreover, when the foundational reality of slavery could have been abandoned, around the time of the 1787 founding of the United States, most powerful white men in charge decided to go with the political and economic choice of greatly expanding the enslavement of African Americans, the large-scale slavery system, rather than to abandon it—in part, of course, to increase their own families' wealth.

Once these critical societal choices are made, the system of oppression has a strong *inertial* force keeping it in place. The first law of physical motion, the famous law of "inertia," asserts that an object at rest will continue at rest, or an object in motion will continue moving in one direction, until an unbalancing counter-force is exerted on it. Applying this to the social realm, one observes a very strong tendency for racial oppression's exploitative mechanisms, resource inequalities, norms, and buttressing attitudes to remain in force and substantially unchanged until a major unbalancing force challenges that oppression. However, the everyday operation of racial oppression, its routine and stable equilibrium, is only occasionally disrupted in a significant way. The racist system does sometimes change in order to meet important external shifts and environmental pressures, often significantly, but so far without altering much of its deep racist structure. Important societal turbulence over racial matters can make it seem like there is more social change that there really is, and thus disguise and hide the underlying deep structure from all but the most savvy observers.

Reacting to social turbulence, those whites in power prefer to make *ad hoc modifications*, rather than to significantly change the deep racial structure. For example, when U.S. slavery was finally abolished—in part because of great pressure from black and white abolitionists and much everyday resistance from those enslaved—elite white actors chose to keep as much of the old oppressive system in place as possible by moving to the near-slavery of Jim Crow segregation rather than to just abandon the racial oppression. When our system of racism does finally change somewhat, a "law of social inertia" seems to operate that keeps the society more like it was in the past than like the supposedly changed society that many often celebrate.

CHAPTER 3

Creating a White Racial Frame

The First Century

As European Christians spread out across the Atlantic world, in their minds and practices they usually positioned themselves socially and mentally higher than other peoples with whom they came into contact. They often saw themselves as exceptional, as "charged with a special spiritual and political destiny" whose task was to build a "New World" as a societal model for all Christians.[1] After developing an extensive colonial system involving land and labor theft across much of the Atlantic basin, the European colonizers worked hard to rationalize, explain, and structure in their minds and writings how it was that they, as "good and virtuous" Christians, could create and maintain such a violent and bloody system of human exploitation and subordination.

Rationalizing the destruction of indigenous peoples and enslavement of Africans in North America apparently seemed essential to the European colonizers. Because of the scale of their genocidal and enslaving actions over the next two centuries, their rationalizing and interpretative framing needed to be strong and comprehensive. Their written histories are useful for understanding this framing of what they did. In their writings colonialism and imperialism are rationalized by proto-racial thinking that from the beginning inclined the Spanish, English, and other European colonizers to dehumanize the "others" that they killed and enslaved as physically and culturally inferior. Their early framing soon became systematically racialized as a distinctive *white racial frame* because these Europeans seemed to need that framing to rationalize and interpret for themselves and others their extensive land and labor theft from indigenous peoples and their labor theft from Africans.

Central Elements of the Frame: The Great Chain of Being

Recall that European colonialism and oppression in North America brought a social stigmatization and denigration of those oppressed. Interestingly, the Europeans' early framing of the latter utilized the image-schema of an up-down ladder with its hierarchy of superior and inferior human groups. (An image-schema is a particular *image* feature of a mental frame that provides understandings of human experience.)[2] In their early group framing, thus, European colonists drew on an older European image-schema, a hierarchical pattern called the "great chain of being" that dates back to ancient Greek thinkers. This is a hierarchical conception of the "structure of the world which, through the Middle Ages and down to the late eighteenth century, many philosophers, most men of science, and, indeed, most educated men, were to accept without question." In this conception of the universe there is an

> infinite number of links ranging in hierarchical order from the meagerest kind of existence, which barely escapes nonexistence, through "every possible" grade up to ... the highest possible kind of creature, ... every one of them differing from that immediately above and that immediately below it by the "least possible" degree of difference.[3]

Long before the colonial era, European thinkers had put human beings at the top of creation because of their reasoning abilities. The higher up the chain of being, the more valued and human a group is, and the lower down, the less valued and human. The Western Christian church accented this cosmology, as it fit their view of a hierarchical society. Christians were firmly above non-Christians, aristocrats above ordinary people, and men above women. In this way a "folk theory" of a *natural* order is mapped onto a *moral* order. Persisting social inequalities are viewed as natural, legitimate, and moral. Prior to its use in framing non-European peoples, the great-chain-of-being frame was an integral part of European patriarchal thinking that placed men above women in the human hierarchy. When they imposed their colonial rule on indigenous and African peoples in North America, English colonizers already held a strong patriarchal frame and frequently used its family imagery in conceptualizing their new communities as legitimately under the control of European American "patriarchs."[4]

Consciously or unconsciously, Europeans and European Americans soon extended understandings from the old great chain of being model to prescribe and defend societal hierarchies in which they were dominant and in which non-European peoples were aggressively subordinated. Seeking to rationalize what they were doing, the European Christians leading the colonization of the Americas and Africa conceptualized and framed newly conquered non-Europeans as being at the bottom levels of this great chain of being, with Europeans and their colonial descendants clearly at the top. European *men* led these colonial efforts and thus created a legitimating societal frame that was also highly gendered. Thus, European colonialism involved a labor system with a division of labor and social status in which European American men were at the top, European American women well below, and indigenous people and African Americans were at the bottom. For several centuries following North American colonization, European missionaries, government officials, and soldiers imposed these Western views and hierarchical structures across the globe. The European male conquerors were "superior," "powerful," and "manly," while the subordinated peoples, male and female, were "inferior," "weak," and "childlike." Indeed, in this great-chain thinking we already see the close relationships, the intersections, between racial and gender framing by European and European American men.[5]

Early Racial Framing of Native Americans and African Americans

Scholars have debated whether the earliest English and other European colonizers' views of Native Americans and African Americans were "racial" in a contemporary sense. Some have argued that using the idea of "race" here reads back into past history contemporary racial ideas and that the early colonists identified themselves mainly in terms of national identity and religion.[6]

Yet other analysts, however, have shown from data like that presented later in this chapter that the essential ingredients of the modern racial frame did in fact exist in the earliest English American perspective on Native Americans, Africans, and African Americans. Among the important ingredients of this frame are (1) the recurring use of physical characteristics, such as skin color and facial features, to differentiate social groups; (2) the constant linking of physical characteristics to cultural characteristics; and (3) the regular use of physical and linked cultural distinctions to differentiate socially "superior" and "inferior" groups. These frame features are to be found in the earliest colonial thought among the European colonizers, as can be seen in their early tracts, laws, and sermons. Moreover, once these social distinctions of superior and inferior group membership were firmly in place, they served to justify concentrating an array of material and other resources in the hands of the supposedly superior group. The operation of this frame, thus, is clearly to be seen in the everyday practices of European Americans that actively dehumanized Native Americans and African Americans.

To prevent confusion, thus, I will refer to this rationalizing and interpretive European frame in the early seventeenth century as *racial*, though some readers may prefer to consider it to be just *proto-racial* until the last decades of the seventeenth century, when the dominant frame was even more explicitly racialized.[7]

In the first decades of the colonizing invasions, the European master framing of Native Americans and African Americans was already being developed. Each outgroup that was central to capital accumulation in Europe's colonizing expansion was denigrated. Almost immediately, the English American colonists made great use of physical and biological markers in defining and oppressing "Indians" and "Negroes," both labels they borrowed from the Spanish language of earlier European invaders of the Americas. Those subordinated were colorized and biologized, with skin color and other physical features very negatively characterized and connected to their low position at the bottom levels of the great chain of being. These views were, from the beginning, much more than cognitive, for they involved very strong negative images and emotions. The colonists put European Americans as fully human beings at the top of that great-chain-of-being hierarchy, with African Americans and Native Americans as less than fully human at the bottom. Religious-cultural and physical-biological interpretations coexisted, although religion got more emphasis at the early stage and the biological/physical aspect got more attention, and was explicitly named as "race" by the late 1600s. The major defining dimensions of the European American racial frame were already in place by the early decades of the 1600s, albeit dimensions that became ever more systematized over the next century.[8]

Interestingly, today many scholars argue that in the United States racist thinking accenting the biological/physical dimension has been largely replaced by racist thinking accenting the cultural dimension, as though the latter emphasis is relatively new. However, negative biologically-oriented thinking about the oppressed others and negative culturally-oriented thinking about them have been closely linked from at least the early 1600s. From the beginning of this country, European Americans have merged cultural, moral, and physical factors in their minds, both for themselves and for outgroups they have routinely subordinated.

Early Framing of Indigenous Peoples

Conceptions of the "others" encountered and used in the European colonial expansion varied with their utility for European colonizers. In their colonial conquests in Central and South America, the early Spanish conquerors defined and viewed the indigenous peoples as inferior "Indians" and "natural slaves, as subhuman beasts of burden," for that is what the Spanish needed them to be.[9] Columbus himself recorded many details about the lives of the indigenous peoples of the Caribbean islands on which he landed, as he and his men proceeded to subordinate, enslave, and kill them in the thousands. Over their centuries of colonization of the Caribbean, Central America, South America, and parts of North America, the Spanish sought indigenous peoples' lands and labor and in the process brought genocidal wars, enslavement, and European diseases that killed tens of millions of the indigenous inhabitants, evidently the largest "holocaust" in human history.

In North America, in contrast later English colonizers and their descendants were much less interested in using Indians as enslaved laborers, although they did enslave some for a time. The English colonists were mainly interested in stealing the lands of the indigenous peoples. Prior to their arrival, the English colonizers knew little about the "Indians," except what they had gained from Spanish colonizers' writings. The Spanish influence can be seen in the Spanish-derived English words "Indian" and "Negro" (black). As early as 1646, one puzzled indigenous inhabitant of North America asked the English missionary John Eliot, "Why do you call us Indians?"[10] The English had borrowed this term from the Spanish "los indios," one indicating that early Spanish colonizers' had thought they were near Asia. In addition, these English umbrella-type words, "Indian" and "Negro," indicate that the early European colonists often saw few differences among the many indigenous American groups and the many African groups that they had encountered and oppressed. They lumped these culturally diverse groups together into these broad umbrella categories. Such categorizing suggests too that a prototypical visual image and associated set of stereotypes had already become part of early European American framing of those oppressed.

Significantly, most English colonists early defined indigenous Americans as the uncivilized enemy, and wars with the Native Americans who resisted the invasion were important in accenting the sense of European cultural and physical distinctiveness. In the early 1600s the English colonists' framing of "Indians" grew out of a rationalization of warfare with them and of the taking of their land. The first English colony was established on Roanoke Island, off what became the colony of Virginia. English commentaries from this era indicate a variable, even schizophrenic, view of indigenous Americans. The early colonizer Arthur Barlowe landed in this area in 1584, claimed it for "her highness," and penned this account of indigenous people:

> We were entertained with all love and kindness and with as much bounty, after their manner, as they could possibly devise. We found the people most gentle loving and faithful, void of all guile and treason, and such as lived after the manner of the Golden Age. . . . A more kind and loving people, there can not be found in the world, as farre as we have hithertoo had triall.

Soon thereafter, however, the English colonizers attacked these gentle people because they were, as Robert Gray described them, "wild beasts, and unreasonable creatures" or "brutish savages." Moreover, they were not Christians and "worshipped the devil." Thus, as Barlowe recounted, "we burnt, and spoyled their corne, and Towne, all the people beeing fledde."[11]

Thinking in military terms, those who founded the Roanoke colony reported back to England that the indigenous people there were scared of English weaponry and could easily be conquered. "Indian" and "savage" were the most common terms applied to indigenous peoples by these early English colonists, although they also used "infidel," "heathen," and "barbarian," all terms revealing the significant religious dimension of the early framing of indigenous peoples, one that has lasted to the present day.[12] Color and physical characteristics got some attention, but seem less significant in this very early English American framing of Native Americans than in their framing of African Americans—a differentiating tendency that would persist over subsequent centuries.

Later English colonists also wrote of their mostly negative views of indigenous peoples. At Jamestown, Virginia, the celebrated Captain John Smith viewed indigenous groups as uncivilized "savages" and "inconstant in everie thing" and "craftie, timerous . . . very ingenuous." Thus, Smith made it clear that he did not trust the "craftie" indigenous groups that dominated the area at this time. In 1613 the English minister Alexander Whitaker described them as "barbarous people," "naked slaves of the divell," yet still as "industrious in their labour." In 1625 Samuel Purchas described them as "having little of humanitie but shape, ignorant of Civilitie, of Arts, of Religion; moree brutish than the beasts they hunt . . . captivated also to Satans tyrallny in foolish pieties, wicked idlenesse, busie and bloudy wickednesse." In these commentaries we again see the early European framing of Indians as uncivilized, unchristian, and beast-like. Interestingly, a few decades later in 1651, the leading English philosopher Thomas Hobbes would point to the "savage people in many places of

America" as examples of those whose lives are, in his famous phrase, "poore, nasty, brutish, and short."[13] Of course, their shortened and impoverished lives were often the result of the English invasions and military attacks.

The leaders of the Massachusetts colony to the north operated out of a similar imperialistic frame that led them to speak of North America as "unpeopled" and to destroy indigenous communities to secure more land. Indians were constantly referred to as the "common enemy."[14] Much colonial language described the Indians as "wild beasts" who should be "removed from their dens" and killed. As one historian notes, "In times of trouble natives were always wild animals that had to be rooted out of their dens, swamps, jungles."[15] Here we see another important dimension of early European framing of the "other," one that animalized them and thereby placed them well down the great-chain-of-being hierarchy. Significantly, in 1637 one dissenting New England colonist, Thomas Morton, wrote disapprovingly of this colonial framing of Indians in his book *New England Canaan.* He described the "new creed" of his fellow European colonists as holding that the "Salvages [savages] are a dangerous people, subtill, secreat and mischeivous." Morton did not agree: "I have found the Massachusetts Indian more full of humanity then the Christians."[16] A major dissenter from the hostile Eurocentric framing of Indians, Morton himself was persecuted and hounded out of the New England colony for his views and close relationships with Indians.

As we see in most of these English commentaries, the powerful European frame not only focused on the subordinated "others," usually negatively, but also on the oppressors themselves, usually very positively. From the beginning, this dominant frame was not only unidirectional but also quite emotion-laden: The "others" are portrayed negatively and are mainly to blame for intergroup problems, while whites are portrayed as virtuous and rarely to blame for intergroup problems.

At an early point in North American colonization, the dominant framing accented the view that European Americans were "virtuous republicans," to use Ronald Takaki's phrase. Spanish, English, and other European conquerors initially rationalized the oppression of indigenous peoples in Christian theological terms. Early European American colonists' framing of the new society portrayed themselves as rational, ascetic, civilized, and sexually controlled, while Native Americans and African Americans were stereotyped as irrational, hedonistic, uncivilized, and oversexed. Recent researchers have demonstrated the religiously repressed nature of many European colonists, with their obsessive fears of the "dark others," the irrational and unvirtuous non-European peoples who were thought to be the opposite of Europeans. The European Americans who saw themselves as virtuous republicans increasingly resented what they had given up, and thus portrayed Native Americans and African Americans in terms of the things they had given up. The European American thus created a "pornography of his former life. . . . in order to insure that he will not slip back into the old ways or act our half-supposed fantasies."[17] Clearly, there is strong counterpoint thinking here: "The Indian became important for the English mind not for what he was in and of himself, but rather for what he showed civilized men they were not and must not become."[18]

Note here the central importance of the European American notion that it is the "others" who are irrational and emotional. In this view rationality equals emotionlessness, and irrationality equals emotionality. Yet, from the beginning to the present, European Americans' fears, angers, and jealousies about other racial groups have signaled their own powerful and often destructive *emotions*, no matter how much they attempt to repress a consideration of them.

Early Framing of African Americans

Before the colonizing of North America, early European travelers to Africa had returned to northern Europe with views accenting some positive features of Africa and Africans, but also citing what they viewed as their ugly, unchristian, and uncivilized character, the latter two views much like those Europeans had of indigenous Americans. Sexual imagery played a role in early European views as well. For example, just prior to the American colonial era early English mapmakers put images on their maps that would become ever more central in later white racial framing, such as images of large genitals on black male and female figures placed onto their maps. However, as one sees in the sympathetic Othello (African) character in William Shakespeare's 1603 play *Othello*, by the time of English colonization of North America in the early 1600s there was still ambiguity in English views of people of African descent. A fully developed negative inferiorization of Africans did not develop until later, with the colonization of North America.[19]

The first twenty Africans imported into the new colonies were purchased off a Dutch-flagged ship with "victuals" (foodstuffs) by the European colonists at Jamestown, Virginia, in 1619. Their labor became so valuable that the numbers of those enslaved grew rapidly over the next century. By 1650 there were 300 African Americans in Virginia; by 1700, about 6,000; and by the time of the revolution in 1770s about 270,000, nearly half that largest North American colony's total population. In the first two decades of colonial development the early Africans bought off slave ships were sometimes enslaved for life and at other times treated by the colonists more like indentured servants. However, while some were freed after long terms of service in the earliest decades, by the 1660s most were enslaved for life. Indeed, at an early point in time, English servants in the colonies are recorded as insisting that they cannot and should not be made into "slaves" by their masters or political authorities, an argument signaling they saw early on slavery as something only non-Europeans should endure.[20]

Most importantly, even in these earliest decades the social position of the "Negro" workers was *never* equal to that of the European American indentured servants. The sense of European superiority and Negro inferiority is in the legal and other colonial records from the beginning. Early European comments on the dark color of African Americans appear in the comments of Captain John Smith on those first twenty Africans (he called them "negars") imported at Jamestown in 1619, as well as in court decisions and legal statutes soon after that date in the large colonies of Virginia and Massachusetts. As early as 1624, colonial court cases were making it clear that people of African ancestry were framed as socially inferior and physically distinctive in a negative way. The first court reference to a "negro" was in a 1624 court proceeding, when the Council and General Court of Virginia mentioned a certain "John Philip, A negro . . . Christened in England 12 years since," who testified in a court case against an English colonist. Imposed inferiority was clear in European colonists' framing of a man as "negro," a physical color-coded name (from the Spanish for black) and identity assigned to him by the English colonists and not chosen by him or other African Americans. Indeed, the color-coded identity of none of the other trial participants is mentioned in the legal account. That account explicitly indicates that Philip was a Christian, which meant that he had more legitimacy in European eyes. If a negative framing of black Americans as inferior had not already been in place, neither "negro" not "christened" would have been relevant to mention.[21]

Just six years later, in another Virginia case, an Englishman who was found "lying with a negro" was condemned to be whipped "before an assembly of negroes & others for abusing himself to the dishonor of God and shame of Christianity." The man in question, Hugh Davis, was viewed by the court as having defiled himself with someone viewed as physically inferior and thus was punished before African Americans and others. A "negro" woman's inferiority is here clearly and officially indicated, perhaps for the first time in North American history. In another example, an English colonist who had sexual relations with a "negro" was punished for "dishonoring" God by doing public penance in a church. Such forbidden sexual relations were thereby framed as a religious violation. In their laws and court decisions early European colonists made clear their concern, indeed obsession, with intergroup sexual relationships. Strong emotions are also evident in early laws against intergroup sex and marriage, with both considered to be "unnatural" and "abominable." For example, in 1662 Virginia established the first law officially banning interracial sex, and in 1691 a law against interracial marriage was enforced by banishment from the colony. Again, we see the ways in which these early English colonists saw themselves as virtuous and those they oppressed as venal; we also observe a certain repressed sexuality as well.[22]

Laws passed in colonies farther south indicate a similar framing of those enslaved. In a 1690s preamble to a South Carolina colony's slavery law the elite white lawmakers comment on those enslaved: They "are of barbarous, wild, savage natures, and . . . constitutions, laws and orders, should in this Province be made and enacted, for the good regulating and ordering of them, as may restrain the disorders, rapines and inhumanity, to which they are naturally prone and inclined. . . ."[23] Here again the terms "barbarous, wild, savage" serve a double purpose. They not only conjure up notions of African Americans as uncivilized, the early cultural stereotyping, but also views of the latter as dangerous, rebellious, and criminal, a distinctive legal and moral stereotyping relating to emotional white concerns about African Americans rebelling against enslavement, against good "laws and orders." Notice too the clear biological implications of the language of "natures" and "natural." Once again, we see significant similarities in the European American framing of African Americans and Native Americans.

These early legal and political examples reveal that all European colonists, no matter how lowly their social positions, were considered superior to African Americans and were regularly treated as such by laws and political action. As a leading expert on early colonial law, Leon Higginbotham, has shown, the colonial court cases reveal how the concepts of group inferiority and superiority were early and firmly established: make clear English superiority and "negro" inferiority in all things social, punish in public those who violate these understandings, and rationalize these understandings using a strong social framing that accents both physical (color) notions and Christian religious ideas.[24]

Africans and African Americans were early viewed in colonial laws and in other ways as the *personal property* of European Americans. Their large-scale enslavement was rationalized as part of ordinary colonial commerce. European American lawyers, judges, and other high officials did much to create this dehumanized framing of African Americans. Thus, a 1669 Virginia statute asserted it was not a felony for a master to kill an enslaved African American who was stubborn, for that was only a matter of property. In 1671 the General Assembly of Virginia declared that sheep, horses, cattle, and Negroes could be inherited by a white orphan. European Americans framed those enslaved as "ordinary merchandise" and the "personal property" of owners who bought and sold them in the often well-organized colonial markets.[25]

In the first century of colonial development we observe the important naming process that was associated with the growing white racial frame. For example, in 1680 the prominent minister Morgan Godwyn, who lived in Barbados and Virginia, concluded that "these two words, Negro and Slave . . . [are] by custom grown Homogeneous and Convertible; even as Negro and Christian, Englishman and Heathen, are by the like corrupt Custom and Partiality made Opposites."[26] This was certainly the view of established colonial law by this time. (Later on, writing in the mid-eighteenth century, Quaker leader John Woolman similarly pointed out that "whites" of the "meanest sort" would never be enslaved and accented the role of color in whites' enslavement of black Americans: "This is owing chiefly to the idea of slavery being connected with the black colour, and liberty with the white: and where false ideas are twisted into our minds, it is with difficulty we get fairly disentangled.")[27] Not only were the words "Negro" or "black" already in the mid-seventeenth century synonymous with "slave," but the white framemakers had imposed a new sociocultural identity on the culturally diverse Africans. Older sociocultural identities of Africans were partially or totally destroyed by this imposition of an oppressed situation and identity within what was effectively a totalitarian system.

Early European colonists also called those of African descent "negars," "mulattos," and "Moors," in all cases accenting them as physically distinctive and racialized. From 1619 onward the physical features, especially the black "complexion," of African Americans was an increasing obsession in European colonists' minds and in those of their descendants. In 1676 one colonial commentary, thus, insisted that a "blackamoore" was not physically beautiful; and in 1680, Godwyn, the English minister, wrote a pamphlet on slavery in which he noted the importance of skin color: ". . . their Complexion, which being most obvious to the sight . . . is apt to make no slight impressions upon rude Minds."[28] In addition, with more lighter skinned, multiracial African Americans appearing in the last decades of the seventeenth century, whites' framing of African Americans soon adopted the infamous "one drop of blood" rule. All children with any obvious (to whites) African ancestry inherited a parent's condition of racial inferiority, for "God had made them inferior." All black Americans of any shade were thus viewed from the dominant group's framing of them as dark and ungodly.[29]

In contrast, the earliest references to the European colonists are to "Englishmen," "Irish," "Scotch," "Christians," or just "men" and "persons." The term "white" as a color designation for European traders and colonists was in occasional use before the English developed the North American colonies, but its regular use comes only in the later decades of the seventeenth century. Moreover, in the English language of the colonists, prior to the development of African American enslavement, the word "white" had uses that were mostly positive, such as "gleaming brightly," as for a candle, while the word "black" had mostly negative meanings like "sooted." The word "black" had long been used by the residents of England metaphorically, to describe evil and the devil. It was soon adopted by the early English colonists for the purpose of naming dark-skinned Africans.[30]

Over this first century of colonization, legal statutes reveal an increasing use of the word "white" for English Americans, as in this 1691 Virginia law: "whatsoever English or other white man or women ... shall intermarry with a Negro, mulatto, or Indian man or woman ... shall ... be banished from this dominion forever."[31] Both "white" and "black" were not temporary or unattached words, for they were defined and delimited within the ever growing white racial frame. In its racial usage the word "white" was mainly conceptualized in contrast to the word "black"—initially and most powerfully by those who defined themselves as "white." These English language developments were a clear indication of the thorough institutionalization of African American slavery and of its racialized rationalization. Increasingly, the word white defined who European Americans were, and who they were not. Whiteness was indeed a "terrible invention," as W. E. B. Du Bois once put it, one that further solidified European thinking into an extensive either/or framework and that came to symbolize for whites civilization and the "ownership of the earth." While some contemporary analysts view the accentuated solidarity of North American whites as being a more recent social invention—perhaps only after the Civil War—whites were in fact already a distinctive racial group with shared cultural heritage and in a clear racial hierarchy no later than the mid-seventeenth century.[32]

Who Made the Broad Racial Frame, and How?

Numerous scholars and popular analysts have viewed the concept of "race" as "a folk classification, a product of popular beliefs about human differences." Certainly, the thinking of ordinary European Americans about Native and African Americans became increasingly racialized over the course of the seventeenth century, but much of the development and propagation of that racist framing came from the European American leaders in the new society. While most people at all social levels have used racialized categories in sorting out and shaping their everyday experiences, as we have just observed, the elite white leaders such as judges, ministers, merchants, doctors, slaveholders, and government officials have generally been the most important figures in developing, codifying, and propagating strong social categorizations such as that described by the term "race." Since at least the mid-1600s a powerful racial framing has been explicitly, actively, and profoundly shaped by the ruling elite, an elite that has created and consistently communicated this important framing by means of schools, churches, the legal system, and the mass media. As anti-Indian genocide and African American enslavement became ever more important in North American development, European and European American elites aggressively crafted and honed a well-developed white racial frame designed to defend overseas colonialism and imperialism.

European and European American scientists played an important role in shifting the old great-chain-of-being view from a theologically oriented hierarchy with God at the top to a more secular hierarchy that accented "species" or "races" of human beings. Already, by the mid-1600s, these scientists and their associates were designating and writing about dominant and subordinated groups in colonial areas as different "species," which were viewed as part of a natural order to be investigated by the sciences. They were among the first to use the word "race" in English, a word which they borrowed from the Spanish word "raza." In its earliest usage the English word "race" was employed in various ways to classify people and animals, but one of its important uses was for breeding groups and stocks, with a clear linkage to inheritable traits.[33]

By the 1660s and 1670s British, French, and North American thinkers had laid the groundwork for a strong concept of a hierarchy of biologically distinctive "races," which has persisted over the centuries since. Central to this effort in the 1670s was England's Sir William Petty, a leading anatomist, economist, and philosopher. Petty viewed and named "blacks" as physically and culturally inferior to "whites." Drawing on English and other European travelers' and colonists' accounts of the Americas and Africa for data, he began a manuscript on the "scale of creatures" and accented hierarchical gradations among human beings. He speculated that there were unchangeable human "species" or "races" that were breeding groups and were characterized by physical and sociocultural differences. Petty asserted that the Africans who live near the Cape of Good Hope were the most "beastlike" of all the "men with whom our travelers are well acquainted."[34]

The notion of people of African descent being "beast-like" and lower on the "race" hierarchy than people of European descent was a notion that clearly predated Perry, but he was apparently the first to enumerate the array of physical differences in a very detailed way:

I say that the Europeans do not only differ from the aforementioned Africans in color, which is as much as white differs from black, but also in their hair which differs as much as a straight line differs from a circle; but they differ also in the shape of their noses, lips and cheek bones, as also in the very outline of their faces and the mould of their skulls. They differ also in their natural manners, and in the internal qualities of their minds.[35]

Even at this early point in the elite shaping of the white racial frame, the influential Petty, a charter member of the English Royal Society, emphasized much that has persisted in that frame since his time—major physical differences in color, hair, nose and lip shape, facial and skull differences, as well as the concepts and words "white" and "black" for categorizing the groups involved. In addition, like later white analysts, Perry accented intellectual ("qualities of their minds") and cultural characteristics ("natural manners") that he and other English observers then assumed to be closely associated with the distinctive physical characteristics.

A few years earlier in 1665, a summary of the conclusions of French scientists and thinkers about "Negroes" had been published in English, and Perry may have made use of it. Drawing on French experience with Caribbean slave plantations, this scientific account similarly accented certain physical characteristics:

And to shew that the tincture of the skin is not the only particularity observable in Negroes, they have many other Properties whereby they are distinguish'd from other Nations; as their thick lips, saddle-noses, coarse short hair, the horny tunicle of the eye, and the teeth whiter than the rest of men.

The French statement accents strong stereotypes about the mental capacities of Negroes:

Not to mention the Qualities of their minds, which are so ignorant, that though they have plenty of Flax, yet they want Cloth, because they want skill how to work it; they abound with Sugar-canes, yet make no trade of them, and esteem Copper more than Gold, which they barter for the like weight of Salt; and are wholly ignorant of Laws and Physick. Which ignorance renders their spirits more base and servile than those of other Nations; and they are so born to slavery.[36]

In addition, in the 1680s the prominent French scientist, Francis Bernier, was apparently the first to come up with a sorting out of human beings into four differentiated race-like categories: Europeans, Far Easterners, Negroes, and Lapps.

In the last few decades of the 1600s, thus, important members of the British and French scientific elites were accenting an array of physical, mental, and cultural distinctions that differentiated in their minds people of European and African ancestry. In their racial framing they drew on reports from travelers and colonists in North America, and the latter colonists were in turn influenced by this elite thinking as it percolated through their colonial ministers and officials.

Establishing the Racial Frame: The First American Treatises

In this same era the educated white elite of North America was beginning to draft longer treatises that articulated even more clearly the white racial framing of society that had already appeared briefly in the commentaries of judges in early colonial court cases. Let us examine two treatises, one against and one for slavery, by prominent New England judges and entre-preneurs. Their views of African Americans reveal that a strong and well-developed white racial frame was firmly in place in North America by the late seventeenth century.

Very few accounts of the racial views of white colonial leaders and intellectuals have survived from the early eighteenth century, but there are two that are particularly revealing and illustrative. In his 1700 treat-ise, *The Selling of Joseph*, the successful business leader and prominent Massachusetts judge, Samuel Sewall, wrote what was apparently the first attack on slavery by a white American. Citing biblical sources and using human rights language in arguing against slavery, Sewall asserted that, "And all things considered, it would conduce more to the Welfare of the Province, to have White Servants for a Term of Years, than to have [Black] Slaves for Life." In spite of these anti-slavery views, however, Sewall viewed African Americans from a strong white racial frame. He argued that few whites

> can endure to hear of a Negro's being made free; and indeed they can seldom use their freedom well; yet their continual aspiring after their forbidden Liberty, renders them Unwilling Servants. And there is such a disparity in their Conditions, Colour & Hair, that they can never embody with us, and grow up into orderly Families, to the Peopling of the Land: but still remain in our Body Politick as a kind of extravasat Blood.

He later adds:

> Moreover it is too well known what Temptations Masters are under, to connive at the Fornication of their Slaves; lest they should be obliged to find them wives, or pay their Fines. It seems to be practically pleaded that they might be Lawless; 'tis thought much of,

that the law should have Satisfaction for their Thefts, and other Immoralities.[37]

Clearly, the reality of slavery had a great shaping impact on the general worldview of leading white figures early in our colonial history. In these revealing comments from a prominent judge and business leader we observe much about the importance of slavery, even in New England. (About 1715, a full fifth of all those enslaved in the colonies were in the North.) Slavery is important enough in the northern colonies to motivate Judge Sewall to write a pamphlet attacking it. As he continues, however, we see key elements of the white racial frame. He too accents physical differences—especially skin color, hair type, and "blood." We observe the view, shared by Sewall and by slavery supporters as well, that freed African Americans do not "use their freedom well," do not have "orderly families," and are prone to "thefts and other immoralities." Even this white opponent of slavery has trouble understanding how difficult life is for black Americans who are free, or might become free, for they obviously do not have the same resources as better-off whites. Like Thomas Jefferson some decades later, Judge Sewall cannot envision the full social integration of black Americans into the "body" of white America. His inability or unwillingness to analyze the oppressive structural conditions in which African Americans then lived can be seen in the deceptive way ("temptations masters are under") he raised the issue of sexual relations forced by white men onto enslaved black women. From the beginning, this suggests, systemic racism involved gendered racial oppression.

Angered by this anti-slavery pamphlet prepared by Judge Sewall, the Boston merchant, slave trader, and judge on the same court as Sewall, John Saffin, decided a few months later to reply. Also citing biblical passages to support his inegalitarian view of naturally "diffcrent Orders and Degrees of Men in the World," Saffin defended the institution of slavery vigorously and concluded with a vicious poem, "The Negroes' Character," apparently the first anti-black poem in North American history. Saffin attacked the character of black Americans in much the same way that the white frame does today.

> Cowardly and cruel are those Blacks Innate,
> Prone to Revenge, Imp of inveterate hate.
> He that exasperates them, soon espies
> Mischief and murder in their very eyes.
> Libidinous, Deceitful, False and Rude,
> The Spume Issue of the Ingratitude.
> The Premeses consider'd, all may tell,
> How near good Joseph they are parallel. . . .[38]

In this early and strong racial framing, Saffin sounds much like his abolitionist colleague Sewall. He asserted that "blacks" were innately "cowardly and cruel," were "prone to revenge," often have "mischief and murder in their very eyes," hold "inveterate hate," are "libidinous, deceitful, false, and rude," and ungrateful. Saffin, of course, is aggressively and unreflectively rationalizing his legal right to be a slave trader, that is, to take property in black bodies for his own profit. Just in these relatively brief excerpts from the minds of two New England business leaders and judges, we observe key elements of the persisting white racial frame: a heavy accent on physical distinctiveness and strong stereotypes and images of black immorality and crime, family disorganization, cruelty, hate, deceit, and sexuality. Most of these early white stereotypes, images, and interpretations are still part of the modern white racial framing.

Moreover, in the aforementioned treatises by Sewall and Saffin, as well as in some of the colonial court cases, we see that the racial framing of African Americans was religiously sanctioned and circulated broadly to rank-and-file citizens by leading officials in this relatively new country. Very important in this regard were prominent New England ministers like Cotton Mather and Jonathan Edwards, who were among the earliest North American intellectuals to aggressively defend the racist hierarchy. Like other colonists, they viewed African Americans and Indians as inferior and uncivilized. In a 1706 treatise, thus, Cotton Mather argued that whites should try to "Christianize Negroes" in order to save their souls as well as those of their slavemasters. Christianizing Negroes, whom he describes as "creatures" and "barbarians," will make them willing to work harder for their slavemasters and keep them from "magical conversations" with the devil. Mather commented thus:

> What shall I do that this poor creature may have cause to bless God forever, for falling into my hands. The state of your Negroes in this world, must be low, and mean and abject; a state of servitude. No great things in this world, can be done for them. Something then, let there be done, towards their welfare in the world to come.[39]

He then added that those enslaved should be treated as "thy neighbours." This influential religious leader accepted slavery as God-ordained and necessary for African Americans because they were lowly, "brutish," and "stupid" creatures. He viewed a Christianizing education as enabling Negroes to become "men" and not be "beasts."[40] At an early stage, this powerful rationalizing frame was insisted upon by colonial economic, legal, political, and religious elites—men who actively fostered the increasingly omnipresent racial framing by means of communications in white-controlled churches, schools, and newspapers.

In these comments from New England judges and ministers, we see once again that the early racial frame had strong visual, visceral, and emotional dimensions. There were numerous other examples of how complex and detailed this early framing was. For example, writing in the early 1700s, Edward Long, a Jamaican slaveholder whose writings were read in the North American colonies, accented not only the "natural sloth" but also the "bestial or fetid smell" of enslaved Africans. His writings indicate that stereotypes of odor were another part of the early frame. Like Thomas Jefferson later in this same century, Long also viewed those enslaved as close to apes in intelligence and behavior and propagated stories of their having "amorous intercourse" with apes.[41]

White leaders throughout the colonies seem to have held a similarly positive framing of whites and a similarly negative framing of African Americans and Native Americans. Consider Quaker Pennsylvania, the colony where many whites reportedly were opposed to slavery. This colony's treatment of free black Americans made clear how central the white racial frame was there. White officials in Pennsylvania made certain that the officially "free" black Americans there faced severe laws prohibiting such activities as intermarriage and "loitering" (unemployment), for which the punishment was enslavement or reenslavement. While black Pennsylvanians were not numerous enough to present an economic threat to whites, they still were often stereotyped as lazy, criminal, and a physical threat to white women. Here as elsewhere, according to Leon Higginbotham's pioneering research, African Americans also "constituted a psychological challenge to the status of free whites; the greater number of free blacks and the higher their status, the more their presence undermined the status of the general white population."[42]

Unfortunately, assessments of ordinary whites' views of African Americans and Native Americans in this era have to be made mostly on the basis of official laws and public events in newspapers, for we have very few surviving records that directly indicate the views of ordinary whites. There is one 1684 report that has a brief quote purported to be the language used by white plantation overseers for their enslaved workers: "Dam'd doggs, Black ugly Devils, idle Sons of Ethiopian Whores."[43] Even in this fragmentary excerpt we have clear references to an ugly color, devil-like character and idleness, and oversexed women—all emotion-laden stereotypes suggesting that rank-and-file whites shared with the white elite a common racial framing of African Americans.

Summary: Anti-black Framing

Strikingly, the anti-black subframe of the dominant white racial frame was fully in place by 1700, as we have seen in these important commentaries by white scientists, intellectuals, ministers, and other leaders writing between the 1660s and the early 1700s. These white elites are the ones, most centrally, who polished, established, proclaimed, and circulated this white racial frame to the larger population, which in turn used the ideas in their own ways. These elite white commentaries focus on at least these major emotion-laden stereotypes and images of black Americans, who are alleged

1. to have distinctive color, hair, and lips;
2. to be bestial and apelike;
3. to be unintelligent;
4. to have a disagreeable smell;
5. to be uncivilized, alien, and foreign;
6. to be immoral, criminal, and dangerous;
7. to be lazy;
8. to be oversexed;
9. to be ungrateful and rebellious;
10. to have disorganized families.

In the white mind the first four emotion-laden and stereotyped images are thought to be about black Americans' physical and biological character, whereas numbers five through ten are thought to be about their deviant culture and moral character. Collectively, they rationalize the theft of black labor and the brutalities of enslavement. Early on, black Americans are viewed by whites as very different and "unvirtuous Americans." In each case, whites have long viewed themselves as the opposite, as good-looking physically, intelligent, and culturally and morally superior, as the "virtuous Americans." Given these dimensions of their racial framing, whites routinely viewed African Americans as "problematical" for the white-dominated society.

Conclusion

One important question that arises in thinking about this early racial framing is, Why is there such a heavy white focus on just one group, that is, on African Americans? Many categorizations that people make in their important interpretative frames utilize prototypes, that is, they feature a *primary example* for each major category. From the beginning, the white racial frame has made the prototypical "superior" racial group to be white American and the prototypical "inferior" racial group to be black

American. In developing the white racial frame, whites early focused it on black Americans, which is the main reason that they remain central to that frame today, a centrality some call "black exceptionalism."

One reason for this centrality is that African Americans' time of experience with white oppression is the longest for any North American racial group except Native Americans. African Americans constitute the only large immigrant group brought in chains, and they have had the longest history of racial oppression *within* this country's white-controlled economy and polity. Certainly, Native Americans have suffered great oppression at the hands of whites for at least as long a period, but have not been as central to white racial framing and to large-scale labor exploitation *within* white society. From the first decades black Americans have been at the core of the racist system because they are the group whose incorporation and subjugation have been given the greatest attention *by whites*. Whites have devoted enormous amounts of energy to oppressing African Americans—initially for their wealth-creating labor and later for a range of other economic, social, and ideological reasons as well. Indeed, in the Civil War many thousands of southern whites gave their lives, at least in part, to maintain this central oppression of African Americans. In contrast, whites on the whole have put less time and physical and mental energy into exploiting and oppressing other immigrant groups of color, if only because the latter have been in this country in large numbers for much shorter periods of time.[44]

Before the first century of North American colonization was completed, the dominant white racial frame already had targeted Native Americans and African Americans and already had five dimensions that numerous scholars today cite as the important characteristics of the contemporary white-racist ideology in the United States: (1) classification of human groups as discrete biological entities; (2) such groups ranked hierarchically in an inegalitarian way; (3) their outer physical qualities linked to their inner or cultural qualities; (4) such qualities considered inheritable; and (5) each exclusive "race" unalterably differentiated from others by God or nature.[45] I agree with this listing, but close examination of the court cases, treatises, sermons, and books of the white intellectuals, officials, and other leaders in this chapter demonstrates that the white racial frame is about much more than ideological classifications, stereotypes, and concepts. These passages from the early European American colonists clearly illustrate other aspects of the early white framing of the "others" whom they subordinated. They reveal an array of racist images, visceral emotions, distinctive smells, emotion-laden interpretations, and propensities to act—in regard to both virtuous European Americans and the African Americans and Indians who are lacking in virtue.

We can now turn to the further development and use of these elements in the white racial frame over the next two centuries. From the mid-1700s to the late 1800s the white racial frame became ever more developed and spread aggressively from the Atlantic coast across North America as whites expanded westward.

CHAPTER 4

Extending the White Frame

From the Eighteenth Century to the Twentieth Century

During the eighteenth century the North American colonies varied in their framing and discriminatory treatment of African Americans and Native Americans. In some cases the two groups suffered similar types of discrimination within the colonies themselves. For example, in one 1705 colonial statute blacks, Indians, and criminals were all barred from holding office, and deceased Indians and blacks could not be buried with whites. In other cases, colonial whites were clearly more concerned with black than Indian ancestry. Thus, some colonial laws asserted that those with just one black great grandparent were to be considered legally a "Negro," while only those with one Indian parent were considered to be legally an "Indian."[1]

The anti-Indian part of this era's racial framing was also somewhat different from that for African Americans. During this period whites sometimes did assert some positive views of Native Americans and, as we will see in the case of leaders like Thomas Jefferson, they periodically depicted them as human, albeit paternalistically as lesser humans than whites. The white framing of indigenous peoples in this era was still often negative, even viciously so, yet sometimes mixed with positive commentary and thus not as universally negative and denigrating as it was for African Americans. One reason for this is that Native Americans were usually part of distinctive nations rooted in their own territories and regularly fought back collectively, sometimes successfully, against white attempts to take their lands. Some Native American groups made military alliances with white Americans against the British, and Native Americans were much less often in enslaved positions within white communities. Thus, Native

Americans usually had access to the means of collective resistance to enslavement unavailable to Africans who had been torn from their homelands. From the earliest contacts, moreover, European American leaders and intellectuals sometimes offered, albeit often backhanded, compliments about Indian courage, daring, intelligence, and cooperation against the British.

Eventually, many whites even came to frame Indians, especially once they were killed off or forced beyond white-controlled territory, as heroic symbols of the Americas and its natural strengths, while "negroes" were not seen as really American or as having major positive characteristics that should be recognized, but rather were framed negatively as only subordinated labor and contrasting symbols of darkness opposite to dominant whiteness. Indeed, Indian images were added by whites to U.S. money, such as the famous U.S. Indian-head penny and nickel, because Indians were thus viewed as heroic and vanishing symbols of a white-conquered "American wilderness." Such a highly visible "honor" was never bestowed upon African Americans.

Winthrop Jordan has suggested that Native Americans and African Americans were both viewed early on as "primitive peoples" and as "two fixed points from which English settlers could triangulate their own position in America: the separate meanings of Indian and Negro helped define the meaning of living in America."[2] Jordan thus views Indians and black Americans as fixed points against which whites worked out their own social position and identity in North America. There is certainly some truth to this argument, but one should not push it too far. Prior to such contacts the European invaders already had a significant and strong positive identity as Christians and "civilized" Europeans. Thus, it was European Americans' *choice* to create and name the social positions of "Indian" and "black" in their racialized system of oppression and, thus, in their racial framing of society. These were not already fixed positions in their universe. From the beginning whites fully controlled the dominant racial framing for both groups and *imposed* new social identities on them.

Killing Indians: White Unity and Framing in the Eighteenth Century

In the eighteenth-century American colonies the national-origin and religious diversity among European groups—German, English, French, Welsh, Catholics, Quakers, and others—created significant interethnic tensions. Over time, however, all these European groups came to be seen, and to see themselves, as fully white, although this self-framing process was variable by group. Certainly, the seventeenth-century and eighteenth-century European American wars against Native Americans, and later against the

British, were particularly important in solidifying these diverse European nationality groups into one "white nation." Whites' racial consciousness was strongly reinforced during the Indian wars and the late-1700s revolutionary war, and whiteness and white supremacy became very central to the definition of "American." During these numerous wars, most whites came to use the word "Indians" for all indigenous people, and as a result some allied and neutral Indians were killed by white soldiers. Whites frequently grouped diverse Native American societies together as "savage" and "treacherous" and used the collective word "Indians" for them, a racialized framing that, as in previous decades, helped to rationalize white violence against them. In war settings Indians who fought back were asserted to be less than human and depraved murderers, a part of the anti-Indian subframe of the white racial frame. Like their predecessors, eighteenth-century colonists periodically framed Indians as animals—"beasts of prey," as Colonel John Reid put it in 1764 or as "animals vulgarly called Indians" and a "race" who had no right to land, as Hugh Brackenridge put it in the 1780s. Indians who resisted were considered a real danger to the construction of a strong white nation.[3]

In this revolutionary era, the white framing of Indians asserted that there were essential links between their supposedly inferior character and biology and their allegedly inferior culture. Retrospective accounts by white soldiers who had fought in the Indian wars emphasized the biological otherness of Indians. In addition, a shared "white" identity was proclaimed by these soldiers, as well as by white writers in newspapers and in official accounts. Interestingly, white officers in the colonial military units were less likely than rank-and-file soldiers to assert openly their whiteness, but did discuss the color and physical characteristics of the Indians—sometimes terming them "blacks" and thereby making a connection in their framing to black Americans. Ordinary soldiers accented their whiteness as a sign of superiority to Indians, whereas their officers already had a strong sense of class and racial superiority. The ordinary soldiers strongly linked their political rights, such as suffrage, to their asserted white identity, which bridged across the ethnic and religious divisions among them. Thus, the propertied colonial elite had to accept, albeit grudgingly, the idea of universal white male suffrage because of their alliance with ordinary white soldiers in fighting both the Indians and the British army.[4]

The assertion of strong white identity and acceptance of privilege by ordinary whites provide an early example of the "public and psychological wage of whiteness" later described by W. E. B. Du Bois. From this revolutionary era to the present day, most working class and middle class whites have accepted a higher position in the U.S. racial hierarchy and certain racial privileges from the white capitalist elite in return for giving up much class struggle against that elite, a class struggle that would likely have brought them significant economic benefits. Although the white working and middle classes do not have the societal power and resources of the white elite, they have received much in the way of white privileges and socioeconomic resources that stem from their advantaged position in the racial hierarchy. This distinctive psychological wage of whiteness has long been a critical part of white racial framing in this society.

The Declaration of Independence: Officially Framing Indians and Black Americans

Soon after the French and Indian wars ended in the 1760s, numerous colonial political and business leaders decided to revolt against Britain and issued a famous Declaration of Independence. Much has been written about this document, but its highly racialized sections have received relatively little attention, especially the one directed at Native Americans. Two passages in the working draft indicate not only the racial framing of Thomas Jefferson, the Declaration's primary writer, but also of the influential men who signed it. Jefferson sought to include the following passage about the African slave trade in the document, but it was vetoed by his fellow slaveholders:

> He [the British king] has waged cruel war against human nature itself, violating its most sacred rights of life and liberty in the persons of a distant people who never offended him, captivating and carrying them into slavery in another hemisphere, or to incur miserable death in their transportation thither. This piratical warfare, the opprobrium of *infidel* powers, is the warfare of the *Christian* king of Great Britain. Determined to keep open a market where *men* should be bought and sold, he has prostituted his negative for suppressing every legislative attempt to prohibit or to restrain this execrable commerce. And that this assemblage of horrors might want no fact of distinguished die, he is now exciting those very people to rise in arms among us, and to purchase that liberty of which he has deprived them, by murdering the people on whom he also obtruded them: thus paying off former crimes committed against the *liberties* of one people, with crimes which he urges them to commit against the *lives* of another.[5]

In this unusually long passage in the draft of the Declaration, Jefferson hypocritically blamed King George for the slave trade, a trade which he and his slaveholding peers had played a major role in perpetuating. In this white framing of enslaved black Americans, Jefferson expressed fears that the British were inciting them to rebel. Slave uprisings were a recurring concern for the white slaveholders, which is one reason they framed enslaved black men as dangerous and rebellious. Even as these white men cried out for their own freedom, they could not bring themselves to add this passage recognizing that "crimes" were "committed against the liberties" of another people and thus to condemn the slave trade, the latter being much too central to their economic prosperity and racialized social world.

A number of social science and other analysts have paid some attention to this deleted passage that negatively frames black Americans, but very few have analyzed the importance of the racialized passage that actually remained in the Declaration of Independence:

> He [the British king] has excited domestic insurrections amongst us, and has endeavoured to bring on the inhabitants of our frontiers, the merciless Indian Savages, whose known rule of warfare, is an undistinguished destruction of all ages, sexes and conditions.

The Declaration's statement mentioning Indians proclaims emotion-laden racial stereotypes held by Jefferson and his white colleagues in the northern and southern colonies: (1) Indians are not really "adults" but are easily manipulable; and (2) indigenous peoples are viewed collectively and negatively as "merciless Indian savages" who make war immorally on women and children.[6] These racially framed commentaries in a document ostensibly about liberty and equality made it clear that the new country was indeed to be a *white republic*, one where African Americans and Native Americans would not be equal or even citizens.

Over the next few decades Jefferson's views of Native Americans became more complex. In 1785 he published his major book, *Notes on the State of Virginia*, the first ever by a secular American intellectual and one whose racial commentaries were cited by white political leaders and media commentators over the next century—indeed, by white supremacists to the present day. In that book Jefferson's brief comments about Native Americans are rather paternalistic and romanticized. They are said to be noble but lesser human beings: "We shall probably find that they are formed in mind as well as in body" much like Europeans.[7] He does not view indigenous Americans as a separate race or a threat to white racial purity, as he clearly and assertively does for African Americans in the same section of this book. Like George Washington and other U.S. founders, Jefferson even envisions a future blending of white-assimilated Indians and whites into one society, a reality he could not envision for enslaved African Americans if they were ever freed.[8]

In 1813, some years after serving as president, Jefferson sent a letter to Baron Alexander von Humboldt describing his view of the U.S.

treatment of Native Americans. He begins in a paternalistic tone, once again suggesting the possibility of the incorporation of Indians into white society:

> You know, my friend, the benevolent plan we were pursuing here for the happiness of the aboriginal inhabitants in our vicinities. We spared nothing to keep them at peace with one another. To teach them agriculture and the rudiments of the most necessary arts, and to encourage industry by establishing among them separate property. In this way they would have been enabled to subsist and multiply on a moderate scale of landed possession. They would have mixed their blood with ours, and been amalgamated and identified with us within no distant period of time.

But then he shifts back to describing Indians as "unfortunate" men collaborating unwisely with the British enemy in the War of 1812:

> On the commencement of our present war, we pressed on them the observance of peace and neutrality, but the interested and unprincipled policy of England has defeated all our labors for the salvation of these unfortunate people. They have seduced the greater part of the tribes within our neighborhood, to take up the hatchet against us, and the cruel massacres they have committed on the women and children of our frontiers taken by surprise, will oblige us now to pursue them to extermination, or drive them to new seats beyond our reach. . . . The confirmed brutalization, if not the extermination of this race in our America, is therefore to form an additional chapter in the English history of the same colored man in Asia."[9]

In the Declaration of Independence, Jefferson's statement on the "savage Indian" was linked to a rationalization of their extermination, and in this letter he continues with that line of argument. In spite of his periodically paternalistic views, Jefferson here asserts the necessity of government policies aimed at exterminating or fully subordinating the Native American "race." By this time in history Jefferson thought he could see that Indians were vanishing, that is, were being killed off or forced westward as whites aggressively expanded across the continent. This enabled him and later whites to speak sometimes of the "noble" Indian, which became part of complex white imagery of Native Americans that has lasted to the present day.

White paternalism toward Native Americans is also evident in some court decisions that were handed down during Jefferson's era. Shortly after 1800 a prominent judge, St. George Tucker of the Virginia Court of Appeals, issued a decision arguing that the Virginia Bill of Rights did not apply to "a black or mulatto man or woman with a flat nose and woolly head" who had challenged "false imprisonment" in slavery. However, Tucker did rule that the Virginia Bill of Rights applied to a "coppor coloured person with long jetty black, straight hair," by which he meant an Indian, and to "one with a fair complexion, brown hair, not woolly or inclining thereto, with a prominent Roman nose," by which he meant a white person.[10] Tucker's important legal ruling reveals that the relatively few surviving Native Americans had some rights, at least officially in Virginia, while African Americans had none. It also shows just how complex and extensive the white frame was at the time, with its accents on an array of physical characteristics.

More White Framing of Native Americans

From Jefferson's day to the end of the nineteenth century, whites moved westward from the eastern states and engaged in one displacing or genocidal attack on Indian societies after another, until many Indians were killed off and most of the rest were forced onto white-controlled "reservations." This bloody white oppression was, yet again, rationalized with the anti-Indian images of the old white racial frame. Take the example of Colonel Lewis Cass, who led troops against several Indian nations and served as Secretary of War under the slaveholding President Andrew Jackson. (Jackson was famous as a bloodthirsty Indian-killer and creator of the "Trail of Tears" march that forced surviving eastern Indian groups at gunpoint into western areas.) Colonel Cass wrote an article about American Indians in 1827 in which he asserted that all people should value riches, honor, and power, but that there

> was little of all this in the constitution of our savages. Like the bear, and deer, and buffalo of his own forests, an Indian lives as his father lived. . . . He never attempts to imitate the arts of his civilized neighbors. His life passes away in a succession of listless indolence, and vigorous exertion to provide for his animal wants, or to gratify his baleful passions. . . . But he is perhaps destined to disappear with the forests.[11]

Here again we see a member of the white elite articulate with obsessive emotion the old stereotypes of animal-like, lazy, oversexed, and uncivilized Indians. For Colonel Cass and most other whites of the nineteenth century, to be civilized one had to be saturated in Western cultural values.

Later in that century, in a famous paper on "the significance of the frontier in American history," historian Frederick Jackson Turner accented a similar theme and thereby helped subsequent generations of whites to rationalize what they have interpreted as the advance of "civilization"

(Western culture) against "savagery" (Indian cultures) and "primitive Indian life." In Turner's racist framing, there was once a western frontier that was a place of "hostile Indians and stubborn wilderness." Indigenous peoples appear in his analysis as natural objects, like mountains, that whites had just reason to conquer and replace with their supposedly superior society.[12]

However, as historian Richard Drinnon has explained, some three hundred years of Indian wars perpetrated by whites generated a white racial framing that mostly hid the obvious truth about Native American humanity and hardened European Americans to their brutally oppressive actions. This enabled them to engage in "dispossession and extermination or uprooting in an atmosphere fouled by self-congratulation and by sighing regrets over the Native American's utter unworthiness of their disinterested benevolence."[13] The white racial frame served to legitimate the othering process, the theft of indigenous lands, and the killing, which got worse even as the frame became ever more entrenched. Indeed, to the present day, such framing of indigenous Americans has continued to cloud whites' understandings of the reality of the often genocidal conquests whites long engaged in—and in its many contemporary consequences.

The Enlightenment Era: Framing African Americans

The early white racial framing of Indians and African Americans had emerged just before the eighteenth-century Enlightenment era and the rise of modern science, but the scientists and other thinkers of this Enlightenment era adopted and expanded this racial framing with the tools of the new sciences. They joined their natural science interests to the study of human issues, often aggressively linking physical characteristics to human moral and social characteristics. They applied their new scientific methods to placing peoples of color down the human hierarchy. For example, in the 1730s the influential Swedish botanist and taxonomist, Carolus Linneaus, distinguished categories of human beings—white, black, red, and yellow. While he did not use the specific word "race," he clearly did think in racial terms as he directly associated skin color with particular cultural traits, with whites being regarded as superior beings. Like earlier European and American thinkers, he argued that Europeans were "inventive, full of ingenuity, orderly, and governed by laws," but that "Negroes" were "lazy, devious, and unable to govern themselves."[14] He regarded this reality as part of a God-given order of nature, his version of the great chain of being.

This era of the European Enlightenment is typically depicted by historians and other analysts as the beginning of modernity—with its dramatic increase in science and reason, a rejection of old dogmas, and liberating ideas of freedom. Most Enlightenment thinkers, such as Britain's Adam Smith and North America's Thomas Jefferson and Ben Franklin, together with their many acolytes and followers, proclaimed in their speeches and writings that expanded human freedom was centrally important and that individual achievement was the measure of a person's worth—the white liberty-and-justice frame. Even today, encyclopedia articles on this Enlightenment era often do not mention its seamy side—its expanding colonialism, imperialism, and slavery, and its elites' rationalizing these oppressions in important interpretive frames.[15] In fact, the accenting of individual freedom to act created a need for explanations of individual impoverishment and subordination such as slavery. In this era the white racial frame was further emphasized and enhanced, for it continued to explain for whites and others why many people, especially Indians and African Americans, were impoverished or unworthy.

During this era, as earlier, many European Americans, especially slave-holders in the South and the North, aggressively defended the enslavement of African Americans as the only way to develop white wealth in the ever growing American colonies. (By the late eighteenth century African Americans, enslaved and free, made up one fifth of the population.) Arguing that whites could not handle hard labor in the harsh open fields, white apologists for slavery constantly framed the growing numbers of enslaved African Americans as mere property, just as white colonists had done for decades. African Americans were viewed as like the "axes, hoes, or any other utensil of agriculture," to quote one Georgia slavery advocate. Other mid-eighteenth century framing of African Americans carried forward and elaborated yet other emotion-laden stereotypes of African Americans. Numerous proslavery advocates, such as English American navigator and naturalist Bernard Romans, spoke in white-framed terms of inborn flaws in those enslaved, viewing "treachery, theft, stubbornness and idleness" as "natural to them and not originated in their state of slavery."[16] In addition, the stereotyping and imaging of black women as oversexed and dispens-able was often dramatically presented. In the 1730s, for example, the white editors of a Charleston, South Carolina, newspaper published a notice directed to white men that arriving soon were "African ladies . . . of a strong, robust Constitution . . . able to serve them by Night as well as Day. When they are Sick, they are not costly, when dead, their funeral Charges are but [little]."[17] In addition, the white view of black men was still, as earlier, that they too were oversexed but dangerous because they lusted after white women.

The first white abolitionists in some colonies were Quakers, and they sometimes recorded the views of their kinfolk and friends. Anthony Benezet, a Pennsylvania Quaker, wrote that slavery supporters held "in their Minds, that the Blacks are hardly of the same Species with the white men, but are Creatures of a Kind somewhat inferior."[18] John Woolman, also a Quaker abolitionist, spoke of African Americans as "our Fellow creatures," yet also as "far from being our Kinfolk" and as "of a vile stock."[19] In this era, as earlier, African Americans were viewed by a great many whites as a separate species, and were distanced as "vile" even by some white abolitionists.

The Founding "Fathers" Frame African Americans

In the late colonial era and the early United States, the reality of slavery continued to have a great shaping impact on the racial framing of most whites, including those with power and influence. In white leaders' framing the color and physical features of enslaved African Americans received much attention. In the 1750s Benjamin Franklin, the most famous liberal intellectual of the founding era, framed his conception of white virtuousness with an obsessive concern for the country's demographic composition:

> The number of purely white people in the world is proportionably very small. . . . Why increase the sons of Africa, by planting them in America, where we have so fair an opportunity, by excluding all blacks and tawncys, of increasing the lovely white and red?

He further argued that the number of mixed-ancestry Americans would likely grow with an increased slave trade, and white "amalgamation with the other color" would produce "a degradation to which no lover of his country, no lover of excellence in the human character can innocently consent."[20] Franklin not only framed African Americans negatively in cognitive terms, including a stereotyped view of their character, but also revealed a strong aesthetic bias and an obsessive fear of their skin color eventually degrading his highly prized whiteness. Stereotyping, imagery, and racialized emotions once again appear together. Note too that, although history books rarely record it, Franklin was at this time a slaveholder. He and his family enslaved African Americans for decades before he became an active abolitionist later in life.

Other major U.S. founders such as Thomas Jefferson, James Madison, and George Washington were also slaveholders and framed African Americans as racially inferior. Thomas Jefferson, the major framer and intellectual whose views have influenced many whites since his time, was himself influenced by the earlier scientific work of men like Sir William Petty, including their views of black Americans. In Jefferson's *Notes on the State of Virginia*, he articulated a well-developed white frame with strong racist images, cognitive stereotypes, and emotional arguments: Black Americans smell funny, are natural slaves, are less intelligent, are physically ugly, are lazy, are oversexed, are ape-linked and animalistic, are musically unsophisticated, cannot think well, and cannot if freed ever be socially integrated into white American society. If freed, they must be shipped out of the United States. Founders George Washington and James Madison did not write as much about their views of African Americans, but they too shared Jefferson's highly racist framing of those whom they enslaved.[21]

In the peak era for the U.S. slavery system, the late eighteenth century and first six decades of the nineteenth century, the production and circulation of racist ideas continued to emerge substantially from leading slaveholders and their associates, as they aggressively justified slavery for the new United States. A well-developed racial frame was constantly supported by the legitimating discourse of the elite whites who controlled major institutions, including the economy, law, politics, education, and religion.

It is quite ironic, as I noted in Chapter 1, that white Americans' conceptions of their own freedom and of justice developed fully within a societal system grounded in the oppression of Native Americans and African Americans. Over the decades before and during the revolutionary war with Great Britain, white Americans, who were mostly of British ancestry, crafted a liberty-and-justice frame that they articulated aggressively as they pursued their break with a mother country considered to be oppressing them and suppressing their liberties. Yet much in this white liberty-and-justice frame contradicted their strong racist framing, which defended and rationalized the oppression of African Americans and Native Americans. This contradiction does not seem to have bothered most white colonists. Observations of the enslavement of African Americans played a role in white minds as the source for a metaphor they regularly applied to their own "enslaved" political situation vis-à-vis the British king. In the revolutionary era, white colonists frequently insisted that they must not be treated as "negroes" or "Guinea slaves" by the British. Near the beginning of the revolutionary war, General George Washington himself asserted that the time had come "when we must assert our rights, or submit to every imposition, that can be heaped upon us, till custom and use shall make us tame and abject slaves, as the blacks we rule over with such arbitrary sway."[22] Numerous other whites spoke in similar fashion. Even the non-slaveholding John Adams, in his 1765 treatise "A Dissertation on Canon and Feudal Law," argued that British officials treated American colonists "more like slaves than like Britons."[23]

A major part of the ideological effort directed by the American revolutionaries against the British included the explicit construction of a liberty-and-justice frame. This important framing, which has persisted now for centuries, was articulated ever more aggressively after the mid-1700s as the white colonists sought to break away from the British empire. This perspective was perhaps most famously asserted by Patrick Henry at a March 1775 meeting of Virginians considering revolutionary action. Henry gave his speech to urge white Virginians to fight the British. This is a portion of his speech that was preserved:

> For my own part I consider it as nothing less than a question of freedom or slavery; and in proportion to the magnitude of the subject ought to be the freedom of the debate. . . . And judging by the past, I wish to know what there has been in the conduct of the British ministry for the last ten years, to justify those hopes with which gentlemen have been pleased to solace themselves and the House? . . . Are fleets and armies necessary to a work of love and reconciliation? . . . Has Great Britain any enemy, in this quarter of the world, to call for all this accumulation of navies and armies? . . . They are sent over to bind and rivet upon us those chains which the British ministry have been so long forging. . . . If we wish to be free—if we mean to preserve inviolate those inestimable privileges for which we have been so long contending—if we mean not basely to abandon the noble struggle in which we have been so long engaged, and which we have pledged ourselves never to abandon until the glorious object of our contest shall be obtained, we must fight! . . . There is no retreat but in submission and slavery! Our chains are forged! Their clanking may be heard on the plains of Boston! . . . Is life so dear, or peace so sweet, as to be purchased at the price of chains and slavery? . . . I know not what course others may take; but as for me, give me liberty, or give me death![24]

Assuming this version of his speech is roughly accurate (it was first printed by his biographer only in 1817), we see much here that supports the idea that Henry was one of the leading "radicals" in the American revolution, a man willing to give his life for the ideals of freedom. He constantly asserted such views in speeches and letters and was later a strong supporter of adding the Bill of Rights to the U.S. Constitution. Yet, there is also much irony in Henry's language. He counterposes "freedom" to "slavery" and repeatedly uses the metaphor of "slavery and chains" to describe the conditions faced by the white colonists. Yet, at this point in his life, Henry had been a slaveholder for years, and he left some 65 African Americans enslaved at his death. Clearly, the white founders' frequent references to their "enslavement" reveal how central African American slavery was to the colonial society and to whites' deep and defensive framing of the racially oppressive society they maintained and profited from.

The U.S. founders' views were fundamentally hierarchical and increasingly made use of the new term "race" in its modern sense. They were influenced by the ideas of some European thinkers, who were in their turn influenced by the racial framing of white American thinkers and the reality of African American slavery and Indian wars in North America. In Europe the late eighteenth century Enlightenment was anything but enlightened on racial matters. Leading Western thinkers such as Immanuel Kant and David Hume advocated and enhanced the white racial frame. Hume viewed "negroes" as inferior "breeds of men." The West's most celebrated philosopher, Immanuel Kant, taught social science courses explicitly articulating very racist ideas. He asserted that "humanity exists in its greatest perfection in the white race" and that there is a hierarchy of "races of mankind" with superior whites at the top.[25] Like Jefferson and other U.S. intellectuals, Kant used the concept of "races" in the sense of biologically distinct, hierarchical categories. Similarly, the prominent German anatomist, Johann Blumenbach, developed a hierarchical "race" classification with those he named "Caucasians" (Europeans) at the top, and Mongolians (Asians), Ethiopians (Africans), Americans (Native Americans), and Malays (Polynesians) down the ladder.[26]

In this long Enlightenment era, new North American and European scientific and philosophical traditions were aggressively grounded in influential ideas about whites' biological, cultural, and social supremacy. Drawing on these scientists and philosophers, moreover, the popular writers who provided much entertainment and instruction for ordinary people in North America and Europe often adapted and elaborated the white-framed ideas from these traditions for the general white public. The popular media that aggressively circulated this now well-articulated white racial frame in the late eighteenth century and early nineteenth century were mostly newspapers and other printed materials, with a growing number of cartoons communicating vividly the negative imagery of Native Americans and African Americans. Although the general literate public was the target of these media presentations, the white elite was still in control of these media outlets.

The Mid- to Late-Nineteenth Century: More Racist Thinkers

In the mid-nineteenth century slavery continued to substantially shape the political-economic worldviews of leading figures in this era. In the North and the South, white officials and intellectuals proclaimed their versions of the dominant white frame in defending each region's political and economic interests. White southerners emotionally and aggressively insisted on their system of slavery as creating a much better regional civilization. In an 1837 speech in the U.S. Senate, the influential southern Senator John C.

Calhoun, a former vice president, articulated with great emotion the rather preposterous view that southern slavery was a "positive good" for African Americans:

> Never before has the black race of Central Africa, from the dawn of history to the present day, attained a condition so civilized and so improved, not only physically, but morally and intellectually. In the meantime, the white or European race, has not degenerated. It has kept pace with its brethren in other sections of the Union where slavery does not exist. . . . I appeal to all sides whether the [white] South is not equal in virtue, intelligence, patriotism, courage, disinterestedness, and all the high qualities which adorn our nature. But I take higher ground. I hold that in the present state of civilization, where two races of different origin, and distinguished by color, and other physical differences, as well as intellectual, are brought together, the relation now existing in the slaveholding States between the two, is, instead of an evil, a good—a positive good.[27]

Calhoun operates out of a strong version of the white racist frame with its language of the "black race" and "white race" and a rationalization of slavery as improving supposedly uncivilized Africans, who are aggressively stereotyped as physically and intellectually inferior.

Moreover, during this era official reports reveal that white officials often worked to declare a disproportionate number of free black Americans to be "insane." Those black Americans who were free were listed as insane at a rate eleven times greater than those who were enslaved, and much more often than whites as well. Drawing on such official records, defenders of slavery like Calhoun often argued that black Americans were much better off in slavery than in freedom, which supposedly inclined them to personal insanity. Again, we observe a racial framing that accents freedom for whites only.[28]

In this era an anti-black framing was not confined to the slaveholding South, but was widely shared across the United States and in Europe. Writing extensively about his 1830s travels in the United States, the French official and influential analyst of U.S. democracy, Alexis de Tocqueville, was critical of slaveholders like Calhoun who insisted U.S. states had a right to "nullify" federal government acts with which they disagreed. Nonetheless, de Tocqueville routinely viewed U.S. racial matters from a white frame similar to that of Calhoun:

> Among these widely differing families of men, the first that attracts attention, the superior in intelligence, in power, and in enjoyment, is the white, or European, the *man* preeminently so called; below him

appear the Negro and the Indian. . . . The Negro has no family; woman is merely the temporary companion of his pleasures. . . . The Negro, plunged into the abyss of evils, scarcely feels his own calamitous situation. . . . He admires his tyrants more than he hates them, and finds his joy and his pride in the servile imitation of those who oppress him. . . . If he becomes free, independence is often felt by him to be a heavier burden than slavery.[29]

De Tocqueville was respected and influential in the United States and Europe of his day. Moreover, since his insightful book recounting his travels, *Democracy in America*, was published, he has become an icon in U.S. intellectual circles and is often cited as one of the first social scientists. Although critical of some U.S. political and economic institutions, he was unable to transcend the dominant racist framing. This extraordinarily racist aspect of his U.S. analysis has been ignored by almost all social scientists who have cited his work. In de Tocqueville's view, whites were rightly dominant in the racial hierarchy and superior to Indians and "Negroes." He spewed forth old emotion-laden stereotypes: Black Americans have no real families and are oversexed. Holding to an extremely insensitive perspective much like that of other leading whites, de Tocqueville even asserted that black Americans do not feel the pain of their situations, find joy in imitating whites, and cannot manage freedom from slavery. He later added, again parroting age-old racist framing, that the black man's "physiognomy is to our eyes hideous, his understanding weak, his tastes low; and we are almost inclined to look upon him as a being intermediate between man and the brutes." The U.S. racist frame of the day, which de Tocqueville accepted uncritically and rather emotionally, portrayed black Americans as ugly and not quite human. On the future of the racial hierarchy, he agreed explicitly with Thomas Jefferson: "I do not believe that the white and black races will ever live in any country upon an equal footing."

The Continuing White Obsession: African Americans

From the beginning of the nineteenth century to its end, a great many whites, in all social classes, had become rather obsessed with black Americans. In the 1880s the abolitionist and political leader Frederick Douglass, who had been enslaved, made an eloquent speech on this white obsession at a celebration of the twenty-first anniversary of the Emancipation Proclamation:

Go where you will, you will meet with him [the black American]. He is alike present in the study of the learned and thoughtful, and in the play house of the gay and thoughtless. We see him pictured at our street corners, and hear him in the songs of our market places. The low and the vulgar curse him, the snob and the flunky affect to despise him, the mean and the cowardly assault him, because they know . . . that they can abuse him with impunity. . . . To the statesman and philosopher he is an object of intense curiosity. . . . Of the books, pamphlets, and speeches concerning him, there is literally, no end. He is the one inexhaustible topic of conversation at our firesides and in our public halls.[30]

Douglass aptly captured the many ways in which black Americans had become the center of whites' racist thinking, imaging, and emotions. Notice the diversity of white-controlled social arenas where the white racist frame was imbedded and perpetuated. Douglass observed negative images and conceptions of black Americans in treatises of well-educated whites and in plays in theaters attended by ordinary whites. He saw black Americans attacked in large numbers of elite-generated books, pamphlets, and speeches—all ways in which the white elite articulated its racist framing among themselves and to the masses of whites. Douglass also speculated that black Americans were the inexhaustible topics in backstage settings such as white firesides. He found them in broadside pictures on street corners and heard mocking in racist songs in marketplaces. This white obsession was more than mental, literary, and discursive, for African Americans were also being made the targets of violent curses and emotional assaults by whites, virtually all of which went unpunished.

Evidence for this white obsession with black Americans can be found in all decades of the nineteenth century. The print media, the primary mass media of this era, were full of anti-black cartoons and other visual and verbal depictions that constantly reinforced anti-black and pro-slavery views in the North and the South. For example, the prominent artist Edward Clay published a popular series of anti-abolition prints with aggressive caricatures of white-black couples and multiracial children to show whites' disgust with the idea of liberating enslaved African Americans and with the abolitionists' ideal of equal-status interactions between whites and blacks. Like whites before and since, these nineteenth-century whites imaged and framed dangerous black men as regularly lusting after white women. Indeed, this white obsession with interracial sex and marriage led to a new English word, "miscegenation," fabricated by New York journalists strongly opposed to such interracial relationships. An important and very emotion-laden subframe in the white racial frame has long viewed sex across racial lines as somehow unnatural, probably because many whites have viewed black Americans as less than human and interracial sex as a threat to white racial purity. Ironically, this negative framing is profoundly hypocritical, for it has never stopped many white men from forcing sex on black women—from the first decades of colonial development through several centuries of slavery and Jim Crow segregation.[31]

The Jim Crow South after the Civil War was especially marked by a continuing white obsession with racial purity. Numerous new laws stipulated that people with any "ascertainable Negro blood" were to be regarded as and legally segregated as Negroes.[32] Not surprisingly, obsessive white concern over "blood purity" was a major force lying behind the commonplace laws banning interracial marriages. Even into the 1950s, a majority of U.S. states—including all southern and most southwestern states—had laws prohibiting interracial marriages, most specifically marriages between white and black or Asian Americans. From the end of the Civil War in 1860s to the decades of the 1950s and 1960s, the white frame's view of black men as sexual threats to white women was quite intense and often used to rationalize white violence against black men. Moreover, the gendered racism that most whites also directed at black women routinely viewed them as having "jungle bunny" sexual desires and procreative abilities. Some contemporary scholars have even speculated that the preoccupation of many white men with alleged black male hypersexuality reflects some deep white psychological problems, perhaps growing, at least in part, out of collective guilt over the extensive white male role in the rape of black women over centuries.[33]

During the slavery and legal segregation eras, newspapers and other print media were quite important in circulating the dominant racial frame to most white Americans across the country, including to the new European immigrants who came to the United States in ever larger numbers from the 1830s to the early 1900s. In newspapers and magazines highly racist cartoons and drawings, coupled with written portrayals framing African Americans negatively, taught whites of all ethnicities, ages, and classes the white racial framing of African Americans. Cartoons accented "ugly" (to whites) physical characteristics: distinctive hair, skin, lips, and odor. Such physical traits were accented in palpably tangible, visual, and emotional ways and were commonly linked to other negative images of black Americans, including alleged hypersexuality.

Perhaps more important than the print media in spreading old and new aspects of the white racial frame were other forms of popular entertainment, especially minstrel shows and, later, vaudeville shows. A great range of racist imagery, stereotyping, and emotionality was communicated in popular entertainment settings from the early nineteenth century onward. White performers in blackface were popular with large numbers of working class and middle class white men. Such shows spread the white racial frame across the country, especially among the illiterate. The minstrel performances celebrated whiteness by indicating that the audience members, mostly white workers, were not like the "darkies" negatively portrayed on stage. Black men were mocked vigorously as Zip Coon dandies, and black women were stereotyped as sexualized and promiscuous. "Aunt Jemima" imagery originally surfaced in an 1870s minstrel show, later becoming widely circulated on commercial products. Minstrelsy was a critical way that key visual images, stereotypes, emotions, and interpretive understandings of the white frame were spread to illiterate whites, new immigrants, and younger whites.[34]

The minstrel shows perpetuated and reinforced a vicious and tangible version of the white frame and operated across social class lines. They were popular with middle class and elite whites, including U.S. presidents such as John Tyler and Abraham Lincoln. Before and during his White House years, Abraham Lincoln was fond of minstrel shows and the "darky" joking of white performers. He was not the racial saint of historical mythology. While he did oppose slavery, he routinely operated out of and helped to spread the white racial frame, viewing free and enslaved black Americans as racially inferior, supporting Jim Crow laws, and articulating a view of the future United States as an assertively white country. Other influential whites were similarly fond of the highly racist minstrel shows. Not long before his death, for example, Mark Twain expressed great concern for the decline in what he called the "real nigger show," the white minstrel performances. He was typical of leading whites in his era in this favorable view of minstrel shows.[35] The constant media and minstrel portrayals helped to cement negative images of African Americans in the white racial frame as the *counterpoint* to positive white views of whites and whiteness, for all social classes.

Systemic Racism in the North: Violence and Paternalism

The South is too often the main or only focus of sustained commentaries on systemic racism in U.S. history. Yet, before and after the Civil War, the nineteenth-century North was also a difficult and dangerous place for African Americans. Whites' anti-black actions there too were often out of an intense white racist framing of white and black Americans. For example, during the 1840s and 1850s, a relatively light-skinned African American, William Allen, secured a very good education and became a professor at New York Central College, at the time the only U.S. college that had ever hired a black man and one of few with white and black students. Allen became acquainted with a white woman in Fulton, New York, and they decided to marry. In early 1853, when local whites found out about the pending marriage, including most of her family, they were so horrified that they organized to prevent the marriage. Armed white mobs attempted to tar, feather, and kill him, and he was lucky to escape with his life. In a book he wrote about these experiences, Allen notes that at the "announcement of the probability of the case merely, [white] men and women were panic-stricken, deserted their principles and fled in every direction." One town near Fulton even passed a resolution that "Amalgamation is not part of the Free Democracy of Granby." Some newspapers editorialized that Allen should be killed, and some white friends lost their jobs or were otherwise persecuted. Once again, we observe that the white racial frame is far more than a matter of racist stereotypes and ideology, for it includes very strong emotions and inclinations to violence to protect whites' proclaimed racial interests. Indeed, in Allen's stated view, the "so-called free" men and women of color of the North were in bondage to whites and thus as oppressed as those in the South.[36]

In this era, as earlier and later in North American history, much of the white racial frame was quite compatible with various other political and economic frames that were used to interpret society. Thus, even the minority of whites who were critical of slavery, such as the eighteenth century Quaker abolitionists noted earlier, articulated negative anti-black stereotypes. We continue to see this orientation among white abolitionists in the mid-nineteenth century. Even Harriett Beecher Stowe, author of the anti-slavery novel, *Uncle Tom's Cabin*, argued in the 1850s that the "negro race" was very different from the "white race":

> They are possessed of a nervous organization peculiarly susceptible and impressible. Their sensations and impressions are very vivid, and their fancy and imagination lively. In this respect the race has an oriental character, and betrays its tropical origin. . . . When alarmed, they are often paralyzed and rendered entirely helpless. . . . Like oriental nations, they incline much to outward expressions, violent gesticulations, and agitating movements of the body.[37]

What were then considered liberal white views tended to be paternalistic versions of the dominant racial frame and often played up the supposedly childlike qualities and necessary dependency of enslaved and free black Americans. Even the relatively radical Stowe, a fierce opponent of slavery, could not see past her conventional racist framing of African Americans as impressionable and handicapped by bodily expression, which she attributed to their tropical origin.

During this era, moreover, the everyday actions of most white abolitionists reflected paternalism toward and discrimination against African Americans. Thus, in the anti-slavery movement's offices of the 1840s and 1850s, the leading intellectual and activist, Martin Delaney, noticed that he and other African Americans were in a "mere secondary, underling position, in *all* our relations to them."[38]

Extending the White Frame: Other Americans of Color

During the mid-nineteenth century the white-controlled system of racial oppression and its rationalizing frame were substantially extended as white entrepreneurs and political leaders brought in yet more labor and territory of people of color, again mostly for the purpose of generating white wealth. These new oppressions began on a large scale in the 1840s with a U.S. military invasion and conquest of northern Mexico, which brought new lands and more than 100,000 Mexicans within the new U.S. boundary, and in the 1850s with the importation of Chinese contract laborers by white companies, such as the western railroads. Those European Americans who imported Chinese laborers and annexed large areas of northern Mexico by force already had a strong white racial frame in their heads. That age-old frame, from the beginning centrally focused on white superiority and black inferiority, has long been adaptive and multidimensional, and its central racist doctrines have regularly been adjusted and extended to new social contexts and groups. White political and economic leaders, as well as scientists and intellectuals, quickly imbedded the Mexicans and the Chinese in this society's white-controlled hierarchy of exploitation and in its expandable rationalizing frame, both of which were at that time more than two centuries old.

In the southwestern United States few white colonizers invading northern Mexico in the 1830s and 1840s viewed the Mexicans as white, but placed them down at the bottom of the hierarchy with Native Americans and black Americans. For example, one white land agent wrote that Mexicans were "swarthy looking people resembling our mulattos, some of them nearly black." The famous Texas politician and slaveholder, Sam Houston, spoke of Mexicans as inferior "half-Indians." Other whites wrote that Mexicans had a "filthy, greasy appearance," a view that likely led to the white-racist epithet "greaser" for Mexicans.[39]

In 1848 Senator John C. Calhoun, the former vice-president quoted previously, was strongly opposed to the annexation of Mexico, but in speaking against it he revealed yet more elements of the increasingly common white-framed perspective on Mexicans:

> We have never dreamt of incorporating into our Union any but the Caucasian race—the free white race. To incorporate Mexico, would be the very first instance of the kind of incorporating an Indian race; for more than half of the Mexicans are Indians, and the other is composed chiefly of mixed tribes. I protest against such a union as that! Ours, sir, is the Government of a white race. The greatest misfortunes of Spanish America are to be traced to the fatal error of placing these *colored races* on an equality with the *white race*. That

error destroyed the social arrangement which formed the basis of society. . . . And yet it is professed and talked about to erect these Mexicans into a Territorial Government, and place them on an equality with the people of the United States. I protest utterly against such a project. Sir, it is a remarkable fact, that in the whole history of man, as far as my knowledge extends, there is no instance whatever of any civilized colored races being found equal to the establishment of free popular government, although by far the largest portion of the human family is composed of these races. . . . Are we to associate with ourselves as equals, companions, and fellow-citizens, the Indians and mixed race of Mexico? Sir, I should consider such a thing as fatal to our institutions.[40]

The influential Calhoun put Mexicans into the "inferior Indian" and "mixed-race" subframes of the white master frame, accenting that they were not white but down the racial hierarchy among "colored races." He feared any attempt at political equality and viewed Mexicans as unintelligent and incapable of participating in a "free popular government," which of course the slavery-centered United States government was certainly *not* at that time.

The racist framing of Mexicans and other Latin Americans was not limited to the Southwest. Just before the 1840s Mexican American war, a Boston newspaper published a poem, "Their Women Wait for Us," that revealed northern framing of people of Latin American (mainly Mexican) descent:

The Spanish maid, with eye of fire, At balmy evening turns her lyre
And, looking to the Eastern sky, Awaits our Yankee chivalry
Whose purer blood and valiant arms Are fit to clasp her budding charms.
The man, her mate, is sunk in sloth—To love, his senseless heart is loth:
The pipe and glass and tinkling lute, A sofa, and a dish of fruit;
A nap, some dozen times a day; Somber and sad and never gay.[41]

Accenting "Spanish" female hypersexuality and male laziness, this stereotyped and emotion-laden imagery is quite vivid and draws substantially on the pre-existing white framing of black Americans. In his language of "pure blood" and "chivalry" the white poet again accents the white superiority that had already been framed thus for at least two centuries.

Whites outside the newly conquered "New Mexico" area of northern Mexico seized in the 1840s Mexican American war tended to view all the new Mexican Americans as not white and inferior, but the handful of powerful whites in that New Mexico area had a somewhat different viewpoint because they were a statistical minority in a large Mexican American population there. Between the 1840s and the 1880s, thus, these powerful white invaders decided to share some political and economic power with the established Mexican elite already there. Because these elite whites sought statehood—which was delayed for decades because the territory was *not* majority white—they developed a perspective that viewed the Mexican elite as inferior to Anglo Americans but still as European and "Spanish." Even though many in the Mexican elite had Indian ancestry, the white elite decided that they were "white enough" to be citizens and to play an important political role.[42]

Moreover, this small Mexican American elite played a coordinating political, and thus oppressive, role between the Anglo whites on the one hand and the poor Indian, Mexican American, and enslaved African American populations on the other. In this era the Mexican American elite emphasized their own relative "whiteness" in order to relate well to the more powerful white-Anglo elite. Again we see the control that powerful European Americans had over the *definition* of U.S. racial groups, including those granted lesser political power. Invading whites from the eastern United States emphasized the traditional white racial framing and defined the Mexican American elite, but only temporarily, as white enough to assist in expanding Anglo control over the new territory. This historical background may help to explain the fluctuating accents on whiteness and non-whiteness in some parts of the Mexican American population from that time to the present. Scholar Laura Gomez accents the longterm significance: the "twenty-first-century legacy of Mexican Americans' history as off-white" is that they are "sometimes defined as legally white, almost always defined [by whites] as socially non-white."[43]

In addition, from the 1850s to the early 1900s the Chinese workers, and later the Japanese and Filipino workers, brought by white entrepreneurs into the West also faced extensive exploitation and other oppression, which was repeatedly rationalized by the dominant racial frame. Thus, when the U.S. economy entered a depression in the 1870s white labor leaders, newspaper editors, and politicians racially stereotyped and framed Chinese American workers for allegedly taking job opportunities from whites. Chinese workers were physically attacked by white workers and verbally attacked by white politicians and editors supporting the white workers.

These Asian Americans were stereotyped as heathen, docile, crafty, and dirty, and called by new white-crafted epithets, such as "Chinks." White leaders and the white public viewed Chinese Americans as an "alien race," as inferior foreigners and not real "Americans." Again we see elements of the older racial frame—heathen, docile, alien in culture, racially inferior—that were developed to negatively frame African and Native Americans now being used to racialize Asian Americans. Somewhat new emphases can be seen in the anti-Asian subframe, especially accents on foreign-ness and deviousness. These negative images spread and reached the highest levels of the U.S. class structure. For example, in the famous 1896 *Plessy v. Ferguson* Supreme Court decision that upheld Jim Crow segregation of black Americans, the one dissenting white justice to that decision, John Marshall Harlan, gratuitously penned this racist framing of Chinese Americans: "There is a race so different from our own that we do not permit those belonging to it to become citizens of the United States. Persons belonging to it are, with few exceptions, absolutely excluded from our country. I allude to the Chinese race." More than a decade earlier, the 1882 Chinese Exclusion Act had been passed by the U.S. Congress, a law that effectively cut off most Chinese immigration to the United States, until its partial repeal in 1943.[44]

Excluded Chinese workers were soon replaced in western states with imported Japanese workers, who were also economically exploited and viewed and attacked again from the dominant white frame. They too were racially stereotyped and emotionally framed as docile, servile, and devious. Around 1900, for example, the white San Francisco mayor attacked new Japanese immigrants as "unassimilable" and threatening white workers' jobs; a Sacramento newspaper editor similarly asserted that the Japanese Americans were "for various reasons unassimilable, and a dangerous element." Other West Coast newspapers generated campaigns against the white-termed "yellow peril"—that is, Japanese and other Asian Americans. Such racist agitation soon forced the U.S. government to negotiate with the Japanese government to prohibit Japanese immigrants. In these cases, the racist framing of Asian immigrants had exclusionary consequences that shaped the demographic contours of U.S. society—that is, this society now has far fewer Asian Americans than would have been the case without this white discrimination.[45]

Note too that the importation of these Chinese, Japanese, and Filipino workers was linked to U.S. military expansion in Asia and the Pacific area. In the 1890s the U.S. military defeated the Spanish in the Spanish American War and added the Philippines to its empire, with the country's white leadership aggressively framing this victory as indicative of white superiority and the "manifest destiny" of whites to expand everywhere. Invasions were then, as later on in U.S. history, justified from the old white frame. In 1899 the British official and prominent U.S. visitor, Rudyard Kipling, celebrated in a prominent U.S. magazine the U.S. annexation of the Philippines and whites' philanthropic burden to civilize so-called uncivilized peoples in his famous poem, "The White Man's Burden: The United States and the Philippine Islands." The first lines demand action:

> Take up the White Man's burden—
> Send forth the best ye breed . . .
> To wait, in heavy harness,
> On fluttered folk and wild—
> Your new-caught, sullen peoples,
> Half-devil and half-child.[46]

Such poetic framing of Asians and others as heathen, demonic, and child-like dependents by an important European official and its publication in a major U.S. magazine indicated the widespread acceptance of this *visual and visceral imagery* in the U.S. and European elites, an imagery linked to the U.S. governments' moves in a global and imperialistic direction.

In this historical era, the contrast between the way in which Asian and Latino Americans were exploited, subordinated, and racialized in the dominant white frame, and the way in which millions of new European immigrants to the United States were treated and constructed is dramatic. For about one generation, numerous European immigrant groups, such as those from Ireland, eastern Europe, and southern Europe, were viewed by native-born, northern European whites as inferior "races" well below the "Anglo-Saxon race" on the U.S. racial hierarchy, but this view changed in a relatively short period of time. As the European immigrants, and especially their children, gave up much of their homeland culture and aggressively adopted many aspects of the dominant U.S. culture of whiteness, they were mostly accepted by the native-born whites into the "white race."

Significantly, from the 1830s to the early decades of the 1900s millions of these European immigrants and their children adopted the white racist frame's negative perspectives on African Americans and other Americans of color as an important part of their incorporation into U.S. society. Entering during the 1830s and 1840s, for example, poor Irish immigrants were viewed from the prevailing racial frame as an inferior "race," and indeed as "not white," by many of the then dominant English Americans. Most of the former, thus, did not initially view themselves as "white," but they soon assimilated to the dominant culture and were taught how to conceive of themselves as white, principally by their ministers, priests, business people, newspaper editors, politicians, and other leaders. In this adaptation process, they were pressured and manipulated by white elites, including their own leaders, into accepting the already dominant racial framing denigrating blackness and privileging whiteness. Most quickly or gradually came to operate out of this traditional racist frame—such as by attacking or excluding free black workers in competing for jobs in the northern cities. Later, at the turn of the twentieth century, Italian and other southern and eastern European immigrants and their children—after a period in which nativist whites viewed them as inferior "races"—assimilated to the dominant white culture and bought aggressively into that dominant racial frame, thereby firmly identifying themselves as "white" and getting out from under the negative racial imagery. Many European immigrants and their descendants pressed for a privileged place in the socially constructed "white race," whose privileges eventually included such things as greater personal liberty, better-paying jobs, access to an array of government programs just for whites (such as homestead lands, better public schools, and, later, home mortgage and veterans programs), and the right to vote.[47]

At the same time, as part of being "white," they now actively framed African Americans and other Americans of color as racially inferior and discriminated against them. Over time the dominant racial frame has been reproduced and transmitted within numerous immigrant groups and across many generations of Americans. This transmission has been particularly important for European immigrants and their descendants, both in the distant past and in the present day.

The Jim Crow Era: Scientific Racism and the Elites' Racial Frame

Indeed, from the middle of the eighteenth century to the middle of the twentieth century, elite physical and social scientists regularly defended and extended the racialized framing and oppression of African Americans, Native Americans, and other Americans of color. For most of this era most white American and European physical and social scientists enthusiastically accepted the view that biologically determined "races" actually existed. For example, during the slavery era, medical researchers and other influential scientists developed a pseudo-scientific terminology to describe black Americans who resisted enslavement as mentally ill or to portray them as naturally inclined by their "blood" to be resistant or problematical. Physician Samuel Cartwright wrote about black runaways as having a disease he called "drapetomania" and of black Americans being susceptible to "dysaethesia aethiopis," a disease caused by "black blood" that in the brain created "ignorance, superstition, and barbarism." Not surprisingly, as with Calhoun's view previously, black Americans were viewed as requiring the lessons of the tough slavery system to improve their diseased mentality.[48]

Systemic gendered racism was part of the scientific-racist frame as well. Some white researchers in this mid-nineteenth century did medical experiments to prove white-racist stereotypes of black women, including the stereotyped notions of a biological propensity for black women to engage in prostitution and of black women having "primitive" sexual drives. Other researchers aggressively experimented on enslaved black women in order to develop new surgical techniques—as the "father of gynecology," J. Marion Sims, did without anesthesia because black women (in a white framing dating back to Jefferson's time) allegedly did not suffer pain.[49]

During the Jim Crow decades after the 1861–1865 Civil War era, there was a significant expansion of the scientific legitimation of the white racial frame, a trend often labeled "scientific racism." Like earlier white philosophers and scientists, most late nineteenth century and early twentieth-century scientists held firmly to the view that there were specific races with distinctive physical characteristics, that these characteristics were hereditary, and that they were arranged in a natural hierarchy of inferior and superior races. That is, these mostly northern intellectuals provided what they considered "scientific" evidence for the pre-existing white racial frame. They developed a scientific view of people of color across the globe as innately and permanently inferior to whites. The broad ideas of these scientific racists were not supported by careful scientific observations of all human societies, but usually by slanted reports gleaned from European missionaries, travelers, and sea captains who had some contacts with selected non-European societies. While presenting themselves as objective observers, these scientists frequently tried to marshal evidence for the significant differences among human "races" that the white imperialist officials in their governments had decided were important to highlight.[50]

The towering scientific figure of the era, England's Charles Darwin, applied his evolutionary ideas to the development of human races. He viewed the evolutionary process of natural selection at work in Europeans killing off indigenous peoples, and for him black people were a species category somewhere between whites and gorillas. In his view, like that of other European and American biologists of his day, the "civilized races" would eventually replace the "savage races throughout the world."[51] Similarly, U.S. social scientists like Yale University's William Graham Sumner adopted a social Darwinist view that viewed humanity as engaged in a life-and-death struggle, one in which the superior white race should and would win out over the inferior darker races. Black Americans were seen by many of these scientific racists as a "degenerate race" whose alleged immorality was genetic and thus a matter of their inferior biology. Indeed, in the United States the social sciences early on developed substantially in connection with white attempts to rationalize the enslavement and Jim Crow segregation of African Americans. In fact, the first explicitly named "sociology" books were written by southerners Henry Hughes (*Treatise on Sociology*) and George Fitzhugh (*Sociology for the South*), both published in

1854 and both aggressively asserting, once again, the white-framed view of black enslavement as a positive good and of slavery as a social system that should be expanded under U.S. government control.[52]

Over many decades of the Jim Crow era, which began aggressively in the 1870s and lasted until the 1960s, much social science analysis accented, reinforced, and legitimated older white racist views of African Americans and, to a lesser degree, other Americans of color. In the North and the South, social scientists used their "graphs, charts, and other paraphernalia to prove the Negro's biological, psychological, intellectual, and moral inferiority."[53] The emotion-laden anti-black images and stereotypes from the centuries-old white racial frame—such as stereotypes about physical deficiencies, low intelligence, moral deficiency, and cultural inferiority— were now legitimated by leading social and physical scientists, as well as by politicians and business leaders. Scientists like Nathaniel Shaler, a prominent Harvard dean of sciences in the late nineteenth and early twentieth centuries, argued that African Americans not only were racially inferior, uncivilized, and an "alien folk" in the United States, but also would eventually and necessarily become *extinct* under the ongoing Darwinian evolutionary processes.[54]

Such views were dominant among U.S. scientists for many decades, including those in the prestigious academic institutions. For example, during the 1920s Carl Brigham, a Princeton psychologist who later helped to develop the famous College Board tests, argued from World War I psychometric tests on draftees that the relatively low scores of black draftees showed that they were of "inferior racial stock." Operating out of an aggressive version of the white racial frame, Brigham envisioned active sterilization of racially inferior Americans as a good government policy for dealing with them.[55] About the same time, Lothrop Stoddard, a Harvard-educated historian, utilized a globalized version of the white frame in his widely read book, *The Rising Tide of Color*. There he insisted with great emotion that the "white race" was, and should continue to be, the "indisputable master of the planet"—even though they constituted a decreasing minority of the planet's population.[56]

Moreover, for many decades during the Jim Crow era, almost all white business and political leaders viewed the world from an aggressive and quite emotion-laden version of the dominant racial frame. Thus, President Theodore Roosevelt (1901–1909) was well-known for his outspoken agreement with numerous tenets of the new scientific racism. President Woodrow Wilson (1913–1921) also advocated the superiority of European civilization over all others, including those of Africa, and acted to increase the racial segregation of black Americans within the U.S. government during his terms. President Warren Harding (1921–1923), a fan of Lothrop

Stoddard's white supremacist book and himself cozy with members of the Ku Klux Klan, rejected "any suggestion of social equality" between white and black Americans. Prior to becoming president, and much like the German Nazi intellectuals in Europe, President Calvin Coolidge (1923–1929) had articulated in popular magazine scientific-racism arguments against racial mixing: "Biological laws tell us that certain divergent people will not mix or blend. The Nordics propagate themselves successfully. With other races, the outcome shows deterioration on both sides."[57] Again, we observe that the dominant racial frame was not something from the margins of a still expanding United States, but rather something arising from its political, business, and intellectual center.

Jim Crow, the Supreme Court, and the Southern Elite

During the slavery and Jim Crow eras, from 1789 to 1967, the U.S. Supreme Court was a clear manifestation of white dominance, for only elite white men ever served on it. Examining the Supreme Court justices' decisions on racial matters during most of the Jim Crow era, one finds that they regularly reflect the dominant racist framing and routinely ignore or dismiss the civil rights counter-frames of Americans of color. In the decades between the 1870s and the 1930s, Supreme Court decisions regularly eroded the civil rights that African Americans had theoretically gained under the 14th and 15th amendments added to the U.S. Constitution in the Reconstruction era. In the influential 1896 *Plessy v. Ferguson* case, a nearly unanimous court (one dissenter) upheld a Louisiana law requiring white-black segregation in public accommodations. Not surprisingly, in this decision the justices asserted that they as white men *knew better* than black Americans what impact Jim Crow had on them:

> We consider the underlying fallacy of the plaintiff's argument to consist in the assumption that the enforced separation of the two races stamps the colored race with a badge of inferiority. If this be so, it not by reason of anything found in the act, but solely because the colored race chooses to put that construction on it. . . . Legislation is powerless to eradicate racial instincts or to abolish distinctions based upon physical differences. . . .[58]

Not only did these justices frame their decision with racist notions like "racial instincts," but they felt a need to lecture black Americans on what they should feel about segregation, thereby ignoring the black experience and counter-frame. In his dissent, Justice John Marshall Harlan argued for civil rights for black Americans. The 13th amendment made unconstitutional "the imposition of any burdens or disabilities that constitute badges of slavery or servitude," which is what Jim Crow did. Nonetheless, even Justice Harlan expressed a paternalistic and white supremacist version of the dominant racial frame in an added comment: "The white race deems itself to be the dominant race in this country. And so it is, in prestige, in achievements, in education, in wealth, and in power. So, I doubt not, it will continue to be *for all time. . . .*"[59]

Gradually, from the 1930s to the 1960s, desegregation lawsuits brought by black civil rights lawyers resulted in scattered Supreme Court decisions that finally paid some attention to the black counter-frame accenting freedom and civil rights for black Americans. In a key 1938 case, *Missouri ex rel. Gaines v. Canada,* white Supreme Court justices *for the first time* in U.S. history openly ruled in favor of the black perspective on Jim Crow segregation—in a ruling against law school segregation in Missouri. Several other such university desegregation cases preceded the famous 1954 *Brown v. Board of Education* decision, one hailed by many as pioneering action on the part of brave Supreme Court justices breaking with the dominant framing and being far in front of the country's citizenry and leadership.[60] Yet, in *Brown* white Supreme Court justices had belatedly taken seriously the civil rights perspective articulated by the NAACP lawyers and rejected Jim Crow segregation in seventeen states. The *Brown* decision was weak, and its years-late delivery reflected resistance from some justices on the Court who had long articulated a white racist framing of segregation. The white Court's action was not on the cutting edge on issues of racial desegregation, for most African Americans were well ahead of the court in counter-framed understandings of Jim Crow and the need for effective legal action against it. Moreover, with the help of well-placed, white supremacist judges and U.S. senators, the legal segregation of African Americans and others in numerous other institutions persisted into the late 1960s.

For a time after the first *Brown* decision, the high court and other federal courts paid some attention, albeit with waffling, to the black civil rights counter-frame and pressed forward slowly with societal desegregation. For example, several Supreme Court justices were fearful about ordering the speedy implementation of their 1954 decision. A second *Brown* decision, the 1955 decision designed to implement the first decision, did not represent the views of most African Americans about undoing the Jim Crow oppression they faced. Instead, in this weak decision the Court's white male judges took a position more acceptable to most whites and the dominant racial frame: They sent back the *Brown* desegregation cases to the district courts "to take such proceedings and enter such orders and decrees consistent with this opinion as are necessary and proper to admit to public schools on a racially nondiscriminatory basis *with all deliberate speed* the parties to these cases."[61] Clearly, neither of the two *Brown* decisions explained to the general public the anti-civil-rights reality and immorality of racial segregation, and neither decision mandated clearly the steps necessary to end actual segregation. The justices' foot-dragging and lack of forcefulness reflected a concern with the racial framing of the white majority; and their dilatory decision, as well as more recent Supreme Court decisions backing off of school desegregation entirely, explain the general failure to meaningfully integrate the majority of U.S. public schools.

The hostile racial framing by many whites in various regions of the *Brown* decisions made clear the continuing power of the dominant white frame. In one dramatic and very emotional response, from the conservative wing of the white elite, congressional leaders from the South issued a "Southern Manifesto." Signed by nineteen Senators and seventy-seven House Members from southern states, the document condemned *Brown*: "The unwarranted decision of the Supreme Court in the public school cases is now bearing the fruit always produced when men substitute naked power for established law."[62] The manifesto points to northern states, which it argues had pioneered in school segregation. Separate but equal, the writers declared, "time and again, became a part of the life of the people of many of the States and confirmed their habits, traditions, and way of life." They then argued that this brutal system of extreme racial inequality in school facilities "is founded on elemental humanity and commonsense, for parents should not be deprived by Government of the right to direct the lives and education of their own children." Here they operated out of a strong white framing they did not seem to recognize, for they meant *white* parents and children. A fifth of the southern population was then African American, yet they wrote their defiant and emotion-filled manifesto as though it represented the general view of the people of the South.

Reacting against *Brown*, these members of Congress drew on numerous racial fictions from the dominant frame, including old ideas about the virtues of whites and the goodness of a racially segregated society. They argued for the myth of happy racial relations in a segregated society: Desegregation "is destroying the amicable relations between the white and Negro races that have been created through 90 years of patient effort by the good people of both races. It has planted hatred and suspicion where there has been heretofore friendship and understanding." Again, theirs is a perspective coming exclusively from the traditional white worldview. Note too that these powerful whites held to a strong "states' rights" perspective, one that assumed that white southerners had the right to veto federal government action—a perspective that, as we saw earlier, was first developed during the slavery era as a way of protecting the anti-democratic interests of elite white slaveholders.[63]

The hostility and single-mindedness of this racist framing can also be seen in commentaries of major journalists after *Brown*. In the 1950s and 1960s, the influential *Richmond News-Leader* editor, and later national columnist, James J. Kilpatrick, asserted that the South had "a sense of oneness here, an identity, a sharing, and this quality makes the South unique"; for him and many others like him the South was a "state of mind."[64] Indeed, he titled his book *The Southern Case for School Segregation*. Yet again, in such widely expressed sentiments the southern advocates of Jim Crow were thinking only in terms of the views of the white majority. What they meant was the "white southern case." Black southerners mostly did *not*, and still do not, share such dreamy views of oneness, sharing, and beneficent white-black segregation that have long been part of the white segregationists' version of the traditional racial framing of society.

Numerous white political and business leaders outside the South did *not* publicly support *Brown*, including then President Dwight D. Eisenhower. They too could not see beyond the dominant white-racist framing of the historical events. Thus, historian Robert Caro describes Eisenhower's racist views and collusion in southern resistance to dismantling the racist system thus: "Not once during those six years [after *Brown*] would Eisenhower publicly support the ruling; not once would he say that *Brown* was morally right, or that segregation was morally wrong." Indeed, Eisenhower openly sympathized with the white segregationists' resistance in private settings with his friends.[65]

Conclusion

It was out of this era of slow and grudging legal desegregation progress that our contemporary era of continuing, and still systemic, racism has emerged. Without the black counter-frame (see Chapter 7) and the civil rights organizations and protests that it spurred, the significant changes in overt and legal segregation in the 1950s–1970s era would almost certainly not have taken place. This era of significant legal and other societal racial change was substantially the result of a great many black Americans being willing to risk their lives and livelihoods to bring down Jim Crow segregation and to set the country once again on the track to becoming a real democracy. Their efforts, and those of the small minority of whites who actively supported them, indeed changed some of the segregated and other white supremacist ways that U.S. society had functioned with since the Civil War. No longer was overt discrimination legally permitted. Schools were officially desegregated. Jobs once off limits to workers of color were officially opened up. Voting was now permitted. Some black politicians were elected. White police officers were supposed to treat black people with respect, and openly violent white supremacist groups were no longer tolerated by the white majority. In addition, other Americans of color, often inspired by the black civil rights movement, also engaged in similar protests that also helped to bring down the most overt signs of racial oppression and to move the country in the direction of real democracy. Since the late 1960s, moreover, one effect of the legal desegregation progress brought mainly by the civil rights efforts of Americans of color has, ironically enough, been a renewed assertion by whites of white virtuousness. Since the 1960s, increasing numbers of whites have repeatedly insisted that they, and the United States generally, are fair, tolerant, and "no longer racist" and that the continuing social, economic, educational, and political problems faced by African Americans and other Americans of color are mainly of their own making. In the next two chapters, we will examine this perspective on U.S. society, which as it turns out is a refurbished version of the old white racial frame.

CHAPTER 5

The Contemporary White Racial Frame

Over the decades since the civil rights movements of the 1950s, white responses to numerous public opinion surveys have suggested that the level of white-racist stereotyping and other racist framing has declined substantially. Survey researchers and psychologists doing lab studies have found that white responses to typical questions about their racial stereotypes and prejudices indicate that in recent years whites as a group have become much less prejudiced toward African Americans and other Americans of color. Such survey results have frequently been interpreted by some white researchers and various white media analysts to mean that for the most part "racism is dead" in the United States.[1]

Is Racism Really Dead?

This interpretation of U.S. society is quite mistaken, and there is much social science data revealing why. For one thing, typical opinion surveys on whites' racial views are phone polls that ask rather brief questions and get similarly brief answers, answers that are usually forced by the pollster into a limited array of possible choices. At best, these opinion surveys give a surface-level reading of white racial views. Even more importantly, such opinion surveys are seriously limited by the fact that many whites give the pollster, a stranger, socially desirable answers that accent white virtue or colorblindness and thus disguise their actual racial framing of society. Psychological research has found that many white respondents alter their comments on racial issues so that they appear unprejudiced. Public

91

opinion surveys target, at best, only a few of the elements of the white racial frame and miss much of its broad framing of racial realities. Psychological researchers who have probed more deeply into the white mindset have found that more indirect and subtle measures indicate that anti-black views and other negative racial subframes are still quite common.[2]

Research data from social science projects using in-depth interviews and other qualitative research methods have come to the same conclusion. Thus, one important study of white students at three top universities found that their responses to brief attitudinal survey items were often different from those they gave during in-depth interviews. For example, while 80 percent of the large sample of white students approved of racial intermarriages on a simple survey item, substantial in-depth interviews with a smaller but similar student group found that only 30 percent consistently stayed with this racially liberal viewpoint, with the others backing off and indicating difficulties they actually had in their minds when it came to the issue of such racial intermarriages.[3]

A diverse array of evidence, thus, points to the reality that the old white racial frame, albeit with some contemporary alterations and refurbishing, remains powerful and pervasive across the contemporary United States. Research shows, indeed, that it is still learned and used at young ages, including by young white children. For example, early in an ethnographic field study at a multiracial daycare center, one of my graduate students, Debra Van Ausdale, observed an incident that illustrates this point well. One day, Van Ausdale observed a white three-year-old, Carla, getting ready to lie down at the school's nap time. The child started moving her cot. When asked why by her teacher, little Carla replied: "Because I can't sleep next to a nigger," pointing to a black child nearby. Carla further explained: "Niggers are stinky. I can't sleep next to one!" Assertively applying a centuries-old racist epithet and old racist stereotyping with significant emotion to a situation in her own way, Carla demonstrated that as a three-year-old she already held important elements of the white racial frame in her head. Later, at a meeting of staff members and her parents, all the adults present insisted that Carla did not learn the racist epithet from them. Her father finally remarked, "I'll bet she got that from Teresa. Her dad . . . he's a real redneck."[4] If her father's view is correct, Carla learned important elements of the dominant racial frame in her social network. In this example we observe the learning and use of the anti-black subframe of the dominant racial frame by a child within her important organizational and networking structures, structures that provide opportunities for performances of that conventional frame and insure its recurring reinforcement for those involved.

As I have argued throughout this book, a racial-analysis paradigm with deep structural concepts such as "systemic racism" and the "white racial frame" is required if social scientists and others are to probe deeply into the ways that whites like little Carla and the adults around her feel, think, and act on important racial matters. We can recall here the important dimensions of the traditional white racial frame as it is revealed in everyday applications. Today, as whites move through their everyday lives, they frequently combine racial stereotypes (a beliefs aspect), metaphors and concepts (a deeper cognitive aspect), images (the visual aspect), emotions (feelings), interpretative narratives, and inclinations to discriminate within a broad racist framing of U.S. society. The contemporary racial frame not only encompasses cognitive stereotypes and articulated values, the important conceptions of what is desirable or undesirable on racial matters, but also important nonlinguistic elements such as racialized emotions, images, and even smells.

Fostered constantly by political and media socialization efforts, especially by white elite efforts, and reinforced by a majority of white parents and peers, the contemporary white racial frame is deep and pervasive, with numerous subframes. This dominant frame shapes our thinking and action in everyday life situations such as that of Carla and the children and adults around her. Where and when whites find it appropriate, they consciously or unconsciously use this frame in evaluating and relating to Americans of color and in accenting the privileges and virtues of whiteness. One need only read carefully a local newspaper for a week or listen carefully to national media broadcasts for a week to observe how the centuries-old racial frame regularly shapes much of what happens in the public and private arenas of U.S. society.

Learning the Racial Frame

Children initially learn, and adults continue to learn, major aspects of the dominant frame by means of everyday socialization processes and regular interactions with others. The frame's key features are transmitted by an often hidden curriculum taught in families and other important social settings. Constant repetition of elements of the frame in everyday interactions like those in the account of little Carla is essential to its reproduction across networks, space, and time. Repetition and imitation, including the intonation of verbal expressions and the style of nonverbal expressions, build group rapport and facilitate interactions with relevant others. The dominant racial frame thereby becomes deeply imbedded in most individuals' minds, in the neural networks of their individual brains.[5]

Over the last century many of the sciences have accented the importance of various types of *relationships* and *networks* in both the physical and social worlds. Clearly, contrary to much public and philosophical discussion, the basic unit in society is *not* the individual, but rather the relationship between two or more individuals in essential and complex relationships and networks. Dyadic interactions, such as the basic one of mother and child, are tangible relationships that are almost always nested in ever larger networks of human relationships, eventually building to the level of communities and the larger society. Today, as in the past, whites do not invent most elements of their personal racial framing but adapt them from, and often perform them in, their most important social networks, which are typically all-white. Indeed, researchers have found that white Americans tend to have much more racially homogeneous networks than people in other racial groups. Research indicates that in literally millions of these kinship and friendship networks negative stereotypes and images of Americans of color are regularly used, refurbished, and passed along —from one generation to the next and one community to the next. Everyday interactions of friends and relatives in these significant networks make up the "muscles and tendons that make the bones of structural racism move."[6]

At an early age, children like Carla learn the white racial frame in everyday interactions in their networks of relatives, friends, and peers. The elements of this dominant frame are learned, not inborn, and are acquired by children at home, at school, at play, and from the media. Families play a central role, and racist lessons there tend to be deeply imbedded and well-remembered. The little research done on white parents suggests that most offer relatively few explicit lessons about the white racial frame to their children. White children mostly seem to learn the dominant frame and how to act out of it by watching parents, other adults, and peers. In one research study, we conducted an interview with an older white woman whose mother had told her some decades back that, if children like her were not "good," the "niggers would come in the night and steal us away and use us for their pleasure."[7] Not surprisingly, this respondent reported being intensely afraid of black men ever since childhood. Moreover, recent research using pictures of white and black faces and good/bad word associations has found that young white children hold anti-black stereotypes and inclinations and that these orientations do not decline in intensity for older groups of children and adults. For example, research using these photo procedures has shown that white preschoolers tend "to categorize racially ambiguous angry faces as black rather than white; they did not do so for happy faces." The important language and understandings of the old white framing of black Americans and other Americans of color are usually learned first in recurring family and friendship settings, and thus become part of a person's inner speech that is used to think about and shape racial interactions and other racial actions.[8]

As they get older, children usually learn to hide certain racial views from strangers—not surprisingly, given societal accents on racial pretense in public. In one study using the Implicit Association Test, some Harvard researchers found that six-year-old white children showed an implicit prowhite and anti-black bias in connecting white and black faces to good or bad words, and that their self-reported racial attitudes showed a similar overt racial bias. In the same study older white children and white adults revealed a similar implicit racial bias in matching white and black faces to good or bad words. However, the self-reported racial attitudes of the older children revealed less overt racial stereotyping than for the younger children, and the self-reported attitudes of the adults studied showed *no* overt racial bias.[9] This study confirms the point made earlier, and documented in a student diary study cited below, that as whites get older, most know much better how to hide their true racial attitudes in public or "frontstage" settings, such as with researchers, pollsters, and other strangers, and to reserve most blatantly racist commentary and action for the private or "backstage" settings with friends and relatives.

The Contemporary Frame: Still Accenting White Virtues

Elements of the centuries-old white racial frame, often refurbished, continue to be commonplace in whites' everyday thinking and actions. Although nearly four centuries old, this frame has changed rather modestly in much of its prowhite and anti-black core over the centuries. Periodically, of course, important new elements have been added, and some elements have disappeared or at least become more nuanced. Yet, if the leading racist intellectual among our founders, Thomas Jefferson, were to come back today he would recognize much of the contemporary prowhite and anti-black stereotyping and imaging, as well as many of the underlying racialized emotions. He would likely be amazed at the many technological, demographic, and economic changes in U.S. society, but not at much of contemporary whites' framing, especially that which emphasizes the superiority of whites and the inferiority of African Americans and others of color.

In assessing the prowhite material that is central to contemporary white framing, one finds much that has persisted over the centuries. Many of these elements accent the virtues, privileges, and power of whites and whiteness. The great-chain-of-being idea did not disappear from this white perspective as the United States moved from being predominantly agricultural to its advanced urban-industrial period today. That old hierarchical notion has continued over the last two centuries as a more or less unconscious cultural model essential to the way most people orient themselves in U.S. society. Today whites as a group remain at the top of the racial hierarchy, and most view that as still appropriate. Important white views, values, and framing remain normative, the societal standards to be adopted by children of all backgrounds as they grow up and by all new immigrants. Indeed, numerous research studies today offer much evidence that the word "American" is often synonymous with "white." In several social psychological studies researchers examined how strongly three major U.S. racial groups were associated with the category "American." In all the studies their subjects saw African Americans and Asian Americans as *less* associated with the category "American" than white Americans. For their white subjects, they also found that the association of "American" with whites was positively correlated with the strength of the subjects' own national identification. In important ways, the most intensive U.S. nationalism has become a type of white superiority orientation. White media outlets and politicians also often treat the term "American" as meaning "white American." Moreover, for most whites today even the often noted "American Creed" is a white-framed creed with historically white interpretations of its rhetorical ideals of freedom, justice, and equality.[10]

Today, whites and whiteness are viewed in positively framed terms by most people who consider themselves white, and often by those who do not. For the most part, whites continue to view themselves individually and as a group to be good and virtuous. This white-framed perspective is mostly unidirectional, with whiteness and whites in the position of mostly being virtuous and the racial "others" as often unvirtuous. As in the past, moreover, the commonplace white narratives of U.S. historical development still accent whites' superiority and courage over the centuries. Implicitly or explicitly, the contemporary white frame accents continuing aspects of this superiority—that is, that whites are typically more moral, intelligent, rational, attractive, or hardworking than other racial groups, and especially than African Americans and other dark-skinned Americans. Today, in most areas of this society, whites as a group are considered virtuous people who act on racial matters mostly in colorblind ways, and mostly without racist malice. In political, economic, and other social spheres, most whites manifest a strong sense of personal and group entitlement to what they have and what they prize. In many social settings where racial matters come up, one still hears whites insisting on their general or historical virtuousness: "My family never owned any slaves," "I have worked hard for what I have," "It's not because I'm white," and "I earned it, it is my right."[11]

An Ever Evolving Frame: The Colorblind Era

Over nearly four centuries of development in North America, the white racial frame has evolved and periodically changed. It is still a flexible worldview that, as it has for centuries, shapes everything from thinking and believing to feeling and acting. Significant changes in a positive direction have taken place only during a few eras, such as during the nineteenth-century abolitionist era and during and after the mid-twentieth-century civil rights movements. Thus, the 1830s–1860s abolitionist movement helped to bring down the slavery economy, a very significant change in the material structure of oppression. Yet the official abolition of slavery in 1865 did *not* result in an end to extreme white-on-black oppression, the dominant racial hierarchy, or the pervasive white racial framing, as we have seen.

Elements of the dominant frame asserting proslavery rationalizations were thus replaced with views of African Americans as still necessarily subordinate to the superior whites, but under new institutional structures of official segregation. The partially reworked white racial frame still vigorously legitimated a system of near-slavery called "Jim Crow," with its array of structures of segregation and other oppression again targeting African Americans—as well as over time yet other Americans of color. Similarly, during and after the 1950s–1970s civil rights movements, which generated the first major civil rights legislation in a century, the dominant racial frame again changed, albeit often slowly, in a number of significant ways.

One change in the common version of the white frame was the removal of the idea of Jim Crow segregation as essential for white dominance and the adding of a linguistic veneer of "we are colorblind" rhetoric. In many ways, however, this new colorblind rhetoric has just papered over what are still blatantly racist views of Americans of color that have continued in most whites' framing of this society. Over the decades since the 1960s, openly segregationist and white supremacist views have gradually become much less acceptable in the white population. Yet many of the old racist ideas and other racial frame elements, as I document below, have persisted in forms that are only modestly changed. In addition, public actions designed to bring change in the structures of racism, such as the great racial inequalities in economic and educational institutions, have been mostly limited to those necessary to maintain social order. When faced with civil rights protests and the need for some change in the racist system, as in cases like the *Brown* decision, white leaders have usually adopted modest interventions and institutional workarounds—that is, they have made changes in official or legal segregation, but at the same time have usually created weak enforcement mechanisms, which guarantee the continuation of the dominant racial hierarchy and much of its rationalizing frame.[12]

Today the contemporary racial frame's accent on most whites as "no longer racist," "post-racial," and "colorblind" provides some new language for what is in fact a very old view of whites as the most *virtuous* racial group, a viewpoint that has been part of the dominant frame since the seventeenth century. As we will see below, this white accent on now being colorblind has been shown by social science research to be misleading and often a coverup of the substantial levels of blatantly racist framing and action in which many whites still engage. Those who say they "do not see race" in fact usually *do* see it, and they frequently act negatively on what they see. Substantial social science research shows that much of the old racial frame remains influential in white thought and commentary on racial matters, both in public frontstage settings and in private backstage settings.[13]

For example, there is still much discussion of racial issues in the mainstream mass media, but often such discussion is forced on media reporters and commentators by current events, such as the recurring police beatings and killings of black men. In such cases the notion of a colorblind United States is temporarily abandoned, although the mostly white reporters and commentators may express discomfort with discussing such obviously racial matters. Various examples come to mind. Consider that most mainstream media reports on contemporary political campaigns that involve candidates who are not white still insist on accenting the candidates' racial identity whether the candidates wish that or not. Candidates who are not white are routinely mentioned as such, whereas if no racial designation is indicated in a mass media account, the reader or listener is assumed to know that the candidate is white.[14] This is an example of *frame assumption*, the assumption that others, especially whites, share one's own racially framed understandings.

In addition, candidates who are not white frequently face racial incidents or controversies that force the media to discuss racial matters. For example, in the 2008 presidential campaign of Senator Barack Obama his racial identity was constantly accented in literally thousands of media commentaries on his presidential campaign, including media reports on public debates over whether he was "black enough" for black Americans or "too black" for nonblack Americans. His racial identity was implicitly signaled too in numerous media reports on the public's or politicians' discussions of whether "real working class Americans," "Joe Six-Pack," and "hockey moms" (typically euphemistic terms for whites) would actually vote for him. These and many other racialized commentaries about this pioneering political campaign by an African American signaled just how fundamental and extensive a non-colorblind racial framing of African Americans still is in the United States. In contrast, there was no such extensive media focus on or problematizing of the whiteness of his opponent, Senator John McCain.[15]

A great many white Americans, inside and outside the media, sometimes exhibit significant discomfort in talking critically about issues of continuing white racism, especially that which is more covert and backstage in the society. Sometimes this is just a colorblind denial that racial hostility and discrimination persist as serious U.S. problems. In other cases, however, this reflects the knowledge that talking seriously about contemporary racism contradicts the omnipresent colorblind ideology. Research by Eduardo Bonilla-Silva and others has demonstrated the array of rhetorical devices that whites use in their everyday conversations, especially in public and with strangers like researchers, to try to portray themselves as colorblind and non-racist.[16] In addition, we often observe examples of this in public commentaries by politicians and media commentators. For example, in his analysis of racial and class issues in the 2008 presidential election, the prominent news commentator, Chris Matthews, argued that Senator Hillary Clinton's recurring and overt comments on the importance of white working class voters to her primary victories was strange and thus that she seemed to be the "Al Sharpton of white people." Matthews added that he himself did not like to use racial and class labels:

> We've known the ethnic and racial issues always get in the way of arguing over issues—real issues. But this conversation as it's turned—I even hate saying things like "white working class voters." I was taught growing up don't even say words like "blue collar"; don't even get into that kind of elitist talk. We're not sociologists, we're Americans.[17]

Notice his accent on the Reverend Al Sharpton, a black civil rights leader who in Matthews' white mindset had become an iconic and stereotyped spokesperson for black Americans. Conspicuously, too, Matthews downplayed contemporary racial issues as *not* "real," yet he still was eager to talk about them in rather aggressive and stereotyped ways. His commentary suggested that the old white racial frame was still a major media figure's way of viewing U.S. society, yet a racial frame that should not be overtly foregrounded and thoroughly discussed in public.

The Persisting Racial Frame: Preoccupied with African Americans

The contemporary white racial frame, as with its predecessor versions over the centuries, still contains many negative elements targeting African Americans and other Americans of color. From the beginning to the present, whites have placed the anti-black subframe at the heart of this framing. Black Americans have long been a central reference point, the racial standard against which most whites have commonly defined themselves. One very dramatic example of this, which operated until the late 1950s in the U.S. legal system, is the presence of defamation-of-character laws that permitted whites to claim in court that they had been seriously defamed if they were labeled as "black." In contrast, it was not possible under the defamation laws for a black person to sue in court for being labeled "white."[18] Significantly too, being called "Mexican" or "Asian" did *not* trigger such defamation-of-character laws, once again signalling the deep reality of the white frame's central focus on the white-black distinction. Note too the obsessive concern with being able to defend one's whiteness against any taint of blackness. To the present day, most whites consider being seriously taken as "black" to be an insult.

Moreover, if asked today about a vague category like "nonwhite people" or "people of color," most whites will likely think and respond with reference to black Americans unless asked to do otherwise. The intense white preoccupation with black Americans in recent decades not only underscores the pervasive anti-black stereotypes, ideas, and images of the dominant frame but also reveals deep racial emotions and inclinations. Relatively few white scholars have recognized the significance of this preoccupation. It is mostly African American writers and scholars who have called attention to it. Recall Frederick Douglass's speech in the 1880s about this white obsession with black Americans: "Of the books, pamphlets, and speeches concerning him, there is literally, no end. He is the one inexhaustible topic of conversation." This is still the case. Nearly a century after the famous Douglass speech, Irene Diggs, a leading African American anthropologist, wrote a similarly insightful commentary:

> Nearly everybody in the United States is prepared to discuss blacks, and almost no one is entirely without an opinion on blacks. Most are amazed at the huge amount of printed material on blacks. A complete bibliography would consist of several thousand titles. The intellectual energy spent on blacks in the United States, if concentrated in a single direction, would move the proverbial mountain.

Like Douglass, she pointed up the great number of words, books, and articles whites in various sectors have regularly expended on African Americans. Then she added that

> blacks are a main divider of opinion in national politics and certainly in local politics. As a secondary problem and as a peculiar influence on all dominant national issues, the presence of blacks has disturbed religious moralists, political philosophers, statesmen, philanthropists, social scientists, politicians, and businessmen. The presence of

blacks is interpreted by many Americans as a menace: biological, economic, social, cultural, and, at times, political.[19]

Over several centuries now, the white racial frame has kept this strong and obsessive focus on black Americans as the dominant issue, menace, problem, and reference point in an array of institutional arenas of U.S. society. Huge amounts of energy have been expended not only on preserving systemic racism, but also on written and oral rationalizations of it.

Most recently, Nobel-prize-winning novelist Toni Morrison has pointed out that African Americans have long functioned as a key metaphor and fundamental referent for white Americans in public discourse and in literature. For centuries, she has noted, African Americans have been a recurring target of discrimination and thus a constant negative reference, implicit or explicit, for whites. White concern with black Americans is present

> in the construction of a free and public school system; the balancing of representation in legislative bodies; jurisprudence and legal definitions of justice. It is there in theological discourse; the memoranda of banking houses; the concept of manifest destiny and the preeminent narrative that accompanies (if it does not precede) the initiation of every immigrant into the community of American citizens. The presence of black people is inherent, along with gender and family ties, in the earliest lesson every child is taught regarding his or her distinctiveness.[20]

The most central details of the structures of U.S. society involve African Americans as a recurring reference point. Interestingly, African American novelists and essayists have often had the most insightful things to say about the dimensions and impact of the intrusive and oppressive of systemic racism. Commenting on the United States in the twentieth century, an earlier and equally prominent African American novelist, Ralph Ellison, added this insight about the white obsession. In his view an African American often feels like "he does not exist in the real world at all. He seems rather to exist in the nightmarish fantasy of the white American mind as a phantom that the white mind seeks unceasingly, by means both crude and subtle, to slay."[21]

Contemporary Evidence of White Preoccupation

There are a great many historical and contemporary examples of this black phantom dominating white minds, for famous and ordinary whites. Take, for example, the legendary Alabama governor George Wallace. As one white reporter and friend has noted, Wallace, long a leading southern and national politician, was constantly obsessed with African Americans and U.S. racial matters: "Didn't talk about women. We didn't talk about Alabama football. I mean, it was race—race, race, race—and every time that I was closeted alone with him, that's all we talked about."[22] In the United States, at least in the South, for many white men "race" has even trumped talking about football and women, two favorite male topics.

More generally, the white preoccupation with black Americans is evident in recent opinion surveys where a majority of whites *greatly* exaggerate the size of the current black population. In these surveys a majority of whites estimate that black Americans make up at least 30 percent of the U.S. population, some two-and-a-half times their actual percentage. This suggests an old emotion-laden conception, dating back to at least Thomas Jefferson, that there are too many African Americans in the population, a demographic situation many whites view as threatening. Such surveys also suggest that a great many whites habitually view their societal position in relation to the presence and number of black Americans. Conceivably, white concerns today with Latin American immigrants may eventually displace African Americans from this demographic centrality in white minds and framing, but this has not yet taken place.[23]

Recent psychological studies have also shown that negative black images and associated negative evaluations and emotions have become deeply imbedded in an overwhelming majority of white minds, including whites with relatively low levels of overtly expressed prejudice. Researchers have found that, when given a test of unconscious racial stereotyping, most whites quickly and implicitly associate black faces (photos) with negative words and traits (for example, evil character or failure). They have more difficulty in linking black faces to pleasant words and positive traits than they do for white faces. Analyses of thousands of tests taken at a Harvard website and other websites have shown that nearly 90 percent of whites signal an anti-black, pro-white bias in these face-reaction tests.[24] Moreover, in studies where whites are shown photos of black faces, even for a few milliseconds, key areas of their brains designed to respond to perceived *threats* light up automatically under medical-type brain scans. Also, the more racial stereotyping white subjects revealed on paper-and-pencil psychological tests, the greater their brains' threat responses were when they were shown the black photos.[25] Such research studies suggest not only that there is significant cognitive stereotyping but also that whites' emotional states, such as fear and anxiety over black images, link to and undergird their white-racist framing and, likely, their discriminatory actions in everyday life.

Yet other research on white thought and behavior demonstrates this centrality of African Americans to the contemporary white racial frame. In recent field studies that I and my colleagues have done, white interviewees and whites who kept diaries for us have revealed that black Americans are central to their and other whites' identity and everyday thinking. In these studies black Americans are the *only* non-European group that obsesses or preoccupies a large proportion of whites. For example, in the next chapter I will discuss in some detail some accounts of racial events recorded by 626 white college students who kept journals for us on their everyday lives. In these twenty-first-century diaries these college students reported that African Americans appear in about three quarters of all the racist commentaries, racist jokes, and other racialized performances that they have observed themselves and other whites doing. All other racialized groups taken together—including Native Americans, Latinos, and Asian Americans —made up just one quarter of the racist performances and other events they recorded. Similar field interview studies by other social scientists also suggest that the racist socialization of whites regarding Americans of color other than black Americans is less thorough and less central to most whites' identity, framing, and practices. Interviewing in racially diverse California, for example, Ruth Frankenberg found that white women in her important study accorded a hyper-visibility to black Americans and a relative invisibility to other Americans of color in their interviews.[26]

In this social science research most whites seem to have a much more developed and detailed framing of black Americans than of any other group of Americans of color. The contemporary Native American, Latino, and Asian American subframes of the white frame are, as we will see later, strong and widely applied, but seem on the whole less fully developed, with somewhat fewer racial stereotypes, images, and emotional loadings than the black subframe. Historically, whites' anti-black subframe is much older than their anti-Asian and anti-Latino subframes. Whites' negative framing of Native Americans, which is also quite old, appears to have become over the last century less central to the white racial frame, perhaps because the majority of Native Americans who survived white violence and genocide were forced into reservations or less populated areas of the West and Midwest. Considering this geographical reality and the lesser attention to Native Americans in the national media, they are not currently an important part of most whites' everyday experiences. After nearly four centuries of continuing white exploitation of and discrimination against African Americans within white-controlled communities in most U.S. regions, and the centuries-old framing rationalizing that oppression, African Americans today still remain central to the dominant racial frame's verbal, visual, emotional, and interpretive dimensions.

Anti-black Stereotyping and Imaging: Animalistic Imagery

We can now examine some specific aspects of the persisting anti-black subframe. Much contemporary research documents the reality of centuries-old racist stereotypes and images of African Americans still remaining commonplace. A great many white and other nonblack Americans believe or assert that African Americans are violent, criminal, unintelligent, lazy, and oversexed, among numerous other stereotypes and images. In this dominant framing, black Americans are "othered" and usually portrayed negatively. In research studies most whites can list the common stereotypes of African Americans, and the level of whites' anti-black stereotyping has been found to be related to their other racist views and to discriminatory actions directed at African Americans.[27]

Among the most egregious stereotypes and images common in the dominant racial frame today is the old view of black Americans as being somehow linked to the animal kingdom, especially to apes and monkeys. This was a view openly articulated by early founders like Thomas Jefferson, and it persists today. Some of the ape and monkey imagery has persisted in especially vicious forms in some areas of white America, as a review of the numerous white supremacist websites on the Internet will reveal. Various white supremacist groups still circulate drawings that depict African Americans as being similar on various biological dimensions to the apes.[28]

Such views are not limited to white extremists. In recent research studies, moreover, social psychologists have found that the association in ordinary white minds between black Americans and apes remains strong and emotion-laden. In one study, white and other nonblack college students who were exposed to black faces were quicker in recognizing hazy drawings of apes than those who were not thus exposed to black faces. In a second study of white students, researchers found that whites who were subliminally primed with ape images subsequently paid *more* attention to black faces than to white faces that they were shown. Those not so primed paid more attention to white faces. In a third study white male students presented with black and Asian faces were again more likely to attend to black than to Asian faces when they were primed subliminally with ape images. The association between black faces and apes was thus shown *not* to be a general white orientation to all nonwhite faces, but mainly to black faces. In a fourth study using overt questions about racial stereotypes, less than 10 percent of the white college students in their sample said that they actually knew about the old apelike stereotype of black Americans, yet these white students were still faster in associating stereotypically black names with apes than with big cats, although the big cats are more associated publicly with Africa and violence than are apes.[29]

In these recent research studies, a remarkably strong association between ape images and black images was found in many white minds. As in previous centuries, black Americans are still often framed, and apparently unconsciously, by whites as somehow animal-like and not fully human, as lower in the great chain of being. Such data also suggest that, while most social scientists now view "race" as a social fiction and social construction, many in the white population still view "race" as, to some degree, a biological or genetic reality.

Anti-black Stereotypes and Imaging: Criminality

The apelike stereotypes and images of African Americans held at some level by many whites frequently link to other emotion-laden stereotypes and images, such as those of black criminality. For centuries now, a central negative image in the white racial frame has been that of the "criminal black man." Not surprisingly, thus, recent psychological studies have shown the blacks-as-apes stereotyping persists in the prevailing racial frame and that it has serious behavioral implications. In one recent study researchers found that white college students' black-as-apes mental connections, subliminally primed by ape-related words presented to them, shaped their willingness to accept more police violence against a black criminal suspect than against a similar white criminal suspect when these subjects were then shown videos of such police violence. Moreover, a content analysis of hundreds of Philadelphia newspaper articles discussing black and white death-eligible criminal defendants found that words eliciting ape-like images in people's minds were more likely to have been used by newspaper writers for black than white defendants—even when controls were applied for crime severity and socioeconomic status. Clearly, animalistic imagery is part of the dominant white frame that helps to legitimate the whites' targeting of black Americans for discrimination, including discriminatory policing. These researchers conclude that the visual and verbal dehumanization of black Americans as apelike assists the process by which some human groups become targets of societal "cruelty, social degradation, and state-sanctioned violence."[30] Notice too in these studies that the racist framing of black Americans need not have been conscious for it to have had negative effects on the way whites think, feel, talk, or act in various social settings.

Much social science and other research shows that many whites automatically connect black Americans as a group with crime, while they do not easily associate whites as a group with crime. The image of black Americans as criminal remains an important part of the contemporary anti-black subframe. We observe this openly racist perspective in the recent comments of William Bennett, former U.S. Secretary of Education who on a radio talk show stated that, "if you really wanted to reduce crime, you could—if that were your sole purpose—you could abort every black baby in this country and your crime rate would go down." After focusing only on black babies, Bennett backed off by saying that such actions would be "an impossibly ridiculous and morally reprehensible thing to do, but your crime rate would go down." Even though the arch-conservative Bennett backed off and said this was a hypothetical he did not agree with (and used the "I am not a racist" strategy), we observe just how firmly imbedded in some white heads, including those of the elite, this connection between African Americans and crime remains.[31]

The mainstream media are partially responsible for perpetuating this framing. The criminality image is constantly reinforced in the media, especially in local news programs that are major sources of news for most Americans. Most local media operate routinely out of the dominant racial frame and thus accent blue-collar crimes by black Americans and other people of color in news programming, commonly ignoring much white crime, especially white-collar crime. One research project on local news programs found that news stories about violent crime that listed a suspect featured black suspects in a much higher proportion than was warranted by their actual arrest rate. Other research on local television stations has found that black suspects accused of crimes are much more likely to be negatively portrayed in on-air photos than are similar white defendants. In addition, in local television news programming whites are greatly over-represented as crime victims, while black Americans and other Americans of color are regularly over-represented among those said to be the criminals.[32]

Gendered Racism: Images of Black Women and Men

Another important dimension of the stereotyping and imagery in the dominant racial frame, in both its past and present forms, has been its gendered-racist character. The dominant frame's negative portrayals of women and men of color, especially black women and men, have important similarities, but they are not interchangeable. Consider the negative portrayals of black women that are commonplace in this society. In a recent research study, social scientists had three groups of mostly white college students view three different videos—with one group viewing a video with a strongly stereotyped image of a black woman as a housekeeper/mammy, another group viewing a strong stereotype of a black woman as a sexually aggressive "jezebel," and a third group viewing a nonstereotypical image of a white man retrieving a morning newspaper. Then the three groups were asked to observe mock employment interviews, one with a black female applicant and another with a white female applicant, both with similar abilities and answers. After this observation of employment interviews, the subjects were asked to determine if a list of positive, negative, mammy, jezebel, and neutral adjectives indicating character traits fit the person in the employment interview they observed. The mostly white subjects who observed the black interviewee linked her more quickly with *negative* character adjectives than with positive character adjectives. The opposite was true for those who had observed the white interviewee. In addition, when asked to assess a black or white job applicant, the subjects who had viewed the jezebel video and also observed the black interviewee responded more quickly to jezebel-type (sexual) adjectives than to other adjectives offered to them.[33]

Viewing one black woman in an employment interview was enough of a cue to stimulate these subjects to draw on the negative sexual image of the black woman, one that has long been part of the dominant racial frame. These quick associations of positive and negative adjectives with white women or black women not only indicate a knowledge of old gendered-racist stereotypes of black women, but also suggest a deep, often automatic, acceptance of them.

Today, the mass media remain central to the perpetuation of this gendered-racist framing of black women. For example, in spring 2007 radio commentaries by the popular talk show host, Don Imus, included blatantly racist comments about a successful and mostly black women's college basketball team. He laughingly called these talented young college students "nappy-headed hos." Famous for his barbed comments, Imus brought the harsh and sexualized framing of black women usually reserved for the white backstage out into the public frontstage, and he got fired. Yet, because radio executives wanted him, he was soon back on the radio. The mostly white and male executives generally decide what blatantly racist elements from the dominant frame can be openly used by media commentators and entertainers on their "news" or "entertainment" programs.[34]

Explicit in Imus's emotion-laden imagery is the centuries-old view that black women are not as beautiful as white women. Recall that early in the development of the dominant frame a hierarchy of human beauty was developed by whites. In the late eighteenth century, for example, Thomas Jefferson made clear in his articulation of the racist frame that white was beautiful and black ugly, a view also asserted by Benjamin Franklin, who revealed a strong aesthetic bias against the color of the Africans and an assertive preference for the "lovely white and red."[35] In contemporary U.S. society black girls and women continue to endure much negative white imaging and commentary on their physical appearance in various settings, including the media, and in recurring advertising that suggests black women's bodies are not as beautiful as white women's bodies. Undeniably, white women have long been the standard for female beauty in North America.[36]

White views of black men likewise reveal aspects of gendered racism, as in the criminality stereotype. For many white and other nonblack Americans, just hearing words like "black man" stimulate an immediate mental image of a large black man with physically threatening characteristics. In research studies even subliminal presentations of black male faces, flashed so quickly that the conscious mind does not notice them, trigger negative white responses more so than white male faces. One research study gave white subjects a dot matrix with very fast presentations of the faces of young black men and young white men looking forward. The researchers found that white subjects gave significantly more attention to black male faces than to comparable white faces. However, in a second study using black faces with averted-eye gazes, the researchers found that these black faces did *not* capture the white subjects attention. Apparently, in this study at least, young black men were especially noticed or considered dangerous only if they were looking at a white person. Overall, the researchers concluded that the white view of black men as threatening is "so robust and ingrained in the collective American unconscious that Black men now capture attention."[37] Notice too that these otherwise savvy researchers fail to make clear here that it is the *white* "American unconscious" that is especially central in this phenomenon. Moreover, our previous historical analysis shows that this white fear of black men is not a biological or evolutionary reaction to the physical environment, but rather a social construction that is an old part of the white racist framing of society.

Significantly, the dominant white standard for what is a "real man" in U.S. society is still white-male and patriarchal. The most famous television program with a strong black male figure in U.S. history was probably the long-running Bill Cosby show. One major research study of this comedy series found that most white viewers who were interviewed liked the positive black family portrayal with its strong male figure (a comedic father figure), yet many of these whites did not change their negative views of black Americans and their families generally as a result of viewing that show. Instead, the majority categorized Cosby's strong father figure and his family as "exceptions to their race" and stuck with the dominant racist framing of black Americans as lazy and as capable of succeeding if they would work harder. Oddly enough, a black television "family" was cited by whites as strong evidence that most black Americans were actually inferior to white Americans.[38] Such reactions are commonplace in many societal settings. The achievements of individual African Americans such as Bill Cosby or Barack Obama, and their personal efforts to counter the dominant frame's racist images, often have little impact on the general racial frame because their achievements are viewed by many whites as just "exceptions to their race," exceptions that to them prove that their racist framing of most black Americans is correct. New information countering the racist frame, thus, seldom changes it in its fundamentals.

The mostly white executives in major U.S. media, entertainment, public relations, and advertising companies obviously work hard to get people to watch or listen to their media presentations and buy their advertised commodities. In so doing they significantly shape trends in popular culture, which is today substantially a mass media culture. When these contemporary trends are racially oriented, this media-influenced "popular" culture typically draws important elements from the dominant white racial frame. Popular culture thus can play a significant role in channeling when and where the elements of that old racial frame get popularly expressed. Popular culture does sometimes shift and periodically tolerate more overt expressions of the old racist frame, but then may retreat from those racist expressions if there is too much public criticism, as in the Don Imus case. Note too that in spite of the presence of numerous entertainers of color, U.S. popular culture is mostly white-controlled through decisions of the top corporate executives. Even leading black entertainers such as Bill Cosby and Oprah Winfrey, as well as major rappers, work for or depend on these top white executives at the major media and entertainment firms that control most of their access to the general public. They all must acquiesce in various ways to the dominant racial hierarchy and its rationalizing racial frame.

More than Words: Strong Racial Emotions

In most examples of contemporary racial stereotyping, we observe that the verbal elements of the dominant racial frame are frequently linked to significant visual imagery and to major human emotions. Today, as in past centuries, an emotional construction of racial realities is usually present where there is a verbal construction. W. E. B. Du Bois once suggested that the color bar is created not only by whites' ill will, but also by more powerful motives, by what he called the "irrational reactions unpierced by reason."[39] What are these emotions? Some are obvious in previous examples, and others become obvious as one reflects on white actions over the course of U.S. history. Over this history one often observes that a greedy and predatory desire for material wealth has from the beginning been an important motivator of whites' racial thought and actions, including the killing and enslavement of other peoples. A strong desire for dominance, often associated with a type of white masculinity, seems common in this history as well. Other motivating emotions for such oppression have included a racialized arrogance or an anxiety over possible resistance from those oppressed. Strongly anti-black actions have also often entailed a visceral hate dimension, what Joel Kovel has called the "madness" of white racism.[40]

In his pathbreaking analysis of white fear, another important emotion we have already noted, Kovel has argued that whites typically reject blackness and black bodies because they project their own fears, often rooted in childhood, into the dark otherness of an objectified black person. In the childhood socialization process, most whites learn, consciously or unconsciously, to associate black people and blackness with dirt, danger, ignorance, or the unknown.[41] For this reason, the black targets of white hostility and discrimination are not seen as "one of us." The racialized others become a general "they" or "you people" to be marginalized, excluded, or otherwise discriminated against. Over time, white racist thought and action also involves a massive breakdown of positive emotions such as empathy, the human capacity to experience the feelings of members of an outgroup unlike your own. Holding back or destroying positive emotions, especially empathy with those across the racial line, seems essential to creating a system of racial oppression like that in North America.

Today, to take perhaps the most conspicuous example, strong racist emotions can be seen in white supremacist groups with which hundreds of thousands of whites are at least loosely affiliated. Some of the fiercely emotional partisans of white supremacy and racial segregation today can be found in white nationalist groups that make effective use of the Internet to peddle their extreme versions of the white racial frame. For example, there is a "Stormfront" website, now the largest explicitly white nationalist site on the Internet with its 129,000 registered users and millions of posts articulating a strong white supremacist framing. In the summer of 2008 this website featured a portrait labeled "Thomas Jefferson, white nationalist," as part of a featured banner at the top of its first webpage. This portrait had a famous quote from Jefferson's autobiography: "Nothing is more certainly written in the book of fate than that these people are to be free. Nor is it less certain that the two races, equally free, cannot live in the same government."[42] These whites accent what they, like Jefferson, view as an absolute necessity for the United States—a complete geographical separation of white and black Americans. The hundreds of thousands of whites who today flock to these websites draw heavily on one of the oldest versions of the white frame, what might even be called a "hyper-frame" because in it one finds overtly proclaimed with much emotion a very strong white racist framing of U.S. and global racial matters.

Other Americans of Color

Continuing Racist Framing of Native Americans

In some ways the oldest North Americans, Native Americans, are today the most invisible of Americans of color. In public discussions of issues like affirmative action or employment discrimination, Native Americans are usually the Americans of color least focused upon and the least considered for anti-discrimination government policy. As I suggested previously, they are not part of most whites' recurring interactions and experiences. Their relative invisibility to influential and ordinary whites today may be in part because a significant proportion of the Native American population is out of the sight of most whites—that is, they currently live in rural areas or in towns and cities away from the East and West coasts. They are also a relatively small group—because of earlier centuries of white genocide, a bloody history erased in much contemporary white memory. Central to maintaining the white frame's image of whites as virtuous involves a *collective forgetting* about how whites historically reduced this important North American population to national invisibility.

Today, numerous old racist views of Native Americans remain in the contemporary white framing, including images of Indians as lazy, drug- or alcohol-addicted, criminal, foreign, and not quite American. One Internet-based study of nearly 45,000 people, using explicit attitudinal questions, found that the majority said that they viewed Native Americans as being "more American" than white Americans. However, when the Implicit Association Test was used to measure the strength of their positive associations with "American," the white faces in the test were found to be more strongly associated with the concept of "American" than were the Native American faces. Strikingly, this implicit bias against Native American faces as more foreign and less American than white faces was found not only for white respondents, but also for people in all other racial groups except Native Americans. The researchers found a sharp contrast between respondents feeling they *should* say that Native Americans were very American in reply to the explicit questions asked of them, yet contradicting themselves with negative evaluations of their American-ness in their unconscious responses to real Native American faces.[43]

Other negative stereotypes and images of Native Americans can be found in the media, school textbooks and popular fiction, and school and professional sports' mascots. For example, in spring 2008 the white host of a North Carolina radio show openly stereotyped Native Americans in his long on-air discussion. Joking with white guests, he mocked Indians as "lazy" several times and claimed his view of Indians was statistically proven. For his likely uninformed listeners, such claims appear as actual "information" that reinforces the old racist framing of Native Americans. The white host and his guests mixed racist joking with serious discussions, including about whether a particular North Carolina tribe had been federally recognized as such and whether Indians would consider the term "sitting Indian-style" as offensive. On the show the host asked a white intern who was marrying a Native American if the latter's grandfather would stand on road with a "single tear," referring to the stereotyped 1970s "Crying Indian" advertisements. Another white man on the program asked the intern if the couple was "gonna have a teepee-warming party?" After listener protests, the show was briefly suspended, but soon returned to the airwaves. As in the aforementioned Don Imus case, this racist stream of consciousness was permitted to continue, with brief interruption, by executives at one of the country's leading mass media corporations.[44]

Recent research studies of elementary, high-school, and college text-books have discovered many negative stereotypes and images straight out of the old white racial frame. These textbooks often deal briefly with indigenous peoples, but as though they are only part of past history —and that history is usually sanitized or described inaccurately. In addition, numerous children's books and children's movies frequently portray Indians with images of Pocahontas-type "princesses," "squaws" (a derogatory term), or male "warriors," dressed in a stereotyped fashion. In this country one also observes continuing and negative warrior-type framing in the sports mascots used by many high school, college, and professional sports teams in numerous towns and cities. Examples of crude racist imagery out of the frame are the Chief Wahoo caricature widely used by the Cleveland "Indians" baseball team, the Indian carica-ture and tomahawk imagery of the Atlanta "Braves" baseball team, and the Indian caricatures used by the Washington "Redskins" (a vicious racist epithet) football team.[45]

Even today, the non-Indian management of these teams, who are mostly but not exclusively white, and many of their supporters see no problem with such extremely racist images and indeed have vigorously opposed significant changes. Indeed, some whites have engineered emo-tional counter-protests against Native Americans who have organized and protested this commonplace pseudo-Indian imagery. The omnipresent, white-generated parodies of Native American images, sacred chants, face paint, headdresses, and drums just for sports fans' entertainment are taken, realistically, by many Native Americans as assaults on them and their cultures, not the least because many of these items have spiritual signifi-cance for them. Notice too that the sports mascots and related fan gestures are usually based on old emotion-laden stereotypes of Indians as wild "savages" or bloodthirsty warriors. That is, they are today viewed much like they were in eighteenth-century framing, such as that in Thomas Jefferson's portrait of "merciless Indian Savages" in the Declaration of Independence. Both Jefferson's racist framing and the contemporary white-controlled framing of Native Americans ignore the historical reality of the truly "savage" European Americans stealing Native American lands by bloody, often genocidal means. Note too that the Indian symbolism chosen by professional and college sports teams frames and accents Indians only as historical groups and thereby ignores their reality as oppressed and marginalized Americans of color on the contemporary scene. The often emotional and successful white resistance to Native American attempts to get rid of this extraordinarily racist imagery reveals yet again that whites as a group continue to have the dominant power in determining how and where the white racial frame operates in contemporary U.S. society.[46]

The Continuing Racist Framing of Asian Americans

Over the centuries whites, especially those in the elite, have been active agents extending the white racial frame, initially developed for rationalizing the oppression of Native and African Americans, to numerous other groups. As we have already seen, during the mid-nineteenth century Chinese workers and Mexican farmers and workers were the first Asians and Latin Americans incorporated into U.S. society and its racial hierarchy and framing. They were brought in as part of the large-scale white expansion in the West, which included recruitment of Chinese laborers for West Coast enterprises like railroads and the imperialistic Mexican American War that brought Mexicans into the union. Each new group thus encountered and exploited by whites was added to the racial hierarchy and to the white racial frame.

Over the last century, moreover, whites have continued this process of expanding the racial hierarchy and dominant white frame to include an array of immigrants of color. We do not have the space to review this process in detail, but we can examine some important examples. As we previously saw in a diary account, the one where students sang a song mocking the Japanese flash-burned on walls during U.S. bombing attacks, whites view Asians and Asian Americans as available targets for racial stereotyping, imaging, and hostility. The dominant white racist frame includes a strong subframe with distinctive language and images targeting people of Asian descent. Over the last century and more, Chinese, Japanese, and other Asian Americans have been imaged and labeled in many areas of society as "the pollutant, the coolie, the deviant, the yellow peril, the model minority, and the gook . . . as an alien body and a threat to the American national family."[47] For example, in movies and other mass media from 1910 to the present day, Asian American characters have periodically been pictured as distinctive foreigners, outsiders, villains, and criminals. In a process led by elite whites in the media and politics, they have been stereotyped as "inscrutable Orientals," poor English speakers, drug dealers, gang members, and dangerous or treacherous.[48] Note too that most such racialized stereotypes and images are variations on preexisting images from the older racist framing of African and Native Americans.

As with other white racist framing, this anti-Asian framing has had significant societal consequences. The negative U.S. framing of the Japanese played some role, albeit one still debated, in the build-up to World War II. From the early 1900s to the 1930s, in the U.S. mass media and in political speeches, moviemakers, writers, and politicians attacked in racialized terms not only the expanding Japanese empire in the Pacific, but also Japanese Americans in California and Hawaii.

The Japanese empire's expansion in the Pacific bumped up hard against the expanding U.S. empire in the same area. In the first decades of the twentieth century, white writers and cartoonists set forth many racist images such as that of a devious, threatening, and buck-toothed "Jap." White leaders argued that the Japanese were immoral, and used the ape imagery for them that had been applied earlier to African Americans. U.S. military and political leaders acted out of an anti-Japanese racist framing that was a subframe of their dominant racial frame. In the middle of World War II, for example, West Coast military commander General John DeWitt aggressively asserted that "A Jap's a Jap. The Japanese race is an enemy race, and while many second- and third-generation Japanese born on U.S. soil, possessed of U.S. citizenship, have become 'Americanized,' the racial strains are undiluted." DeWitt was echoing a racist view widely held in the white population, including the elite. Fearing enemy collaborators in what they had framed as a "large alien population," these white leaders moved most Japanese Americans into what were euphemistically called "internment camps" (actually, *concentration camps*) in inland areas of the western United States. In this extremely discriminatory removal process, most of these Americans lost land and other property they had worked hard for, and some died or were injured protesting discriminatory treatment. Clearly, racist subframes have had serious consequences for Asian Americans.[49]

In recent decades Asian Americans have continued to face much negative racial framing, with substantial stereotyping and mocking, and consequent discrimination. They are often viewed by whites as somehow un-American and culturally inferior or problematical. Their language or speech is frequently mocked, and their physical features are periodically caricatured in visual imagery. For example, the Adidas company recently produced some shoes with a logo that had a negative caricature of a buck-toothed, slant-eyed Asian. Similar white-framed images of Asian Americans are used in many areas of society. In the late 1990s the editors of the widely circulated *National Review* magazine placed a cartoon-like caricature of then President Bill Clinton and Hillary Clinton as slant-eyed, buck-toothed Chinese figures with Chinese hats, an image critiquing them for Democratic fundraising allegedly involving Asians.[50] More recently, a movie animation company created a *Mr. Wong* cartoon with a crude caricature of a Chinese "hunchbacked, yellow-skinned, squinty-eyed character who spoke with a thick accent and starred in an interactive music video titled 'Saturday Night Yellow Fever.' "[51] This mocking of Asian people can also be seen in the puppet movie, *Team America: World Police*, which included a Korean official speaking gibberish in a mock-Asian accent. The movie was "an hour and a half of racial mockery with an 'if you are offended, you obviously can't take a joke' tacked on at the end."[52]

This language mocking and its associated anti-Asian images remain a significant part of the contemporary framing of Asian Americans. Asian American children and adults often are forced to endure hostile mocking such as: "Ching chong Chinaman sitting on a rail, along came a white man and snipped off his tail"; "Ah so. No tickee, No washee. So sorry, so sollee"; and "Chinkee, Chink, Jap, Nip, zero, Dothead . . . Flip, Hindoo."[53] A Toledo radio station's white disc-jockey recently phoned Asian restaurants using mock-Asian speech, including "ching, chong chung" and "me speakee no English." On her talk show prominent comedian Rosie O'Donnell repeatedly used "ching chong" to mock Chinese speech.[54] Such language stereotyping and mocking involve racializing *sounds* and have long been part of the dominant racial frame and have been directed not only at Asian Americans but also at African, Native, and Latino Americans. This hostile language mocking is usually linked to other important racialized stereotyping and imagery that whites hold in their negative framing of those Americans of color. Language researcher Rosina Lippi-Green has noted an essential point about such routinized mocking: "Not all foreign accents, but only accent linked to skin that isn't white . . . evokes such negative reactions."[55]

During the 1960s the "model minority" image of Asian Americans, a significant addition to the contemporary white frame, was added by elite whites in academia, the media, and the political arena. The main reason appears to have been to counter the anti-racist arguments and actions of black civil rights demonstrators in the 1960s civil rights protest era. The model minority imagery, and indeed the term itself, were *not* created by Asian Americans, but by influential whites. The idea was apparently first articulated by social scientist William Petersen, who in a 1966 *New York*

Times article, entitled "Success Story, Japanese-American Style," celebrated some of the socioeconomic achievements of Japanese Americans, which were contrasted to the situation of black Americans, who were then actively protesting oppressive conditions.[56] Some months later, a *U.S. News & World Report* article similarly celebrated Chinese Americans for their hard-work values and argued that if African Americans were like these Asian Americans there would be no need to spend "hundreds of billions to uplift" them.[57] Clearly, white Americans in elite positions in academia, the media, and government agencies have regularly helped to generate or reinforce this new stereotype in the dominant framing of Asian Americans. The model minority image is frequently trotted out when elite whites or their minions wish to put down the efforts or character of people of color who are not Asian.

This serves the interests of whites as the top group in the racial hierarchy. Asian Americans suffer because this imagery conceals the harsh reality of racial hostility and discrimination that they too routinely encounter from whites, which in reality often limits their achievements in society. It also conceals numerous other problems generated for Asian Americans in this white-controlled society, including the significant poverty faced by some Asian American groups. Not surprisingly, thus, one recent summary of research on experiences of Asian American students on campuses shows that the usually white-generated images they face are often quite "negative, such as perceptions that Asians 'don't speak English well,' 'have accents,' and are 'submissive,' 'sneaky,' 'stingy,' 'greedy,' etc."[58] A principal point about both the white-generated model minority and other common Asian American imagery is that whites, especially those with significant resources, have the power to specify how a group of color is framed in U.S. society.

The Continuing Racist Framing of Latinos

Today, Latinos make up the largest group of Americans of color, with Mexican Americans being the most numerous in this umbrella group. At the beginning of white contacts with Mexicans in the 1830s and 1840s, as we have seen, whites viewed the latter out of the old racist frame they had already constructed for African and Native Americans. This pattern has continued over the last century. For example, during the 1920s a prominent white member of the U.S. Congress described Mexican immigrants as an undesirable and "mongrelized" mixture of the Spanish and "low-grade Indians," but with troubling African "blood" added in. Again we see a very negative view of "racial mixing." Similarly, during this era a white Ivy League professor expressed the fear of many whites that they would eventually be eliminated from the United States because of this racial interbreeding and that the "progeny of Mexican peons" would long "continue to afflict us with an embarrassing race problem."[59]

This imagery of being overwhelmed by people "lower" in the U.S. hierarchy remains strong today in the dominant framing of Mexican and other Latin American immigrants and their descendants. We have noted previously the white exaggerations of the size of the U.S. black population, which suggest similarly racialized fears. At one 1990s meeting on Mexican immigration in California, a white state senator expressed opposition to public schooling for children of Mexican immigrants, describing the latter as "on the lower scale of our humanity." Here again, the great-chain-of-being notions about "lower scale" people remains strong in the dominant racial framing. Significantly too, the U.S. Latinos who publicly criticized this white senator's racist comments were themselves attacked in some of the white-controlled mass media.[60] Using more circumspect language, but making a similar point that the U.S. "civilization" was under significant threat from Mexican and other Latino immigrants, the late Harvard professor, Samuel Huntington, wrote and lectured out of a strong white racist framing of Mexican Americans, whom he viewed as having a culture inferior (for example, lacking in ambition) to that of white Anglo-Saxon-Protestants.[61]

Immigrants from Latin America and their children are today stereotyped and framed in various ways. Linguistics researcher Otto Santa Ana has investigated the language and metaphorical imagery used in reporting on undocumented immigrants in a major West Coast newspaper. His analysis of newspaper articles revealed that the mostly white editors and reporters there made frequent use of negative language portraying Latino immigrants as animals, invaders, or disreputable persons. Numerous articles used a framing that animalized immigrants, with some similarities to the animalizing of African Americans we have previously noted. In the newspaper government health and other social programs were described as "a lure to immigrants," and the California electorate was said to have an appetite for "the red meat of deportation." Reporters described federal immigration agents as catching "their quarry" and spoke of the need to "ferret out illegal immigrants." The reporters' use of strong metaphor-linked words such as burden, dirt, disease, invasion, and floods, explicitly or implicitly, conveyed images of Mexican and other Latin American immigrants as threatening, dangerous, and burdensome.[62]

Whites' negative framing of Mexican Americans and other Latinos can also be seen in the ways in which whites have stereotyped and imaged them, much like black Americans, as violent and criminal now over many decades. For example, a 1940s report by a white police officer, backed up by his white superior in the Los Angeles Sheriff's Department, alleged that

Mexican Americans had a desire for street violence that was an "inborn characteristic." Reflecting on the era of the 1940s, one prominent white scholar wrote at the time that the Mexican American was justifiably viewed as " 'lawless' and 'violent' because he had Indian blood; he was 'shiftless' and 'improvident' because that was his nature."[63] This commentary shows how strong the central racist stereotypes of Mexican Americans were in the white racial framing even before recent increases in immigration. Two decades later in the 1960s, a leading historian of the Southwest, Walter Prescott Webb, framed Mexican Americans in a similar way: "There is a cruel streak in the Mexican nature" and that "may and doubtless should be attributed partly to the Indian blood."[64]

The traditional white framing has long accented, often prominently and overtly, notions of "blood," violence, and criminality in assessing most Americans of color, including Latino groups. These negative stereotypes have regularly appeared in movies and television programs. Over recent decades Hollywood films, such as *Dirty Harry* (1971), *Falling Down* (1993), and *Gran Torino* (2008), as well as numerous television crime dramas, have portrayed U.S. Latinos as disproportionately violent criminals, "gangbangers," drug users, and welfare mothers. This negative framing of Mexican Americans and other Latinos, moreover, is found in the views of whites at various class levels. For example, one survey of white college students found them agreeing that Hispanics were more likely than whites to be physically violent, dirty, uneducated, and criminally inclined.[65]

Today, many whites continue to stereotype and frame U.S. Latinos in conventional ways. In this survey of white college students, they also expressed the belief that, compared with whites, Latinos place less value on economic prosperity, learning, and "mature love." In addition, the majority of white respondents in another opinion survey believed that Latinos "tend to have bigger families than they are able to support," while one-fifth felt Latinos lacked "ambition and the drive to succeed."[66] Recently, several researchers have found strong anti-Latino, especially anti-immigrant, views among whites in the South and Midwest, including among whites who live in rural or small town areas. Interestingly, many of these latter places have rather small Mexican American and other Latino populations. This demographic reality suggests how powerful and national the white racial framing of Latinos is, for it is often strong locally even where there are relatively few people targeted by it.[67]

As with other Americans of color, whites have included in the Mexican American and other Latino subframes of the dominant racial frame much language mocking, which is commonly expressed with joking and laughter. Mocking Spanish involves whites, frequently in the middle and upper classes, creating derisive terms like "no problemo," "el cheapo," "watcho your backo," and "hasty banana," as well as phrases like "numero uno" and "no way, José." Such mock Spanish by white English speakers generates, overtly or subtly, a negative view of Spanish, those who speak it, and their culture. Mock Spanish, together with associated caricatures of "lazy" or "oversexed" Mexicans, is commonplace in gift shops, board rooms, and the media, especially in the Southwest. Even though today openly racist talk is often frowned upon by many whites, nonetheless, this mock Spanish is still used by whites in both public settings and backstage settings. It thereby perpetuates negative stereotypes and images of Mexicans and Mexican Americans, as well as other Latinos, in ways that whites may view as harmless. However, as Jane Hill has shown, the significance and impact are indeed quite substantial: "Through this process, [Latinos] are endowed with gross sexual appetites, political corruption, laziness, disorders of language, and mental incapacity."[68] Such repetitive mocking routinely reinforces the anti-Latino frame in the minds of whites and others of all ages and classes.

Throughout much of the contemporary racial framing of Mexican Americans and other Latinos one observes frequent negative references to immigrants. One commonplace view of these immigrants is that they somehow cannot be fully incorporated into U.S. society. That is, they do not want to adapt, or do not adapt well, to the dominant English language and Anglocentric cultural traditions. However, this idea of "assimilation" is itself problematic, because for more than a century this commonplace idea has developed within a strong racist framing of U.S. society. For that reason the idea of assimilation is usually accompanied by an insistence on the one-way adaptation of immigrants, especially immigrants of color, to the white-dominated culture and pre-existing racial hierarchy. Even the scholarly literature on the immigrant incorporation process tends to make use of the term and idea of assimilation uncritically, and thereby to reinforce the dominant racial framing and hierarchy. Indeed, the conventional white racial frame and the U.S. racial hierarchy are often, consciously or unconsciously, assumed by many scholars and media analysts to be part of the normal nature of this society and thus something that naturally has to be accommodated by new immigrants of color. Today, for the most part, whites will reciprocally assimilate only to aspects of new immigrants' cultures that do not threaten white dominance, such as to some immigrants' music or food preferences.[69]

As a matter of everyday reality, thus, Americans of color, including immigrants from Latin America and Asia, are more or less forced to accept much of the white racial frame and hierarchy. The mostly white-controlled media and schools aggressively press them to conform constantly over their lifetimes. They learn that they must more or less conform to many white-normed and white-framed societal realities, so that they can survive in this still racially oppressive society. Indeed, they adapt much more cooperatively to many of these societal pressures, such as in learning the English language, than most whites are willing to give them credit for.[70]

This pressure to conform has numerous negative consequences. One of the striking things about the white racial frame today is how widespread many of its essential elements are across this society. For example, even many new immigrants of color, such as new Latino and Asian immigrants who have been interviewed recently, carry important bits of the white frame in their heads, frequently imbibing them from a now global U.S. mass media even before they have arrived in the United States. They, as well as other Americans of color who have been in the country for a long time, often accept significant parts of the dominant white racial framing— sometimes including negative stereotypes and framing that whites have historically directed at their own Latino, Asian, African, and Native American groups. Americans of color that I and my colleagues have recently interviewed often buy so strongly into white racial framing of yet other Americans of color that they do not trust or relate well to the latter. Such cross-racial framing makes intergroup collaboration and cooperation in the struggle against white racism much more difficult. Once again, a key consequence of the white racial frame is the maintenance of white privilege and dominance at the top of the racial hierarchy.[71]

Conclusion: Some Scholarly Impacts

The white racial frame is amazingly pervasive throughout U.S. society today. One finds it operating in both obvious and unexpected places, influencing much in the domestic society and indeed in global society. Even white scholars, researchers, and others with much education often think and write, consciously or unreflectively, out of a strong and unexamined version of the white racial frame.

For example, biology professor Joan Herbers has recently pointed out how certain words or concepts from older versions of the white frame are still used in the physical sciences. She notes that biological scientists and writers still use the terms "slave-making ants" and "negro ants" because of the behavior of a specific type of ant that preys on other ants. Like the U.S. founders who used slavery as a metaphor for their political oppression at British hands, even today some scientists reference the enslavement of black Americans in their scientific naming and discourse, likely without a thought to the larger frame from which it comes. Herbers thus argues to her colleagues that "using the slavery metaphor today is anachronistic, and I submit that it is time to discard it altogether." One reason to do this is because regularly using this slavery metaphor may possibly trigger subliminal links in some minds to the historical enslavement of black Americans, and thus may subtly help to normalize both that historical reality and its contemporary racist manifestations.[72]

Periodically, various researchers in both the biological sciences and the social sciences have revealed that they think, talk, and act uncritically out of this old white racial frame. Take the case of the white researchers, Richard Herrnstein and Charles Murray, who in the 1990s made influential arguments that paper-and-pencil "intelligence" test data demonstrated conclusively that black and Latino Americans were intellectually inferior to whites. In their view, which has been picked up by numerous popular analysts to the present day, certain black-white genetic differences account to a substantial degree for racial differences in these conventional test scores.[73] Some might argue that this 1990s perspective on white-black intelligence is something no scientists still accept, yet one of the most distinguished physical scientists, James Watson, co-discover of the double-helix structure of DNA and Nobel prize winner, argued in 2007 that IQ-test data indicated that black people were less intelligent than whites. He noted that, "All our social policies are based on the fact that their intelligence is the same as ours—whereas all the testing says not really."[74] However, the scholars and popular analysts who make such arguments never seem to recognize that they are thinking out of an uncritical white frame of reference. They write as though there is no other way to view the group data on the conventional skills tests (inaccurately termed "intelligence" tests) that they review other than their negative racial framing of the supposedly lesser intelligence of people of color. They do not critically analyze the fact that for the most part these tests were created by and normed on whites, nor the fact that much of the substance of the tests directly or indirectly reflects the knowledge and culture of those who made up what are actually "skills" tests.

We might note too that some years earlier in 2000, James Watson hypothesized that because research data on melanin (which creates skin color) suggest that extracts can enhance the sex drive that dark-skinned people have a greater sex drive than lighter-skinned people. This unreflective, white-framed approach to the biology of "race" is an old approach that most scientists of all types used in the early, more overtly racist, decades of the twentieth century, but which the substantial majority of physical and social scientists have since abandoned in recent decades.[75]

Moreover, in analyses of U.S. history some white historians have periodically, if unconsciously, revealed an uncritical white racial framing of society. For example, the otherwise insightful white historian, Winthrop Jordan, has written frequently and unreflectively like this: "By 1790 . . .

Americans had been transformed into a free people, dwelling in an open land under an ordered government constructed on principles which were the antithesis of hierarchical."[76] Yet, at that time, a great many Americans had not been thus transformed, especially African Americans and Native Americans (and, indeed, white women). Even for the otherwise savvy Winthrop, thus, the word "Americans" often means "whites." Writing in the 1960s, Jordan also viewed "races" as biologically real, although changing with environmental conditions. Numerous recent scholars continue this insensitivity to the language they use in otherwise critical analyses of U.S. society.

Clearly, the white racial frame permeates not only the thinking of ordinary Americans today, both those who are white and those who are not white, but also many of the most savvy scholars and influential analysts in the United States.

CHAPTER **6**

The Frame in Everyday Operation

From the beginning racial oppression has been part of the deep structure and longterm development of this society. To make sense out of this systemic racism, we need to consider not only its early material development and rationalizing frame, but also the ways in which it continues to operate in this society. Today, as in the past, the dominant white racial frame continues to shape, structure, and rationalize an array of racially exploitative and discriminatory actions by whites, and sometimes others, in this society. A central aspect of the white racial frame is its persistent interpretive and motivating power in generating everyday actions, which is one way we know the shape it takes in human minds. Whites routinely engage in racial performances and discriminatory behaviors motivated by the racist stereotypes, images, narratives, and emotions of that frame. The dominant racial framing does not exist apart from actions. Indeed, it was originally created to rationalize an array of discriminatory actions. Thus, today the dominant racial frame both generates, and is reinforced by, a myriad of discriminatory actions in everyday life.

The Frame in Everyday Operation: The Backstage

Much contemporary research shows the still severe and destructive reality and consequences of systemic racism. Psychological researchers have found that virtually all whites are aware of major elements in the dominant racial frame, especially the age-old anti-black stereotypes, no matter what their personal inclinations to act on them may be. Automatic mental processing brings up commonplace racist stereotypes in the minds of most people whenever an appropriate stimulus appears, such as a member of a racial outgroup. However, this research also indicates that very prejudiced people are more inclined to act on the activated racial stereotypes, while less prejudiced people often engage in mental processing that ignores or rejects all or part of the triggered stereotypes.[1]

Research studies have found that those who show an implicit racial bias on measures like the Implicit Association Test (of different faces) are more likely to engage in overt racial performances and other types of racist action, including discrimination against people of color. Studies at Rutgers University found that white and other nonblack subjects who revealed greater implicit bias toward black Americans on psychological tests were more likely than other subjects to report engaging in discrimination such as hurling racist slurs, excluding black people, and threatening physical harm to black people. Moreover, in assessing hypothetical university situations, white students with strong racial biases were also more likely to recommend budget cuts for black, Asian, and Jewish student organizations (that is, potential economic discrimination).[2] Clearly. the dominant racial frame is so deeply entrenched in society and in individual minds that most whites do not realize how routinely they act out of it.

Given that most of the social psychological studies we have examined reveal a strong racial bias for a substantial majority of whites, it is not surprising that field studies also show a substantial level of racist performances and other racial behavior. In our in-depth interviewing and other field research, my colleagues and I have found that much blatantly racist thought, commentary, and performance has become concentrated in the social "backstage," that is, social settings where only whites are present. Much less is performed in the social "frontstage," social settings where there are strangers or people from diverse racial groups present. This is because of pressures to be socially correct ("colorblind") in frontstage areas such as workplaces and public accommodations.

For example, examining these two faces of white racism today, Leslie Houts Picca and I recently analyzed journals from 626 white students at more than two dozen colleges and universities in several regions. These students were asked to record their observations of everyday events in their lives that exhibited racial issues, images, and understandings. In relatively brief diaries (on average, 6–9 weeks) these white college students gave us *thousands* of accounts of blatantly and obviously racist commentary and actions by white friends, acquaintances, relatives, and strangers—much of it in the backstage areas. In addition, some 308 students of color at these same colleges gave us several thousand more diary accounts of racist events that had happened to them or friends and relatives of color.

The white journal accounts offer many insights into how the white racial frame operates in whites' everyday lives. Let us examine a few examples that show the range of racial performances and other actions. In one journal excerpt a white female student at a midwestern college comments on a recent trip with two white friends on Halloween:

> I rode in the car with my best friend Abby and her new boyfriend Todd. It takes a little over an hour to get to . . . the Haunted Trail . . . so Todd decided to put in a little music. I'm not really sure what types of bands played this but it wasn't real music. They were songs about black people and they were very harsh and very gross. The lyrics said things about hanging, and they were good for nothing, and shooting, and such. Todd thought it was hilarious, he loved it! Abby and I were disgusted, I couldn't believe that he actually liked this, and that people would actually seriously say these things. We finally asked him to turn it off and to play the radio. He turned the radio on but he seemed rather reluctant, it seems that he was enjoying what we had been listening too. We asked him if he was racist and he said, "Hell yeah!" I don't remember exactly what he said now but he talked about how he thought that black people were only good for the sports they played in, how he hated the fact that they all smoked and pretended to be cool. I was surprised that Abby would date someone like this, because we have a few black friends from her school. I know that he wouldn't have said that around just anyone, cuz he would probably get his ass kicked. Other than these comments and his bad choice of music he seemed like a fun guy to hang out with.[3]

Unmistakably, the anti-black aspects of the white racial frame are not something only to be found in decades past, for they are still routinely expressed and acted on by many whites. Here a strong racist framing is aggressively expressed in an everyday social interaction. Notice two categories of actors—a central protagonist and two mild dissenters who tolerated the extreme anti-black performance for some time. This account is in an interactive backstage where only whites are present. The protagonist is aggressively white-centered, and he enjoys supremacist music and obviously feels that he can impose his negative framing of African Americans on white friends. It takes a while for the women to get the music shifted to something else. Many whites enjoy or tolerate such white-oriented music, and clearly the mostly white executives who run the U.S. music industry provide the production and distribution facilities to circulate musical versions of the dominant racial frame in both its blatant and more subtle forms.

Notice too that the diarist describes the male protagonist as knowing when and where in his various social settings to accent racist views. Whites often speak and act differently in the all-white backstage and the diverse frontstage. There is an interesting rationalizing phenomenon here: If whites do not articulate racist ideas in public, if they keep them to themselves or just express them in the backstage, then they or their white friends and relatives often do not see them as seriously "racist." Articulating blatant elements of the racist frame in private settings seems to be at least acceptable, probably because in their view no one is "really hurt" by that tactic. What is particularly striking here and in numerous other student diary accounts is how the participants describe friends who do these blatantly racist performances as "nice," "fun to hang out with," or "not a racist." An accented view of *white virtue,* a very old concept in white racial framing, seems to override the actual reality of racist performances in many of the diary accounts. Also, numerous journal entries reveal that these college students do not want to describe their friends or relatives as "racist," or as doing racist stuff, even when that is obviously what they are doing. This is an important part of the colorblind version of the contemporary white racial frame—the view that one should play down or not see the actual racist behavior that one engages in, or that one's friends and relatives engage in.

In their diaries most of the students and their friends and relatives do not appear as extreme white supremacists like the young man in the previous account, but they still demonstrate much strong anti-black framing in the everyday accounts. Here is a typical example of a white performance of the anti-black subframe, in this case from a diary entry by Hannah, a white student who reports on a night of drinking at a northern college:

> Three of my friends (a white girl and two white boys) and I went back to my house to drink a little more before we ended the night. My one friend, Dylan started telling jokes. . . . Dylan said: "What's the most confusing day of the year in Harlem?" "Father's Day . . . Whose your Daddy?" Dylan also referred to black people as "Porch Monkeys." Everyone laughed a little, but it was obvious that we all felt a little less comfortable when he was telling jokes like that. My friend Dylan is not a racist person. He has more black friends than I do, that's why I was surprised he so freely said something like that. Dylan would never have said something like that around anyone who was a minority.[4]

Rather old anti-black stereotypes targeting black families, and using the ancient animalizing imagery, pervade this white performance. The emotion-laden stereotypes have an impact because of their frame resonance: The youthful listeners also have a deeply imbedded racial framing that resonates with these racist commentaries and thus enables the latter to have much more impact on their thinking and action than they otherwise would have. Indeed, a similar joke about whites would not have had this strong impact, because there is no negative antiwhite frame in white minds for such commentaries to resonate with.

Later in her diary Hannah provides reflective commentary that is rather unusual in these college student journals:

> It is this sort of "joking" that helps to keep racism alive today. People know the places they have to be politically correct and most people will be. However, until this sort of "behind-the-scenes" racism comes to an end, people will always harbor those stereotypical views that are so prevalent in our country.

In her perceptive commentary Hannah offers a rare recognition of how different white performances often are in the "behind-the-scenes" backstage. She recognizes how such performances in backstage settings maintain the dominant racist framing, and thus systemic racism. Nonetheless, even the perceptive Hannah is unwilling to classify her friend as "a racist person." Note too that the dominant racial framing is here performed in an intensely social and interactive setting. The performances emerging out of the dominant racial frame are frequently essential in integrating white networks, which makes implementing anti-racist changes more difficult. Researching an all-white country-and-western group, sociologist Nina Eliasoph discovered that overtly racist performances among them, like those of these students, helped to integrate the group socially. Ending racially framed conversations would likely have contributed to its breakup. Knowing the dominant racial frame well includes knowing "how and where it is appropriate to speak about it."[5]

The college diarists wrote numerous accounts about similar performances by relatives also operating out of a blatantly racist framing of African Americans. Note this journal entry from Tiffany about a well-framed performance by her father, in a midwestern home setting:

> We were watching the news and my father (white male in 40s) noticed that most of the stories they were telling had to deal with primarily black people. Once he started that the negative black jokes poured out of his mouth. He had some customers in the house (we own our own . . . repair shop) and he was still telling the jokes. He never thought twice about it. He never thought about what his customers might say or do. Some of the jokes were along the lines of "Why is Tylenol white? Answer: Cause if it was black it wouldn't work!" Everyone in the room was laughing and they all had their own

responses to the jokes. One lady (around 30 years of age) said "Yeah . . . that is true."[6]

Here too we have an important social setting, one in which racist commentaries seem to provide a type of "social glue." As they are in three quarters of all the student diary accounts of racist performances, African Americans are again primary targets of this performance, in this case in a backstage setting with white family members and customers. The central protagonist implies white virtue and asserts a four-centuries-old anti-black stereotype. Notice again the frame assumption. In many examples like this, white racist protagonists make the (usually reasonable) assumption that most other whites, in this case white customers, will agree, or at least not object, to overtly racist performances. Apparently, they did not object, as all were laughing and at least one agreed openly with this father's racist joking.

Judging from the college student diaries, frequent repetition of racial stereotypes, racialized jokes, racialized language, and racialized images is characteristic of many all-white private gatherings. The referents and symbols they use in their racist "joking" and related racist performances in backstage settings and, less often in frontstage settings, are generally emotion-laden and linked to a shared white racial frame. They use stereotypes, language, and other negative material regarding black Americans and other groups that dates back centuries, including the omnipresent N-word. The categories of racialized performances in our thousands of everyday accounts show us white protagonists, cheerleaders, and passive bystanders, but extremely few active white dissenters. Backstage events like these thus operate to regularly build and routinely reinforce the white racial frame and the important social relationships and performances among whites that sustain that frame.

The Normality of Everyday Racism

In the many accounts of racial events provided by these college students, whites frequently take material from the centuries-old racial framing and sometimes use it creatively, such as in the case of the student in the diary account in Chapter 1 who made a greeting card with the kittens and the N-word. Yet, no matter how creatively it may be performed, such racist framing is usually that which is, or would be, familiar to their parents, grandparents, and more distant ancestors. The array of racialized actions in the diaries is extensive. Not only do whites of various ages regularly make racist jokes, but they also call black Americans and other people of color the old racist epithets, make greeting cards with epithets, play supremacist music, mock black entertainers and leaders, yell racist epithets on the street, show racialized fear when black men are near, cross streets to avoid black people, make racist comments to black "friends," and mock any person who takes exception to their actions. In these many and diverse performances we see just how the white racial frame is much more than about thinking and believing racist "stuff," for it also involves imaging, feeling, talking, and acting as well. All this signals a well-established white worldview.

One of our significant findings from this journals' research is the distinction students make between backstage and frontstage settings and performances. These well-educated whites periodically comment that many whites will not do their backstage racist routines in the frontstage with strangers because they fear that someone might object or that they might be "misinterpreted" and inaccurately viewed as "racist." When whites engage in numerous racist performances like these, some do seem aware of how these performances reinforce the racist system and yet still do them intentionally, but many appear to be, at most, only half-conscious of the fact that their actions play a central role in maintaining that system. Certainly, a majority of whites do not seem to view most racist joking, commentaries, and other routinized racist actions out of the dominant racial frame as morally wrong. Such actions tend to be viewed as harmless and "no big deal," indeed often just good interactive "fun."

This no-big-deal viewpoint prevents most from perceiving how such racialized performances cause substantial harm, and it also links to a common defensiveness when they are asked about their racist commentaries. When challenged, most whites will feel defensive and assert their virtuousness. Many will say something like, "No, of course we don't intend our jokes to hurt anyone," "They're just jokes," or "You people are too sensitive." This reaction is a contemporary version of the old notion that whites are morally superior. Even when they do racist performances targeting Americans of color, the old racial frame accents that they, as whites, still should be considered to be "good" and "decent" people. The dominant racial frame not only provides the fodder for whites' racist performances, but also one means of excusing those performances. For most whites, at least some white-racist commentaries and performances are just part of the normality of U.S. society. For that reason, most people do not reflect much on them.

The Diverse Frontstage: The Frame's Negative Impact

The white student diaries and other sources we have examined reveal that the dominant racial framing of African Americans and other Americans of color remains strong and commonplace. The white frame's habitual expressions are rarely challenged when whites are with other whites, especially in backstage settings. Not surprisingly, thus, this racial frame operates to motivate and shape many discriminatory actions by whites in a diverse array of frontstage settings. People's everyday lives involve a series of encounters among individuals, and in this racist society there are often negative encounters between white Americans and Americans of color. In many such encounters racist stereotypes, images, and emotions from the dominant racial frame play a significant role in generating an array of types of discrimination by whites, which discriminatory actions in turn reproduce white interests and continuing racial inequality.

We also need to examine and emphasize what happens on the other side of white discrimination, on the other side of the racial frame in its individual and institutional expressions. The targets of racial discrimination are of course real human beings with lives, feelings, and responses to recurring racial hostility and discrimination. Interviews with African American adults that I and others have done typically reveal that over their lives they have had, literally, thousands of negative experiences, ranging from subtle to covert to blatant discrimination, with white Americans of both genders and various ages and classes. Today, most African Americans have to live everyday lives that are to a substantial degree geographically or socially segregated, substantially because of critical choices made by elite and rank-and-file whites in the past and the present to separate and subordinate them. For example, surveys indicate that a majority of African Americans would prefer to live in mixed-race areas with a significant white population, but many cannot do so because whites historically have made that difficult through discriminatory control of real estate, banking, and political institutions, as well as by individual choices by white homeowners and renters. Even many middle-class African Americans have few, or no, white neighbors. Certainly, the deeply pathological reality of a still racially segregated U.S. society, with sharp racial differences in economic assets and continuing housing discrimination, needs to be brought forcefully into contemporary analyses of racial matters and dealt with aggressively by government anti-discrimination policies.[7]

Recently, the Pew Research Center released results of a survey of the racial views of white and black Americans. More than 80 percent of the black respondents reported widespread racial discrimination in at least one major societal area. Two thirds reported that African Americans always or often face discrimination in jobs or in seeking housing. Fifty percent said the same for shopping and restaurants. The Pew report also listed the results of a vague question about black progress: Only a fifth of the black respondents felt things were better today for black Americans than five years ago and just 44 percent felt that life would be better for them in the future. Also significant was the survey's finding that a majority of whites *denied* the black view of significant societal discrimination and the black perception of no recent gains. White respondents were twice as likely as black respondents to "see" black gains in recent years, and a majority thought the future would be better for black Americans. A majority of whites deny the painful and continuing impact of systemic racism endured by Americans of color.[8]

White denial of this extensive and severely negative impact has been part of the white racial frame for centuries. We see this clearly, for example, in Thomas Jefferson's famous 1785 treatise, *Notes on the State of Virginia*, in which he confidently asserts that enslaved black Americans do not feel pain as much as whites: "Their griefs are transient. Those numberless afflictions ... are less felt, and sooner forgotten with them."[9] Such an insensitive view of oppression's impact seems essential to the white racial frame, in its past and contemporary forms, and is closely linked to the white-virtuousness (now "colorblind") perspective white Americans have long asserted.

Everyday Racism in Frontstage Settings

Today, the expression of racial hostility and discrimination by whites takes an array of damaging forms, from blatant discrimination to more subtle and covert discrimination. Whites who are very racially prejudiced are likely to fully embrace the old racial frame and justify use of it with overtly racist explanations. Those who are more racially liberal may internalize much of the frame, yet are more likely to be aware of the parts of it, feel guilty about some parts, and/or try not to act on aspects they believe to be false. Some may draw on the racial frame's material for openly hostile actions, while others may use similar material but in a paternalistic fashion to "help" those who are racially targeted. Many, especially liberal, whites may select elements of the dominant frame to disagree with, and sometimes act assertively out of a counter liberty-and-justice framing of society. Thus, people can hold several frames relevant to a particular social setting in their heads simultaneously. As I suggested previously, they are "multiframers."

Unfortunately, blatantly discriminatory actions motivated by the white racial frame are by no means disappearing from society. Indeed, many African Americans still speak of encountering a "plantation mentality" among white Americans who act as though they should have substantial authority over them. One example of blatant discrimination can be seen in this recent diary account from a black college student attending a historically white college:

> This is one of those sad and angry nights for me. Tonight marks the third time since the beginning of the school year that I've been called

a nigger by a bunch of white students on a . . . weekend. . . . At first I used to wonder where they actually take the time in their heads to separate me from everyone else by the color of my skin. I used to just blame alcohol consumption for their obvious ignorance and racist attitudes, but I have since stopped trying to make excuses for them. I have to admit that at times like this . . . I don't understand how such a system of hate could exist. . . . Sometimes it seems that if I am around all white people, then I become nothing more than a token Black "exhibit" for their amusement. I guess that even I have to be careful not to judge all based on a few bad examples, which more often then not is the fate of many in the black community today. The saddest thing however, is that these people, these college students are supposed to be the supposed crème de la crème, the future business and political leaders.[10]

In racially diverse frontstage settings this black student has had to deal with barbed epithets hurled by presumably well-educated whites—indeed, as he says, our "future leaders." Black Americans have a long history of racial oppression, and such strong racist epithets can cause, as here, much personal harm. Racist epithets in the present often trigger individual and collective memories of past discrimination. Note that this student diarist, like many African Americans, has a savvy counter-frame that includes his own distinctive sociological analysis of the recurring oppression he faces. He has thought much about the white racist mindset. At first, he blamed whites' racist actions on alcohol, but has since stopped exculpating them. In these everyday experiences, he is viewed by discriminatory whites, not as another human being, but in terms of the racist stereotypes, images, emotions, and language that date back several centuries.

Older African Americans still report much discriminatory treatment by whites. This is often blatant, but also takes subtle and covert forms. Consider these encounters with active white racial framing by two professors in different college settings. The first is an African American professor at a predominantly white institution, who recounts how a white student

went to the [my] department and he talked to some white male professors, and he told these white male professors what I had said in my class. And one of the white male professors had said to him that I was right, that such a thing had happened and had occurred. . . . He comes back and tells me that he was having trouble believing what I said, and that he went over to [my] department to see if he could get that documented and validated. And I said, "And?" And he said, "Well, I asked some professors and they said that such a document existed and that you were telling the truth." . . . Some students don't believe what I have to say and they will have to go and ask somebody white before they believe it.[11]

One of the oldest stereotyped notions in the dominant frame is that relating to black intelligence and incompetence. We see this in the eighteenth-century writings of founders like Thomas Jefferson, who argued that black Americans were very inferior: "Comparing them by their faculties of memory, reason, and imagination, it appears to me, that in memory they are equal to the whites; in reason much inferior . . . and that in imagination they are dull, tasteless, and anomalous."[12] This old racist stereotype of black Americans as less intelligent and creative than white Americans had been in the white racial frame for more than a century before Jefferson's time, and it has remained in the dominant frame ever since. Here even a Ph.D. from a major university is not sufficient to head off the white student's aggressive questioning of a black professor's abilities. We notice too the negative impact such overt questioning, which she indicates is recurring, has on those targeted by it.

As we have seen previously, the white racial frame today includes important subframes targeting other Americans of color. In the next example a Latino professor at a historically white institution makes this clear in talking about a long period of teaching in predominantly white settings:

> Ironically, in my two decades of teaching, it has been the naive White student who, more often than not, needed the safety to ask potentially offensive questions without being made to feel ignorant or malicious. Typical of the initial questions posed by both graduate and undergraduate students are, "Oh, Professor Bonilla, but you don't look Latino." or, "How long have you been in this country? You don't even have an accent!" Today, these kinds of questions present opportunities to enlighten them that not all Latinos look or sound alike. . . . Early in my teaching, my frosty reply to such questions tended to be the not so noble, "How many Latinos do you know?" or, "Well that's nice, I can barely tell you have an accent either." I took their inquiries as unwelcome reminders of my relative isolation. . . . They can be so immersed in the "normality" of their White cultural milieu that they neither see it nor understand it.[13]

Once again, we observe the aspect of dominant frame use that involves frame assumption. White students assume that their way of viewing society, in this case Latinos, and their racialized actions inspired by that view are normal and unproblematic. Because he does not fit their frame's image of what a Latino should look like—presumably he should be darker—he is grilled and questioned. The white framing of Latinos frequently assumes speech and accent "problems," including an inability to speak "good English" or the presence of what whites consider a problematical accent. (All speakers of English speak with an accent.) We observe too the negative and isolating impact of that white-framed action, as well as significant counter-framing and well-honed resistance to such recurring discriminatory actions. While these examples of frontstage interactions across the color line stem from college settings, events like these are well-documented for numerous other institutional settings for most Americans of color.[14]

Moreover, when it comes to everyday hostility or discrimination emanating from whites, the dominant racial frame not only reveals itself in these blatant ways but also in subtle or covert guises. For example, much subtle mistreatment is accomplished by means of significant facial, postural, and other nonverbal signals from whites. By such signals even liberal whites communicate much information about their stereotyped racial framing to those they target. In a long conversation we have had about subtle discrimination, one savvy African American professional recently described to me just a few of his everyday experiences with whites operating out of the racial stereotypes and emotions:

> I see it in daily interactions (i.e., the lady at the counter who refuses to touch your hand and take your money, especially when you just witnessed an alternative behavior with the white patron before you). Then there is the cashier who tosses the money to me as I am waiting to receive change. Also, I was asked at a store just before I was to hand my money over, "Are you paying with cash or food stamps?" I asked the so-called gentleman why he asked me this question when he did not ask the white person before me. . . . Then there is the constantly asking me if I need help in a store when I am alone. When I am with whites, I do *not* get asked at all or very little.

He continues thus:

> I see it when the lone Asian or white female breaks their neck to walk a mile away from me on the sidewalk as I pass. I see it when one white male and I are the only ones in a public bathroom; his nervousness and awkward body language tells me a lot. I see it at work—daily challenges in terms of one's intelligence level—such as voice tones when discussing your ideas that contradict theirs. I see it when white people see me reading academic books at the gym, and I am asked why am I reading that particular book. When I answer, I get a puzzled look on their face as if something does not compute

in their rationale of what I am supposed to be doing as a black man with muscles who enjoys working out. I see it when I am walking with a white woman (regardless of personal status), the white eyes begin to follow you. It is as if you are wearing the "Scarlet Letter" for the white villagers to see.[15]

Notice here the great array of ideas and emotions that whites communicate, often nonverbally, in this brief account of just a few of a black man's everyday experiences: (1) the emotion-laden fear of touching a black hand, probably out of some white stereotype of "dirtiness" or "danger"; (2) the stereotyping of a black man as too poor for customary courtesy; (3) the obsessive white stereotyping of a black man as shoplifter by clerks (who should know most shoplifters are white); (4) the emotion-laden fear of being alone with a black man signaled by nervousness in body language or movement away; (5) the stereotyping of black intelligence at a gym and work—with an aggressive response to a challenge to whiteness signaled in tone of voice; and (6) the hypersexualizing of a black man walking with a white woman revealing old white fears of "racial mixing."

Extremely blatant discrimination is not necessary for whites to communicate their racist thinking and emotions or to create much lasting harm. Targets of the dominant white framing know that it is present even when whites are not hurling a series of explicit racist insults. Holding that racial frame in their heads, but trying to suppress overt actions reflecting it, whites frequently send powerful nonverbal signals as real feelings, the emotions central to that racial frame, leak out into cross-racial interactions. Just a brief listing of recurring events facing one black professional reveals numerous aspects of the *centuries-old* white-racist framing of black men—criminality, dangerousness, black dirtiness, hypersexuality, fear of their resistance—in a remarkably comprehensive and ugly contemporary display. Note too that there is nothing particularly new about most of this white-framed hostility and discrimination.

Such normal behavior by whites is not just discriminatory and very painful to endure, as we can tell from the tone of his comments, but points up how everyday racism is an isolating and alienating phenomenon. People do not experience racism abstractly, but in concrete everyday relationships. The persisting white framing of Americans of color does not exist suspended in the air, but is involved in millions of face-to-face interactions. It divides people from one other and severely impedes the development of a truly common consciousness.

This alienating racist system creates much damage to those targeted by it. W. E. B. Du Bois once eloquently described being black in the United

States as being a person looking out of a deep mountain cave. A black person views

> the world passing and speaks to it; speaks courteously and persuasively, showing them how these entombed souls are hindered in their natural movement, expression, and development; and how their loosening from prison would be a matter not simply of courtesy, sympathy, and help to them, but aid to all the world. . . . It gradually penetrates the minds of the prisoners that the people passing do not hear; that some thick sheet of invisible but horribly tangible plate glass is between them and the world. . . . They may scream and hurl themselves against the barriers, hardly realizing in their bewilderment that they are screaming in a vacuum unheard and that their antics may actually seem funny to those outside looking in. They may even, here and there, break through in blood and disfigurement, and find themselves faced by a horrified, implacable, and quite overwhelming mob of people frightened for their own very existence.[16]

The cave metaphor sharply accents the alienating reality of oppression. In this narrative, being black is often like being an entombed soul trying to get the attention of white passers-by, but to no avail. The wall of separation is too great. Even hurling themselves against the racial barriers gets little serious attention and, if they should break through at great cost, the white mob outside may be very afraid and retaliate.

Today, social science studies regularly demonstrate the many severe effects that this racial dehumanization has on the health of African Americans and other Americans of color. In several interview studies African American respondents who are questioned about the impact of discrimination on them list many effects—from hypertension and stress diabetes to stress-related headaches and heart and stomach conditions. Moreover, the impact of racism is more than physical, for it often has serious psychological effects ranging from anxiety to depression to anger and rage. Today, as in the past, anger over racial discrimination remains commonplace and that anger can in its turn generate physical health problems, emotional withdrawal, and an array of other individual and family costs. Clearly, there are numerous domino effects from particular discriminatory events. The personal pain of discrimination in one's workplace may generate chest pains and headaches, which can in turn create a significant loss of energy. That energy loss can mean less energy for family interactions and parental obligations. Even church and other community activities can become more difficult.[17]

White outsiders, even sympathetic ones, typically view anti-black discrimination as just an individual matter. But the everyday assaults of white hostility and discrimination have effects not just on individuals but also on their social networks, for the pain and trajectory of discriminatory acts are commonly shared with close relatives and friends.

Everyday Interactions: Symbolic Racial Capital

In these accounts of backstage and frontstage actions by whites, we see much evidence of the significant racial capital held by most white Americans. As I suggested previously, this racial capital includes not only economic, political, and educational capital, but also important *symbolic* capital. This valuable capital is at best half-consciously recognized by most whites. Among other features, it encompasses the shared assumptions, understandings, and inclinations to interact in certain traditional ways that whites have mostly learned in families and other networks. Symbolic capital, including white skin privilege, is a central part of the dominant racial frame and operates to relate and link both white acquaintances and white strangers. Perceiving and accenting white skin privilege in daily interactions is one outcome of holding that dominant frame in one's head.

The backstage and frontstage interactions among whites and others that we examined previously reveal the use and abuse of this symbolic racial capital. For example, when whites interact with other whites, they usually receive significant privileges unavailable to people of color. Whites do *not* have to say explicitly to other whites that "I am white like you and need to use my racial capital to gain privileges" in order to get privileges and benefits. Symbolic capital enables whites to avoid many interactive problems, such as police profiling and similar official harassment, and it facilitates positive interactions among whites in many social settings, such as in party settings, job interviews with white interviewers, or gaining access to white political officials. Messages of "I am white like you" are routinely sent out by the physical and cultural markers of whiteness. Living in a society where the dominant framing constantly maintains the prized white identity, and denigrates the identities of racialized "others," a white person is typically taken as having positive symbolic capital and thus worthy of racial privileges. This symbolic capital makes it much easier for whites to interact in most societal arenas, and it often shapes how decisions are made and what their outcomes will be.[18]

The everyday use or operation of this symbolic capital is often subtle and hard for many whites even to see. For example, people of color who are employees in historically white institutions often report that many whites there have significant difficulty or awkwardness in relating well to them. White men, who dominate most meetings of managers in historically white organizations, usually relate reasonably well to each other, drawing on shared experiences, socialization, and language. Indeed, this is the reality described by the common phrase "good old boy network." Such settings are usually fairly comfortable places for most white men to interact. In contrast, white managers often relate awkwardly with the few managers of color in such historically white workplaces, both in meetings and in hallways. Little previous contact with people of color, especially on an equal status basis, is one cause of this awkwardness. Recent research on two major law schools by Wendy Moore reveals a similar pattern. Her data show that these law schools are mostly *white spaces* in terms of a majority of their occupants' characteristics and their imbedded normative structures, racialized spaces where whites rarely think about that discriminatory reality. White students in these law schools related relatively easily to each other and to the mostly white faculty members—because of shared white experiences and white frame assumptions. In contrast, students of color frequently found the experience to be alienating and isolating, and that the white students and faculty were often awkward or discriminatory in relating to them.[19]

Indeed, one liability for whites stemming from the dominant racial frame in our era of increasing demographic diversity is that it requires a kind of social isolation from the experiences and understandings of those who have historically been oppressed, those groups whose numbers are currently increasing significantly both nationally and globally.

The Frame in Institutional Operation: Bureaucratization of Oppression

Human beings too easily rationalize oppression. Gilles Fauconnier and Mark Turner have explained how in the human mind accepted views of the oppression of groups of people are easily blended with an ordinary bureaucratic frame to produce a concept in oppressors' minds of this oppression being just a routine organizational operation. This makes it easier for such societal oppression to be rationalized by the dominant group, both collectively and individually. For the most part, large-scale systems of oppression are not carried out by wild-eyed extremists with major psychological disorders, but by ordinary people in their daily routines. During the slavery and Jim Crow eras, most whites viewed blatant and bloody forms of racial oppression as normal and supported it with indifference or with some type of everyday collaboration.[20]

This general indifference and collaboration remain true for today's serious patterns of racial discrimination and inequality, which are typically seen as more or less normal by the majority of white Americans. The dominant racial frame still views whites as a group to be generally superior and people of color as groups to be generally of less social, economic, and political consequence. One important aspect of this still-dominant frame is that its racial understandings get imbedded deeply in societal organizations and institutions. A majority of whites view most U.S. institutions as normally white-controlled and unremarkable in that whites therein are unjustly enriched and disproportionately privileged. Another common frame notion views local bureaucratic organizations such as a public school or government agency as properly white-controlled, white-normed, and slanted toward white interests.

For a system of oppression to persist it is necessary to develop not only a strong rationalizing frame but also to build that frame's ideas, notions, images, and emotions into the everyday operation of important organizational structures of society. In earlier chapters we have seen how this institutionalization of a racist framing operated in connection with the genocidal actions against Native Americans and the enslavement and Jim Crow segregation targeting African Americans. Today, the system of racial oppression remains highly organized and institutionalized and continues to operate in tandem with our modern economy, strong national government, extensive private and government bureaucracies, and complex legal system.

U.S. Legal and Political Institutions

The U.S. legal and political system is often celebrated as the world's finest and fairest. Today, a typical statement about the U.S. Constitution by prominent U.S. leaders—including politicians, judges, and law professors—is very positive and uncritical, such as "the greatest Constitution that was ever written." Many everyday references to the U.S. Constitution by leaders and ordinary citizens assert it to be an extraordinarily liberty-oriented and freedom-guaranteeing constitution. Typically such statements accent the liberty, equality, and justice rhetoric that the U.S. founders used in their colonial struggle with the British king, rhetoric that has asserted widely and ritualistically since that time.[21] Usually forgotten in such praise for the U.S. Constitution is, as I have shown in Chapter 2, the fact that our foundational document was shaped throughout by the strong racist framing in the minds of the white founders and, thus, by their desire to protect the assets and power most had gained from an economy grounded in land theft and slavery. At the time of the Constitution's making, a majority of the population—African Americans, Native Americans, and white women—did *not* live under a system providing them with real liberty, equality, or justice.

From the founding era in the late 1700s until the 1960s, moreover, most federal court decisions on racial matters, including those of the U.S. Supreme Court, interpreted the Constitution from a very strong version of the white racist frame and thereby perpetuated over the generations most elements of the old system of extreme racial oppression. Racialized apartheid did not officially end in the United States until 1969, a bit more than a generation ago. To the present day, the U.S. Constitution and the Supreme Court decisions interpreting it—almost all made by elite white men—have greatly shaped the basic contours of the U.S. legal and political systems, as well as other important societal institutions.

Important changes in the system of racial oppression, such as the official ending of Jim Crow in the late 1960s, have come *only* when many whites have believed those changes to be in their interest—that is, when there is what legal scholar Derrick Bell has called an "interest convergence" between the interests of the oppressed and the interests of whites, especially those of the white elite.[22] Consider what is probably the most famous Supreme Court decision of the last century, the 1954 *Brown v. Board of Education of Topeka* decision that we discussed previously. That decision was forced on the high court by black lawyers suing to end Jim Crow. The Supreme Court school decision was only grudgingly supported by several of the white justices who were under pressure not only from the black civil rights movement, but also from white officials in the U.S. state department who were worried about how the former Soviet Union was using images of black civil rights demonstrators being beaten and attacked by southern whites in its propaganda circulated to countries across the globe. Here we observe two factions of the white elite contending politically and legally with each other.

The ruling elite in North America has always been overwhelmingly white and male in composition and has for centuries been divided roughly into two socio-political camps—a very *conservative* camp that is unsympathetic to populist and expanding-democracy ideas, and a more moderate camp that is more receptive to some populist and expanding-democracy ideas. The *moderate* wing of this ruling elite dominated the small group of founders that gave us in 1776 a Declaration of Independence, with its ringing rhetoric about freedom and equality, while the more conservative wing of that elite dominated the small group of founders that gave us in 1787 a U.S. Constitution accenting property rights, one initially without a Bill of Rights.[23] These two branches of the elite are disproportionately represented in various regions of the country, with more conservatives in the southern elite and more moderates in the northern and western elites. As a result, the factions of the dominant white elite have periodically found themselves in some socio-political tension and conflict, such as in state and national political contests.

Consider the shaping of U.S. political parties, a process that is centrally about the white racial frame and the divisions within that white elite. For much of the era between the early 1800s and the more recent 1960s, southern white members of the ruling elite, who were mostly from its conservative wing, dominated the Democratic Party (originally the Democratic-Republican Party). Long before the 1860s Civil War, powerful white southerners, often slaveholders, secured disproportionate influence in that Democratic Party, and as we have seen in previous chapters these white southerners gained much control over the operation of the U.S. Congress and the other branches of government until the Civil War. After that war and a brief Reconstruction period, when they lost national political power, the southern white Democrats again regained control of southern political institutions and imposed legal segregation on African Americans. They also regained disproportionate influence in national political institutions, most prominently in the U.S. Senate, where they were able to block for decades *all* significant attempts to end legal segregation and expand civil rights for African Americans, indeed until the 1960s.

After long decades of protests by African Americans, and a World War II in which white Americans found themselves fighting a highly racist German government, some progress in ending segregation and expanding civil rights began during the 1940s and 1950s. Breaking with the past, and representing the *moderate* wing of the white elite, President Harry Truman (1945–1953) supported a strong civil rights plank in the 1948 Democratic Party platform. This action marked a gradual but significant shift in the dominant white racial frame; rigid Jim Crow segregation was viewed by growing numbers of whites as no longer necessary to preserve white power and privilege. However, this Democratic Party civil rights plank resulted in the creation of a States Right's Party by southern Democrats committed to an arch-segregationist version of the white frame. They left the Democratic Party because of their hostility to expanded civil rights. Their almost unanimous commitment to the Jim Crow version of the white frame persisted for two more decades. Recall from Chapter 4 the "Southern Manifesto," the aggressively white-framed statement of opposition to the U.S. Supreme Court's 1954 *Brown* decision that was signed by almost all Senators and House members from southern states—all of whom were white and Democratic.[24]

Eventually, the 1960s civil rights movement, the new civil rights laws, and international pressures led to significant shifts in the composition and tactics of the major political parties. With the right to vote now legally guaranteed, black voters in southern and border states began actively participating in local, state, and national politics, and principally in the Democratic Party. Over recent decades, thus, the Democratic Party has become increasingly more diverse, with a large percentage of its member-ship today being African Americans and other Americans of color. However, over these decades this increased diversity of the Democratic Party has triggered the movement of many whites into the Republican Party, most conspicuously in southern and border states. Since the 1950s the southern and border states have increasingly become states divided between a Republican party centered in white residential areas, especially white middle-class areas such as suburbs, and a Democratic Party that is multi-racial and centered in urban working-class and lower middle class areas. From the late 1960s to 2006, the U.S. Republican Party came to dominate much of the U.S. political scene at local, state, and federal levels.

Over these decades almost all major leaders in this resurgent Republican Party have been white, and they brought about the Party's resurgence from the late 1960s to the present day by using a politics that frequently has directed overt or subtle appeals to the white racial frame, and especially its anti-black subframe, in the minds of white voters. The usually white Republican politicians generally deliver to working class and middle class whites a strong racial framing, a framing that accents white interests, a white-oriented political rhetoric, and white-run governments. To a substantial degree, this Republican resurgence has been accomplished by making great use of racist appeals, advertisements, speeches, and code-words. As early as the latter years of the civil rights movement, in the late 1960s, presidential candidate Richard Nixon and his white advisors suc-cessfully used the white backlash against the black civil rights movement and resulting civil rights laws and policies (especially affirmative action) that Americans of color had gained.

Then as now, many white voters have feared expanded black political power and black elected officials—and what they see as too black-oriented government programs. This backlash provided the Republican Party with the necessary white votes to put into operation for several decades the goal of remaking the political face of the United States into one with strong white-Republican Party influence. Republican political actions taken dir-ectly out of the white frame were often obvious and overt. In 1980, for example, Republican Ronald Reagan began his presidential campaign with a pro-states-rights speech in Philadelphia, Mississippi, a city where three civil workers had been killed some years before by violent white supremacists. In his two 1980s elections, Reagan easily won the electoral votes of southern states "with thinly disguised appeals to segregationist sentiment, while Democrats were ever more firmly linked to civil rights and affirmative action."[25] Other Republican appeals to white voters have been somewhat more subtle, such as in the central and recurring attacks on "big government." Recall that, while there are several sources of anti-government rhetoric over the centuries, a major source has been the fear of slaveholders and Jim Crow segregationists—and their white descendants in recent decades—that federal government agencies might interfere with their "freedom" to dominate "those people," that is, African Americans and other Americans of color. Yet, rarely do these white Republican leaders oppose the many "big government" actions, such as huge military expenditures in their districts, that benefit them and their white constituents.

In practice, since the 1940s, the Republican Party has been the "white party" of the United States, with relatively few Americans of color strongly committed to it. By 2006 more than 40 percent of Republican Party members in Congress were from the South. Moreover, at the 2008 Republican national convention in St. Paul, Minnesota, which nominated two whites for president and vice-president, only 7 percent of the delegates were people of color (and only 1.5 percent black), compared to the 33 percent of delegates who were people of color at the Democratic Party's convention that year in Denver, a convention that nominated the first African American candidate ever from a major party.[26] Thus, the white-conservative political shift that has dominated much of the U.S. political scene from the late 1960s to the early 2000s is a direct result of the *white backlash* against the black-led civil rights movement and, from then to now, against the gradual advances by African Americans and other Americans of color into major institutions from which they were once excluded. This political backlash is substantially motivated by the traditional anti-black elements in the old white racial frame that is still dominant in a great many white minds.

In addition, we might note one other political consequence of the dominant racial frame in recent political campaigns. The conventional white racial frame is so institutionalized that all mainstream media outlets routinely and unquestioningly operate out of some version of it. One example can be seen in the 2008 presidential election, during which the white supremacist groups—and later most mainstream media and many Republican political groups—focused intensively, for months of the primaries and final election, on a story about then Senator Barack Obama's former African American minister, Dr. Jeremiah Wright, because of what the media regarded as his "radical" views of U.S. society (see Chapter 7).

This mainstream media story lasted so long because the image of a supposedly "radical" black minister resonates loudly with the dangerous black man image in the centuries-old white racial frame. In contrast, a somewhat similar story about the controversial views of an archconservative, anti-Catholic minister who was a friend and supporter of

Senator John McCain, did not last very long in the same mainstream media. An Internet search of media outlets and various news websites at the time indicated that the McCain's minister story received less than one tenth of the coverage on Internet websites than the Wright story received. The main reason is likely that there is no common framing in most white minds of white men as dangerous and radical for McCain's minister to resonate with. So the story about him and the Republican candidate died after a few days. It is also important to note that Dr. Wright, a recipient of seven honorary doctorates from U.S. colleges and universities, has published several books of well-crafted sermons that are studied by white, black, and other seminarians at major U.S. divinity schools and was voted by *Ebony* magazine as one of the fifteen leading ministers in the United States. At the time of the media and other attacks on him, Dr. Wright had been a minister for a long time in a predominantly white Protestant denomination, the United Church of Christ, one that had been founded in part by the Pilgrims. At no point, as of this writing, has any mainstream media outlet done a critical examination of the role of the media's white-racist framing in these highly distorted attacks on a leading U.S. minister and theologian.[27]

The Frame and Unjust Enrichment: Justifying Institutional Processes

One function of the white racial frame is to justify the great array of privileges and assets held by white Americans as the group at the top of the racial hierarchy. As we have seen in previous chapters, unjust enrichment and unjust impoverishment have accompanied racial oppression from the beginning. The huge resources and wealth gap is substantially the result of the social processes of the reproduction of unjust enrichment for white Americans and unjust impoverishment for African Americans and many other Americans of color over centuries of systemic racism. These social inheritance mechanisms are disguised by the "whites are virtuous" images of the dominant frame to make the intergenerational transfer of resources and privilege appear fair, when in fact this frequently represents the longterm transmission of *unjust* enrichment across many generations of oppressors and oppressed. This type of societal inheritance has often enabled later generations of whites to provide better educational, housing, and other socioeconomic opportunities for their children than the later generations of black Americans and other Americans of color whose ancestors, many over 8–10 generations, did not secure access to such important resources because of massive white-imposed discrimination and segregation.

How, when, and where the critical realities of racial oppression are reproduced do vary across major institutions and do fluctuate with the particular actors making decisions within them. Yet, the effect of white actors operating in public and private organizations in ways that reproduce or enhance white privilege and power has been to keep the overall system of racial oppression and inequality in operation now for four centuries. Sociologist Robert Merton introduced a term for the significant process of resource accumulation and increase over time, what he called "the Matthew effect."[28] (The term is drawn from a Bible verse: "For unto every one that hath shall be given, and he shall have abundance: but from him that hath not shall be taken away even that which he hath.") The Matthew effect is central to the operation of many types of societal inequality that increase dramatically over time.

Small initial differences in racial, class, or gender inequality tend to build up to very large inequalities over time, like the compound interest that accumulates on money savings. For example, recent research on gender inequality in U.S. workplaces has shown how small initial advantages accumulate to larger advantages over time. In important workplace meetings, thus, women employees are less likely than male employees to have their comments taken seriously by senior managers, who are usually men. In turn, this leads the women to participate less actively in subsequent meetings, which means that they are less likely than their male peers to accumulate small but important job-related advantages over months and years. Successful job advancement in most workplaces involves gradually parlaying small initial advantages over other employees into bigger advantages, ultimately leading to significant advances.[29] In one project, researchers did a computer simulation of workplace promotions up an eight-tier ladder of jobs. They began with equal numbers of male and female employees at the entry level and assumed a certain percentage would be promoted at each of the employment ladder rungs. The researchers discovered that a very small initial bias in favor of men, one providing only *1 percent* of the initial variability in promotion factors, had huge longterm effects. After numerous rounds of promotions, the small initial advantage resulted in male employees making up two thirds of those at the highest job level.[30]

This substantial advancement for male employees just from the accumulating effects of small initial patterns of gender discrimination is very similar to what results for white workers from the typically much larger pro-white bias that has advantaged white workers in most U.S. workplaces and numerous other societal settings over past and present decades. In addition to suffering current discrimination, employees of color often come into the workplace settings with initial disadvantages, small and large, from large-scale past discrimination against them and their families. Moreover, in many institutional sectors, the Matthew effect has regularly worked against African Americans and many other Americans of color over centuries by making the seemingly modest *racial* advantages that most ordinary white families have historically secured—such as a few hundred acres of farmland given by the government to white families to homestead from the 1860s to the 1930s (but kept from most black families by segregation and violence)—into large later advantages for them and their descendants.[31]

The dominant racial frame plays an essential role in rationalizing and legitimating the many Matthew effects across the society. Most whites do not know, or do not wish to know, how this ongoing Matthew-effect process has historically privileged them and their ancestors in many ways over nearly four centuries. The frame allows them to celebrate their own white virtues and to blame the racial "others" for their supposed lack of such virtues.

The White Frame and the World Racial Order

Centuries of European and U.S. colonialism and neo-colonialism have created a *world racial order*. Since the fifteenth century, numerous European countries, and later the United States, have expanded globally in imperialist and colonizing ventures that created colonies and military outposts across the world. In the first century of this overseas colonialism, as we have seen, the white racial frame became very important in rationalizing the wholesale theft of asset-generating resources from or within colonized countries. This process continued for centuries more. Once this global system of labor, land, and resources theft was in place, the rationalizing white racial frame shaped people's actions in many sectors not only of the colonizing countries but also of their colonies, including their economies, religious and educational systems, and political institutions. As noted previously, this frame was from the beginning highly Eurocentric and Orientalist in its accent on the West as superior to all other global regions.

The ever pioneering W. E. B. Du Bois was again among the very first to evaluate this globalizing oppression from a critical historical perspective, and he noted well the patterns of bloody and racialized subordination that came to many people of color everywhere. In his pathbreaking book on Africa, Du Bois summarized the impact of European colonialism and imperialism in this manner:

> There was no Nazi atrocity—concentration camps, wholesale maiming and murder, defilement of women and ghastly blasphemy of childhood—that the Christian civilization of Europe had not long been practicing against coloured folk in all parts of the world in

the name of and for the defense of a Superior Race born to rule the world.[32]

Much of this destructive colonialism was rationalized by a "superior white race" framing, and important aspects were often intentionally forgotten by the colonizers. In this overseas labor and land theft, one indigenous society after another was destroyed or reshaped by the impact of the European and U.S. invaders and their military, economic, political, and religious organizations. This plundering colonization was defended in imperialistic countries, as well as by white elites in colonized countries, in terms of a strong framing that accented white racial and civilizational (usually Christian) superiority and that denigrated the colonized residents and their cultures as racially inferior and uncivilized.

After several centuries of direct European colonialism, and half a century now of decolonization, the colonizing and colonized countries have remained inextricably interrelated. Today, continuing poverty and related economic problems in the former colonies are closely linked to continuing prosperity that has persisted over several centuries now in Europe and the United States. In major ways the stolen labor, land, and resources of these countries continue to be one substantial reason for contemporary prosperity and wealth in Europe and the United States, while leaving these former colonies with lasting poverty and other socioeconomic problems often not of their own making. Even with the demise of direct colonial control in the mid-twentieth century, economic neo-colonialism has continued the process of extensive resource exploitation of the former colonies. Neo-colonialism means that white-run European and U.S. corporations are still largely in control of a continuing process of labor, mineral, and other resource extraction in most of these countries.[33]

Since declaring their independence, many of these former colonies' governments have become controlled by local elites that have substantially collaborated in the neo-colonialism process and even have adopted significant elements of the white racial frame to rationalize this process. Most especially, we see among numerous elites in the former colonies a worshipful stance toward a supposed white superiority in markets, technology, education, and political institutions. For the last century, many governing elites in these former colonies have adopted substantial elements of this white-superiority worldview and have, thus, sought thereby to please powerful white officials in the European and U.S. governments, in international economic organizations, and in multinational corporations. Moreover, during and after the colonial era various private agents, such as white missionaries and business entrepreneurs, from the United States and Europe have created new white-oriented institutions—churches, schools, businesses, and media organizations—in numerous formerly colonized countries. As these Western actors and organizations have become influential overseas, they have greatly shaped a strong pro-white and anti-other racial framing of much that goes on in the world and, in many cases, helped to form or reinforce a Western-type racial hierarchy internationally.[34]

Today, this world racial order involves a multi-tiered complex of relationships. Numerous European, North American, Central American, South American, and South African countries have within them a traditional Western-type racial hierarchy that places white people, or lighter-skinned people with significant European ancestry, at the top and darker-skinned peoples, usually with substantial African or indigenous ancestry, toward the bottom of that racial hierarchy. In countries with a Western-influenced racial hierarchy, the hierarchical racial order of local communities is often linked to that of the surrounding nation state, which is in turn linked to the global racial hierarchy seen in the international economic and political spheres. Indeed, there is now a world racial order that links more than 200 nation-states together, with nations of color in that global order generally subordinated in numerous ways to the most powerful nations, which are still mostly those controlled by whites.

An array of international corporate, nonprofit, and governmental agencies provide the important organizational linkages that in the present day perpetuate this world racial order. For example, today the maintenance of major elements of this white-dominated international racial hierarchy is substantially done by global economic institutions, such as international corporations, the World Bank, and International Monetary Fund, and by agencies within international political institutions such as some agencies of the United Nations.

Today, the large capitalistic corporations and major government organizations operating globally out of European and U.S. headquarters are mostly racialized in their internal employment and other economic structures. These major international organizations and the markets they have created are substantially controlled by white (mainly male) corporate executives in the United States and the European Union, with some increasing input now from Asian executives, especially in Japanese, Chinese, and Indian corporations. In the present day, the majority of these powerful decisionmakers, even many who are not white, view the world substantially from some contemporary version of the old white racial frame. Moreover, since whites still play the central role in shaping the norms and structures of international markets and many international political institutions, these are often oriented to white European and U.S. interests, especially major corporate interests. In their internal and external operations, Westernized global organizations and institutions not only reflect the racial hierarchy and much of the white framing of dominant Western nation-states, but also periodically take actions that shape nation-state and community racial orders within and beyond their own borders—such as by stimulating or reducing the movements of immigrants of color in various regions across the globe.[35]

With recent economic upheavals, especially since the near-depression economic crises of 2008–2009 across the globe, many in the world's non-Western elites have been rethinking their acceptance of Western frames of market economics, Western-dominated international relationships, and white-Western superiority. The dominant role of the white racial frame and related class and gender frames in the global political-economic order is now under great pressure to change in significant ways. The future global order is not likely to be white-dominated.[36]

The Frame and U.S. Foreign Policy

U.S.-generated systemic racism has had an extensive and lasting impact on U.S. foreign policy and resulting international relations. As we have seen, slavery and Jim Crow segregation were in effect for the first 180 years of the U.S. nation, thereby routinely and greatly affecting the way U.S. politicians looked out at the larger world, especially that huge part of it that is not white. In 1789, soon after the U.S. Constitution was approved, the U.S. Department of State was established and from its beginning reflected the interests of those controlling the country's slavery-centered economy, including the major slaveholders and early presidents George Washington, Thomas Jefferson, James Madison, James Monroe, and Andrew Jackson. Similarly, when the U.S. Foreign Service was finally established in 1924, the country's national government was aggressively committed to and supportive of legal segregation in southern, border, and some northern states. Thus, for nearly two centuries the U.S. government's most important foreign policy agencies were established and its broad foreign policy approaches were developed in the societal context of extreme racial oppression, an openly advocated racist hierarchy, and an openly proclaimed white-racist frame accenting slavery or Jim Crow segregation and white supremacy. The result, not surprisingly, was the creation and maintenance of an openly racist global order.

This global racial order has persisted into recent decades, indeed to the present day. As historian Irene Diggs has noted, "United States foreign policy has been colored by the racial composition of countries with whom it has relations, tending to minimize the importance of the largely nonwhite part of the world."[37] For example, as recently as the 1980s Ronald Reagan administration, the U.S. government flagrantly ignored the views and

aspirations of peoples struggling to break free of extreme forms of racialized oppression. The Reagan administration was a strong supporter of the
extreme racial segregation (apartheid) of the country of South Africa.

Today, more than 80 percent of the world's people are not white, yet the
majority of the world's countries have only recently been taken seriously—
and not yet seriously enough—by the mostly white ruling elites of the
United States and Europe. Most of the white corporate and governmental
elites clearly view the global scene from some version of the white racial
frame, which generally means a condescending or paternalistic view of
countries made up principally of people of color and a strongly positive
view of Western superiority and Western global dominance. For example,
in an important book attacking the idea of racial equality, the influential
Time journalist and Pulitzer Prize winner, William Henry, has argued
that the European conquests and colonialism overseas were successful
in dispersing "superior cultures" to other cultures, and that it is good
that the latter have had to assimilate and accommodate to the former.
Many other European and U.S. analysts have aggressively articulated a
similar version of this old idea, one accented so conspicuously in Rudyard
Kipling's late nineteenth-century idea of the "white man's burden" to
carry Western civilization to the "uncivilized" of the world. Not surprisingly, thus, from the late nineteenth century to more recent decades, this
framing of "civilization and democracy" has legitimated dozens of U.S.
military invasions of countries in Asia, such as the Philippines, and in
Latin America, such as Cuba.[38]

Operating in the minds of many U.S. corporate executives, government
officials, and foreign policy experts, the dominant racial frame, coupled
with Western class and gender framing, continues to shape significant
aspects of U.S. foreign policy. Conceptualizing those countries and peoples
that are not white as somehow inferior in culture, civilization, or religion
is often a way of using much in the old racial framing without speaking
explicitly of "race." Top white officials still often operate with an attitude
of moral and civilizational superiority, thereby making it easier for them to
rationalize the U.S. or other Western invasion, occupation, domination, or
subversion of countries more recently, such as in South Vietnam, Nicaragua,
and Iraq. Discussions of yet more overseas interventions in non-Western
countries periodically appear in the political news of the United States and
European countries. While blatantly racist views of people of color were
openly expressed by U.S. foreign policymakers and advisors until the
1960s, today these racist views are usually hidden behind a façade of paternalistic "concern" over the lack of commitment of "underdeveloped"
countries to "civilized values" or to "democracy," or over too much commitment to "extremist religion" or threatening moral values.

Today, U.S. foreign policymakers often operate from a nationalistic perspective with an imbedded white racial framing of other countries and their actions. "American," still typically meaning white American, virtue, morality, and superiority are routinely assumed. Indeed, the U.S. government is the *only* government across the globe to give an annual report card about other countries' human rights behavior. Yet, leading members of this same U.S. government tend to get angry when the U.S. human rights record is even modestly questioned by international organizations or non-Western officials.

For example, U.S. government officials withdrew in protest from a 2001 World Conference Against Racism authorized by the United Nations General Assembly and held in Durban, South Africa. U.S. reparations for U.S. slavery and colonialism, as well as the issues of Zionism and Islamaphobia, were on the agenda. The official reason for this early U.S. government departure was because the conference was considering a resolution that criticized Zionism as an example of racism. Yet, there was also a great reluctance by U.S. officials to engage in serious discussions in this international forum of reparations for Western involvement in the Atlantic slavery system and to discuss continuing racial discrimination in the United States. A white framing of the globe in the minds of many U.S. officials may also explain the relatively weak U.S. commitment to the United Nations, especially in recent decades. This commitment has appeared especially weak when the United Nations general assembly or a major United Nations agency, influenced by the world's population majority of people of color, has made decisions that U.S. political leaders consider contrary to U.S. interests.[39]

Indeed, a frame-influenced nationalism and ethnocentrism are still strong in the United States. Rank-and file Americans, and most especially rank-and-file white Americans, mostly share their leaders' assertive framing with a strong nationalism and ethnocentrism that not only accent U.S. cultural and political superiority, but also typically see no need to learn much about other countries and peoples. This nationalistic framing views the United States not only as the world's "best country," but also as not having significant competition for that honor. Thus, a recent Harris poll found that nearly two thirds of 2,400 Americans agreed with the statement that "overall the U.S. is better than other nations." Just 3 percent chose "worse," and only 27 percent chose the option of the United States being "a country like any other, and is no better or worse."[40]

This very ethnocentric perspective inclines a majority of Americans, including powerful white Americans, to mostly ignore many important world events and to stay poorly informed about most of the world outside the United States. We see this in their views of global history and of the present global scene. For example, even U.S. and west European historians often celebrate what they view as the central role of their countries' armed forces in bringing down the German Nazis and their armed forces during World War II. However, fully 75 percent of all Germany's land and air forces were concentrated in the Eastern front fighting the ethnically diverse armed forces of the Soviet Union. This Eastern front was the central defining front of World War II, the area where eventual German defeat became guaranteed. Today, the ignorance of U.S. citizens about this critical global history—as well as about contemporary world geography, politics, and religion—continues to reveal an ethnocentric, U.S.-centered perspective that is both white-framed and influential in foreign policy circles. Indeed, even as the U.S. government was still occupying Iraq with its military forces in 2008, a survey of the public in that year revealed that only a small minority (one in seven) of Americans could even find the large country of Iraq on a map of the Middle East. As one India-born U.S. journalist has noted, U.S. residents "speak few languages, know little about foreign cultures, and remain unconvinced that they need to correct this."[41]

Spreading the Frame Globally: The U.S. Mass Media

For more than two centuries now, U.S. individuals, agencies, companies, and other organizations have been very active in spreading the white racial frame internationally. For centuries, U.S. and other Western colonizers, missionaries, and soldiers have done much to spread the pro-white and anti-other aspects of that frame, but today that influential frame is effectively circulated across the globe by a great and diverse array of organizations—including, perhaps most effectively, U.S. and other Western media corporations.

Today about sixty large media corporations control most of the world's major media operations, including, newspapers, magazines, books, television stations and production, cable networks, record production, and motion picture production and theaters. Much of the material circulated throughout this white-dominated global media system is U.S.-based, and significant portions reflect white-oriented cultural productions and the white racial framing. Most of the world's countries are now important markets for U.S. media productions that periodically make substantial use of racially stereotyped conceptions, understandings, and images. Across the globe hundreds of millions of households daily get significant information and entertainment from old and new U.S. movies, cable television programs, videos, and Armed Forces radio and television stations. In this manner hundreds of millions, probably billions, of the world's people encounter important elements of the dominant white racial frame, including negative images of African Americans, other Americans of color, and, indeed, people of color in other countries.[42]

It is likely that a substantial proportion of the world's population now holds some racial views that are shaped by the white racial framing that originated in the United States or allied European countries. For example, one small study interviewed fifteen rural residents of the island of Taiwan off the coast of China and found that most of these Chinese respondents held racially stereotyped views of black Americans as self-destructive, dirty, lazy, unintelligent, criminal, violent, and ugly—all features of the old white racial frame. The respondents indicated that their racist ideas and images mostly had been drawn from U.S. television shows, movies, and music videos that had been imported to Taiwan from the United States. A similar impact has been reported for Latino immigrants to the United States from Central America. They too often hold negative views of African Americans even before they enter the United States because of the racist images and ideas in U.S. movies and television programs that they have watched in their home countries.[43]

The mostly white and male corporate executives who control these globally powerful mass media generally accent a consumerist individualism and usually play down important civic values and marginalize local efforts aimed at significant local and international reforms. As one journalist has noted, international journalism, even at its most developed, tends to be "pitched to the business class and suited to its needs and prejudices; with a few notable exceptions, the journalism reserved for the masses tends to be the sort of drivel provided by the media giants on their U.S. television stations."[44] Light escapist entertainment is emphasized, and little that is critical of racial, class, and gender oppression in any country is ever presented.

Conclusion

It is hard to overestimate the centuries-old impacts of the white racial frame on societal institutions. This dominant framing has both shaped, and in turn been shaped by, the systemically racist institutions of U.S. society. Even as this frame has evolved to include new or refurbished old emphases, such as relatively recent accents on a colorblind and post-racial America, the deep structures of racial discrimination remain in workplaces, housing markets, banking, policing, and political institutions. Even as advances are celebrated, such as the election of the first black president of the United States, the racist structure constantly reveals its reality in these institutions to those who are willing to see this reality. Research reports indicating continuing and institutionalized discrimination routinely contradict these

Pollyanna assertions of a post-racial era. Indeed, even as the first black president, Barack Obama, officiated over his first year in office, the powerful U.S. Senate had only one African American (and he was a temporary appointment) among its one hundred senators. Moreover, as we move well into the twenty-first century, much of the traditional white racial framing still remains evident and influential globally in a variety of institutions across most of the world's countries, as well as in dominant international institutions.

CHAPTER 7

Counter-Framing

Americans of Color

So far, we have examined the dominant white racial frame and the way that it has developed and impacted this society and others across the globe. In this chapter we consider a few other important frames that have also developed over the last four centuries, frames that provide alternative or countering perspectives to the dominant white framing. As I noted previously, most people carry several perspectival frames applicable to particular situations in their heads at the same time. They are multiframers. In examining the contested history of the white racial frame, we discover at least these four important categories of frames in everyday operation: (1) the dominant white racial frame; (2) a white-crafted liberty-and-justice frame; (3) the anti-oppression counter-frames of Americans of color; and (4) the home-culture frames that Americans of color have drawn on in developing their counter-frames.

The Liberty-and-Justice Frame

The second category here, the white liberty-and-justice frame, is quite significant in U.S. history because most white Americans, as well as most other Americans and some Europeans, have articulated some version of this frame, at least since the seventeenth century. This critical framing appears in the essential founding documents of the United States, the same documents that made sure that the slavery system would thrive. Notice the centrality of this framing in the "life, liberty and the pursuit of happiness" language in the Declaration of Independence, as well as in the "establish justice" and "secure the blessings of liberty" language of the preamble to the U.S. Constitution. Liberty, freedom, equality, and justice were well-known concepts for the white founders of the United States.

Where did these founders get their ideas of liberty and justice for this important framing? Certainly, they sought their own freedom from the British king, and the actual circumstances of their conflict with Britain contributed to their goals and views of personal liberty and societal justice. In addition, they drew on various European and North American sources for ideas. Today, the typical scholarly discussion accents European sources, including political philosophers such as John Locke and Jean Jacques Rousseau. In a famous 1690 treatise on government, the political philosopher read by some U.S. founders, John Locke, asserted his view of social "justice" as a universal concept that is part of natural law: "Justice gives every Man a Title to the product of his honest Industry, and the fair Acquisitions of his Ancestors descended to him." For Locke, justice includes the idea that people have a natural right to the product of their labor, including a right to pass that to subsequent generations. In his writings Locke also emphasized the importance of what he termed "life and liberty." U.S. founder and secular intellectual, Thomas Jefferson, was directly and indirectly influenced by Locke and other European Enlightenment thinkers, as we see in the "life" and "liberty" language Jefferson put into the Declaration of Independence.[1] It is significant, however, that in significant areas Locke, like Jefferson, did not live by his ideals of justice and liberty. He was a major investor in the Royal Africa Company, a leading slave trading company, and served on English councils that supervised North American slavery.

Strikingly, the European and U.S. leaders' professed understandings of liberty, freedom, and justice were contradicted by the bloody enrichment of white Americans at the expense of indigenous Americans and enslaved Africans. Their hypocrisy on these matters is a major feature of European and North American history. Indeed, recall the eloquent Patrick Henry's famous lines, "for my own part I consider it as nothing less than a question of freedom or slavery," "there is no retreat but in submission and slavery," and "give me liberty, or give me death." I noted earlier the sad irony of this most famous of the founders' speeches: that it was given by a well-off southern slaveholder who left many people enslaved at his death. It is also clear that white American understandings of what freedom and liberty meant were acutely sharpened as they observed millions of enslaved human beings in their society whose lives had little or no freedom. They could see in the tears and words of those enslaved and in their frequent resistance to slavery, as well as in comments of free black leaders and abolitionists, just what freedom and liberty really meant for human beings.

From the American revolutionary era to the present, most whites have held in their minds a cherished liberty-and-justice frame, albeit one that is mostly rhetorical and hypothetical when it comes to challenges by Americans of color to institutionalized racial oppression. When it comes to everyday interactions, the white racial frame routinely eclipses the liberty-and-justice frame, which tends to be most openly celebrated in rhetorical speeches at ceremonies and on holidays. This was certainly true for most white Americans during the long and bloody decades of U.S. slavery from 1787 to 1865 and also during the long and harsh decades of legal segregation from the 1870s to the late 1960s. All too often, this is true today as well. At any point over the four centuries of contact and oppression, the European colonizers of North America and their descendants could as a group have broken completely with the white racial frame, conformed to their own best ideals of liberty and justice, and fully implemented those ideals for the lives of Native Americans, African Americans, and other Americans of color, but they never have.

Yet, as I pointed out previously, over the centuries some whites have taken this liberty-and-justice frame very seriously and worked to end racial oppression, in the form of slavery, Jim Crow, or contemporary discrimination. For example, the early Puritan dissenter, Roger Williams, was substantially influenced by contacts with Native American leaders in New England and wrote respectfully about Native American culture. He lived with Native Americans for a time, rejected much racist framing of them, sought for white colonists to be fair in land dealings, and used his knowledge of Native Americans to argue for fair treatment. Interestingly, over time such advocacy of multicultural respect and cultural diversity influenced the early and distinctive North American philosophy called "pragmatism," a perspective that has accented the importance of everyday experience as the best test of human ideas.[2]

By the mid-1700s, moreover, a small group of white Quakers were articulating strong abolitionist views and developing a more authentic liberty-and-justice frame in regard to African Americans. The Quaker leader, John Woolman, wrote incisively about the negative impact of African American enslavement on the minds of white Americans: "Being concerned with a people so situated that they have no voice to plead their own cause, there's danger of using ourselves to an undisturbed partiality, till, by long custom, the mind becomes reconciled with it, and the judgement itself infected." Woolman was an early "social constructionist," for he saw what systemic racism did to all people in society, especially those oppressed:

Placing on men the ignominious title, slave, dressing them in uncomely garments, keeping them to servile labour, in which they are often dirty, tends gradually to fix a notion in the [white] mind, that they are a sort of people below us in nature, and leads us to consider them as such in all our conclusions about them.[3]

Woolman recognized the moral contradictions. On the one hand, whites were taught Christian morality and a liberty-and-justice framing of society. On the other hand, they were taught how to implement and rationalize racial oppression. He is sensitive here to the negative impact of slavery on whites.[4]

Woolman also pointed out that white Americans never enslaved their own kind, yet had no trouble enslaving black Americans. He was one of the very first to analyze sociologically the connection of skin color to slavery: "This is owing chiefly to the idea of slavery being connected with the black colour, and liberty with the white: And where false Ideas are twisted into our minds, it is with difficulty we get fairly disentangled."[5] Woolman further accented the way in which racial oppression becomes normalized as white minds imbed "false" and "fixed notions" about those who are black and "becomes reconciled" to their oppression. In white framing liberty was color-coded: whiteness encompassed liberty, while blackness did not. Here Woolman is early moving in the direction of a central idea developed in this book: a dominant racial frame held deeply in white minds routinely rationalizes racial oppression.

Since Woolman's day, some whites have periodically joined with black Americans and other Americans of color to accent the liberty-and-justice frame and to act assertively on it. Historically, this can be seen in the anti-racist actions of the white abolitionists in the mid-nineteenth century and the white civil rights activists in the mid-twentieth century. In the next chapter we will return to this role of whites in trying to assist Americans of color today in bringing down the centuries-old system of racial oppression.

Black Resistance: Anti-racist Counter-Frames and Home-Culture Frames

There are two other categories of perspectival frames that are quite useful in making sense out of systemic racism and the resistance to it: the anti-oppression counter-frames of Americans of color; and the home-culture frames that Americans of color have drawn on to develop effective anti-oppression counter-frames. Over the long centuries of racial oppression, African Americans and others targeted by oppression have frequently developed important counter-frames designed to fight back or to just survive. Not surprisingly, this North American resistance framing began in the first century of European colonization in the Americas. Leaders of racially oppressed groups have long honed a strong counter-frame, as have most ordinary people, the "grassroots intellectuals" in racially oppressed groups. Although counter-frames were initially developed for survival, over the centuries many elements have been added that strengthen and enhance strategies of everyday resistance. Counter-frames have provided important tool kits enabling both individuals and groups to effectively counter recurring white hostility and discrimination.

In the North American colonies and, later, in the United States, pressures on African Americans to conform to the dominant Eurocentric culture forced them as a group to become significantly *bicultural*, that is, to know the dominant white-determined culture as well as their own home-culture. From the first decades of the slavery system, African Americans have created and sustained a critical home-culture that incorporates cultural features from their African background, as well as aspects of European culture, all of which are refined and shaped in the fiery crucible called North American racism. In spite of the great oppression they faced and constant pressures to abandon African cultures, the very diverse groups among those enslaved—the Yorubas, Akans, Ibos, and many others—became an African American group with a home-culture that imbedded many of the family values and moral elements from the African cultures. With important African infusions, these enslaved Americans created their own religion, art, and music, as well as their own perspectives on social oppression and social justice.

Nonetheless, since the seventeenth century, African Americans have often been restricted by whites in how much they could make overt use of many positive elements of their Africa-influenced home-culture and its alternative framing because of retaliatory repression from whites. Those enslaved typically faced aggressive reculturalization: Africans and their descendants in North America were forced to accept much European American culture, including the English language, but they still passed along valuable African-origin understandings and other cultural elements through oral and written traditions over many generations. Because this home-culture and its alternative cultural frame predated white oppression, enslaved Africans, and their African American descendants to the present day, have drawn on this background regularly for positive cultural elements that assist in crafting a successful counter-frame and its anti-oppression strategies.[6]

Consider the religious orientations of African Americans as an example of this process. For a great many African Americans, past and present, the home-culture and its alternative framing of society have been infused throughout by a positive religious and spiritual imagination that, among other aspects, has affirmed the common humanity of all people and the sacred importance of justice and equality. This religious home-culture has influenced the development of the black counter-frame of resistance and protest actions growing out of it. Historically, the discourse of most oppressed groups has included counter-framed critiques of oppression that are not discussed publicly.

For example, enslaved African Americans frequently drew both on their African religious traditions and on Christianity—the latter initially forced on them by white slavemasters—to resist white dominance. In religious services where whites were present, enslaved African Americans frequently pretended to accept Christian teachings about such things as obedience. However, when whites were absent, they often blended their African religious understandings and their version of Christianity in order to accent ideas of freedom from slavery. Conceptions of God that many held in mind—for example, the emphasis on God's having led the Israelites *out of slavery*—were not what slaveholders had envisioned. In the counter-framing of those enslaved, the "Promised Land" could mean the northern states or Canada and thus freedom, and heaven might be seen as a reality where white oppressors would be punished. This was true for African American men like the enslaved Baptist preacher, Nat Turner, a religious man who had recurring visions from God. These visions of deliverance inspired him in 1831 to lead a violent rebellion by seventy enslaved people in Virginia. Many whites were killed before white soldiers put down these black freedom fighters, who clearly had a strong framing of "liberty and justice" in their minds. Indeed, they had originally planned to begin attacks, as Turner put it, on their "enemies" on July 4 (Independence Day). The white reaction was fierce. Turner's body was beaten, beheaded, and quartered; and some 55 other black Americans were executed for allegedly participating in the rebellion.[7]

Those enslaved African Americans who participated in the numerous efforts to revolt against slavery clearly took seriously aspects of the principle of "liberty and justice for all." Thus, hidden in the apparently Christian symbolism of their music there was often a strong yearning to be free. Optimistic and humanistic religious insights and resources from the African American home-culture have been important to the development of strong counter-frames of resistance, from the slavery era to the present day.

In addition, from the beginning this distinctive African American Christianity has provided some organizational settings within which to critique oppression and through which to try to transform systemic racism. Religious gatherings and organizations during the slavery era, including churches of free African Americans, were important places where they could critically assess the realities of a racially oppressive society and develop a strong counter-frame with its array of resistance ideas and strategies. Enslaved African American men were usually allowed by slave-holders to preach, with the result that some became important resistance leaders. Ever since, to the present day, African American religious organizations and their leaders have played a very significant role in major protests against racial oppression, as we have seen in the civil rights protests of more recent decades that played a central role in bringing down Jim Crow segregation.[8]

Early Assertions of the Black Counter-Frame

From the days of slavery to the present day, African Americans have a long history of overt and covert resistance to racial oppression. No later than the mid-1600s, whites in colonial America were worried about violent insurrections by those who were enslaved. White leaders such as Virginia's influential William Byrd, a major slaveholder himself, spoke out about the dangers of insurrection that might come from the greedy actions of white slavetraders and slaveholders who were then increasing the numbers of enslaved Africans. Indeed, in 1710 Virginia's governor, Alexander Spots-wood, cautioned the Virginia Assembly that their weak militia should be concealed from "our slaves" lest their "desire of freedom may stir those people" to rebel.[9] White fears of black Americans drawing on their own liberty-and-justice framing and rising against slavery were already obvious, and such fears accelerated as the number of those enslaved increased dramatically over the next century. Whites had good reason to fear rebellions; over the long slavery era African Americans engaged in an estimated 250 slave revolts and conspiracies to revolt, averaging about one a year for just those that were recorded. Most such conspiracies to revolt did not proceed as far as that of Nat Turner's revolutionaries, but were discovered and put down by whites. Nonetheless, they indicated a significant level of collective black resistance and thus frightened many whites, thereby contributing to the "dangerous black man" imagery in the dominant racial frame.

During the nineteenth century African Americans frequently protested, individually and collectively, first against slavery and later against its oppressive replacement, legal segregation. Before the Civil War there were hundreds of protest meetings and demonstrations by black and white abolitionists targeting the institution of slavery. It was in this era, in 1829, that David Walker, a young abolitionist working in Boston, published what seems to be the first extended statement of an anti-oppression counter-frame in U.S. history. In his bold pamphlet, *Appeal to the Coloured Citizens of the World*, Walker crafted a manifesto for *full* human equality. He specifically wrote to fellow African Americans with revolutionary arguments couched in an anti-oppression framing and aggressively circulated it in the North and the South, so much so that southern slaveholders put a large $10,000 bounty on his head. Indeed, because in 1830 Walker died young and under suspicious circumstances, some analysts have suspected that he was murdered by whites. If so, this indicates well the very strong investment whites had in suppressing any type of assertive black counter-frame.[10]

Walker's anti-oppression manifesto lays out elements, critical ideas and resistance strategies, that one still finds in the black counter-frame today. He explicitly analyzes the slavery system, and the segregation of free African Americans, with blunt language accenting the injustice of these structures. Most whites are "cruel oppressors and murderers" whose "oppression" will eventually be overthrown. They are "an unjust, jealous, unmerciful, avaricious and blood-thirsty set of beings." In his aggressive counter-framing the white oppressors are defined as problematical. His critical counter-frame thus incorporates a *countersystem* analysis, one that examines the institutionalized and systemic character of white racial oppression and calls for its replacement with a new social system. Walker is perhaps the first U.S. writer to accent the concept of unjust enrichment: Whites seek for African Americans to be slaves to them "and their children forever to dig their mines and work their farms; and thus go on enriching them, from one generation to another with our *blood* and our *tears!*" Enslaved African Americans are there "to enrich them and their children. . . . the same as a parcel of brutes." In addition, Walker takes on the stereotyping of the anti-black frame. He notes that whites emotionally stereotype black Americans as "ungrateful," but replies to this white framing with historical analysis: "What should we be grateful to them for—for murdering our fathers and mothers? Or do they wish us to return thanks to them for chaining and handcuffing us, branding us . . . or for keeping us in slavery . . . to support them and their families." He specifically critiques Thomas Jefferson's extensive negative framing of African Americans in *Notes on the State of Virginia*—for example, by explaining that Jefferson's argument that enslaved blacks have limited abilities and are thus naturally inferior to whites makes as much sense as saying that a deer in an iron cage can "run as fast as the one at liberty."[11]

In his sharpest critique, Walker points up the contradictions between the extensive racial oppression of African Americans and whites' own rhetorical liberty-and-justice frame. He quotes the words "all men are created equal" from the Declaration of Independence, then challenges white readers:

Compare your own language above, extracted from your Declaration of Independence, with your cruelties and murders inflicted by your cruel and unmerciful fathers and yourselves on our fathers and on us—men who have never given your fathers or you the least provocation! . . . I ask you candidly, was your sufferings under Great Britain one hundredth part as cruel and tyrannical as you have rendered ours under you?[12]

Walker does not stop with a critique of the white racist framing, but also accents a positive view of African Americans: "Are we *men*!!—I ask you, O. my brethren! Are we *men*?" Here he builds on what must be one of the oldest elements of black resistance framing. I have tried to discover even earlier statements of this perspective, but the very earliest counter-framing of those enslaved is only indirectly recorded. One rare example is seen in a 1684 book by Caribbean slaveholder Thomas Tryon, titled *Advice to the Gentlemen Planters of the East and West Indies*. There he described an enslaved black man as insisting, "we are not Beasts . . . but rational souls."[13] Like his predecessor, Walker accents the humanity and strengths of African Americans. In the *Appeal* he also chides African Americans for not taking more assertive action against oppression and calls on them to actively refute the racist claims of white Americans. Throughout the *Appeal*, Walker accents a vigorous social justice framing of U.S. society.

In David Walker's brave and revolutionary analysis we see that black Americans already had a strongly developed counter-frame to the dominant white frame: (1) a strong critique of white racial oppression; (2) an aggressive countering of the negatively stereotyped framing of African Americans; (3) a positive assertion of the full humanity of African Americans; (4) a clear assertion of the American-ness of African Americans; and (5) a strong accent on liberty, justice, and equality for all Americans.

A few years later in 1843, an admirer of Walker and prominent abolitionist, Henry Garnet, gave a famous speech, titled "An Address to the Slaves of the United States of America," at a National Negro Convention in Buffalo. Speaking like Walker primarily to his fellow African Americans, Garnet's fervent counter-framing is very aggressive in arguing that those enslaved must assertively rebel against the racial oppression they face. In his speech he offers a structural analysis using the term "oppression" and asserting that the white "oppressor's power is fading." Like Walker he aggressively argues that African Americans like "all men cherish the love of liberty. . . . In every man's mind the good seeds of liberty are planted." He then calls on those enslaved to take revolutionary action: "There is not much hope of redemption without the shedding of blood. If you must bleed, let it all come at once—rather *die freemen, than live to be slaves*." After presenting vivid images of black Americans as free men and women, he concludes with a strong call to rebellion: "Brethren, arise, arise! Strike for your lives and liberties."[14] In spite of some critical reaction, Garnet's address was subsequently published and widely disseminated.

In the early 1850s another prominent African American abolitionist, Martin Delaney, wrote in detail about his anti-racist counter-frame. In a book directed at all Americans, he fervently points out the contradictions between the white liberty-and-justice frame and whites' everyday practices: The "United States, untrue to her trust and unfaithful to her professed principles of republican equality, has also pursued a policy of political degradation to a large portion of her native born countrymen, and that class is the Colored People. . . . There is no species of degradation to which we are not subject." In addition to assessing the oppression faced by African Americans, Delaney makes clear that his resistance framing builds on and extends the ideals of the old white liberty-and-justice frame: "We believe in the universal equality of man, and believe in that declaration of God's word, in which it is positively said, that 'God has made of one blood all the nations that dwell on the face of the earth.' " In his analysis he also takes on the negative stereotyping of black Americans in the dominant racial frame. He argues that the "absurd idea of a natural inferiority of the African" was only recently in human history dreamed up by "slave-holders and their abettors in justification" of African American enslavement.[15]

Delaney attacks such racist stereotypes and images with a detailed listing of the important achievements of numerous free and enslaved African Americans across many areas of U.S. society. He lists business entrepreneurs and professionals who have been successful among free African Americans. He describes how enslaved African workers brought very important skills in farming and animal husbandry to North America that the European colonists did not possess. Without these agricultural and related skills, cotton, tobacco, and other important agricultural production would not have been possible in colonial America or the United States. In his view black workers are the "bone and sinews of the country." Indeed, the very "existence of the white man, South, depends entirely on the labor of the black man—the idleness of the one is sustained by the industry of the other." He turns the tables on slaveholding whites, asserting that they are the ones who lazily profit off the labor of others. In addition, once again, we see the idea of the unjust enrichment of whites as part of the black counter-frame. Throughout his book, Delaney accents the point that African Americans are old *Americans* and do not seek to emigrate to Africa, a common idea among whites in his day, but rather seek liberty and justice within the U.S. society they helped to build. "Our common country is the [1850s] United States . . . and from here will we not be driven by any policy that may be schemed against us. We are Americans, having a birthright citizenship."[16] The black counter-frame, at this early point in time, was not just about beliefs, for it was asserted with much imagery of freedom and much fervor for liberation from slavery. The counter-frame was linked by some to calls for a new American revolution against slavery.

Resisting Slavery and Legal Segregation

Nat Turner acted on his counter-framing and took aggressive action against slavery. Martin Delaney too acted aggressively out of his counter-framing. In May 1858, he and the fiery white abolitionist John Brown gathered together a group of black and white abolitionists for a revolutionary anti-slavery meeting just outside the United States, in the safer area of Chatham, Canada. Nearly four dozen black and white Americans met and formulated a new constitution to govern what they hoped would be a growing band of armed revolutionaries drawn from the enslaved population; these revolutionaries would fight aggressively as guerillas for an end to the U.S. slavery system. Delaney was also among the abolitionists who in the 1860s pressed President Abraham Lincoln to recruit African Americans, both those who were free and enslaved runaways, for the Union army. As a result of this successful recruitment by Delaney and others, during the last years of the Civil War several hundred thousand African Americans, the majority formerly enslaved, served as Union soldiers and support troops— and thus did much more to free enslaved Americans than did President Abraham Lincoln's famous 1863 Emancipation Proclamation.[17]

Like the black abolitionists, most of these Union soldiers and support troops undoubtedly held some version of the black counter-frame in their minds. For example, the formerly enslaved John Washington, who ran away and became part of the Union Army's support troops, described his new situation thus:

> Before morning I had began to feel like I had truly escaped from the hands of the slaves master and with the help of God, I never would be a slave no more. I felt for the first time in my life that I could now claim every cent that I should work for as my own. I began now to feel that life had a new joy awaiting me. I might now go and come when I please This was the *first night of freedom*.[18]

Another formerly enslaved member of Union support troops put it this way: "The next morning I was up early and took a look at the rebels country with a thankful heart to think I had made my escape with safety after such a long struggle; and had obtained that freedom which I desired so long. I now dreaded the gun, and handcuffs and pistols no more."[19] For formerly enslaved men and women, liberty and justice were much more than rhetorical abstractions. Their sacrifices on Civil War battlefields and behind the lines helped not only to free those enslaved, but also to put the United States on track to become a freer country.

Although they had the chance to implement key features of their own liberty-and-justice frame after the Civil War, most members of the powerful white elites in the South and the North refused to do so. They encouraged or allowed whites in all social classes in the southern and border states to establish an extensive system of Jim Crow segregation that was backed by lynchings and other anti-black violence, while encouraging or permitting significant de facto segregation of black Americans to continue in northern states. Over time, this legal and de facto apartheid generated individual and collective protests from African Americans, including more honing of a strong resistance frame.

For example, the ever perceptive, formerly enslaved black leader, Frederick Douglass, developed an extensive counter-frame, first during his enslavement in Maryland, then as an anti-slavery abolitionist, and later during legal segregation after the Civil War. In 1852 after he had become an abolitionist leader, Douglass made an eloquent Fourth of July speech in Rochester, New York: "What, to the American slave, is your Fourth of July? I answer: A day that reveals to him, more than all other days of the year, the gross injustices and cruelty to which he is the constant victim. To him your celebration is a sham."[20] Once again, we observe important counter-framing that accents the hypocrisy of the white liberty-and-justice rhetoric, coupled with a strong emphasis on the great injustice done to African Americans.

For decades after the Civil War, the courageous Douglass gave many speeches that counter-framed the oppression of Jim Crow segregation as a new type of enslavement for African Americans, as in this 1880s speech: "It meets them at the workshop and factory, when they apply for work. It meets them at the church, at the hotel, at the ballot-box, and worst of all, it meets them in the jury-box." Most African Americans had moved from being the "slave of an individual" to now being the "slave of society."[21] A few years later, also during the early decades of legal segregation, two important black social scientists, Ida B. Wells-Barnett and Anna Julia Cooper, began to develop the idea of *gendered* racism, a view accenting how gendered the dominant racial hierarchy was in practice. They were among the first to analyze empirical data on the oppressive segregation faced by African American men and women, as well as the discrimination faced by women in general, and they made explicit use of counter-frame ideas and terms like "oppression," "subordination," and "repression" in their analyses. Working as a researcher and an activist dealing with violent expressions of racial oppression at the turn of the twentieth century, Wells-Barnett developed key sociological ideas about how white oppression is grounded not only in the material reality of economic exploitation, but also in the brutal gendering (with related violence such as lynchings) of black men as dangerous to white women and of black women as oversexed. In the decades before and after 1900, these and other black female social scientists were among the first to emphasize the overlapping of institutional racism and sexism.[22]

Working about the same time, and also drawing on a centuries-old black resistance frame, sociologist W. E. B. Du Bois developed fully a counter-framed view that the United States was pervaded by institutionalized racism. In *The Souls of Black Folk*, he described the difficult black consciousness that is created by having to deal every day with racial oppression: "It is a peculiar sensation, this double consciousness, this sense of always looking at one's self through the eyes of others. . . . One ever feels his twoness—an American, a Negro; two souls, two thoughts . . . in one dark body, whose dogged strength alone keeps it from being torn asunder."[23] This sense of twoness, and the dual roles flowing out of it, have from the beginning been imposed on African Americans by systemic racism. It was early the case, and often still is, that a black American could not openly express his or her true self without risking significant white retaliation. Du Bois made clear that countering whites' framing means not only knowing the black counter-frame well, but also constantly reinforcing it in backstage settings where it can be safely expressed.

Du Bois implemented his counter-frame ideas in actions, such as by helping to found the National Association for the Advancement of Colored People (NAACP) just after 1900 and by being a leader in that organization for decades. He extended his counter-framing to the global sphere and as the leading advocate of pan-African nationalism. His globalized counter-frame emphasized the common conditions of, and need for uniting, colonized people of African descent across the world. In 1919, near the peak of the Jim Crow era and over objections from the U.S. State Department, Du Bois put together the first Pan-African Congress. Attended by delegates from fifteen countries, the Congress pressed for the final abolition of all slavery, an end to colonial exploitation, and democratic treatment of people of African descent everywhere. This Congress was considered a radical challenge to white dominance and white racial framing by leading white officials in the U.S. State Department and White House.[24]

By the 1930s and 1940s, the pioneering African American sociologist Oliver Cox was also developing a counter-framed analysis of U.S. racism as fundamentally structural and institutionalized. In his counter-framing, the sustained exploitation of black Americans for centuries had created in the United States a hierarchical structure of racial classes with whites firmly at the top. The white seizure of African labor in overseas colonialism and in North America created a deep structure of institutionalized oppression. He rejected the mainstream social science accent on individual bigotry. For him, U.S. racism was not some "abstract, natural, immemorial feeling of mutual antipathy between groups, but rather a practical exploitative relationship with its socio-attitudinal facilitation" of "only nascent race prejudice."[25]

The Civil Rights Movement: Action Out of the Counter-Frame

It took several decades for black organization and protests against Jim Crow segregation to become substantial and successful, but they eventually did. Over the last century African Americans, and some other Americans of color, have created numerous civil rights organizations that have asserted and implemented an anti-racist counter-framing. One example is the NAACP, which early in the twentieth century inaugurated major law-suits against Jim Crow segregation, lawsuits that eventually led to the 1954 *Brown v. School Board of Topeka* Supreme Court decision. As suggested previously, both black leaders and black Americans generally were far in advance of the white leadership on desegregation issues, indeed many decades in advance. Centuries of anti-black oppression have made a major-ity of black Americans into "everyday intellectuals" who are forced by their harsh circumstances to develop an institutional-racism framing of U.S. society and who have long sought to destroy that racism. As early as the 1930s and 1940s black organizing and voting in the North were sub-stantially responsible for the northern white elite's (and Supreme Court's) increasing concern with taking action against Jim Crow. By the end of World War II, the NAACP alone had some 1,000 local organizations and a half million members. Moreover, many black veterans returning in the late 1940s from World War II, a war fought "for democracy," were aggressive in articulating the need for desegregation and joined confrontational civil rights organizations.[26]

From the 1910s to the 1950s, an indication of the increasing expression in action of an anti-racist counter-frame could be seen in the millions of black Americans who had abandoned southern states for northern cities, where many could vote for Democratic presidential candidates like Franklin Roosevelt and Harry Truman. As presidents, both men were pressured by black civil rights organizations to take action against U.S. apartheid. During World War II, under pressure from African American leaders planning a march in the nation's capital to protest discrimina-tion, President Franklin Roosevelt issued an executive order reducing discrimination in employment and setting up a Fair Employment Practices Committee. After the war, President Harry Truman even took more aggressive action, desegregating the U.S. Armed Forces and establishing a Committee on Civil Rights.[27]

By the 1950s, the black civil rights movement's protests and development of a strong anti-racist counter-frame had created a serious legitimation crisis for the country's white elite. The desire of this elite to protect its national and international legitimacy, including the respect of other world leaders and world opinion, in the face of increasing black protests against Jim Crow was important to the success of civil rights protests. Without aggressive pressuring by African Americans, the white elite would likely not have moved toward racial desegregation. Important too was the "Cold War" setting in which the U.S. ideology of democracy was proclaimed against undemocratic enemies (especially the Soviet Union) everywhere by the U.S. government. In addition, the wars of the civil rights era—World War II, the Korean War, and the Vietnam War—required substantial mobilization of black workers and soldiers for success, which made it easier for the voices of black leaders and protestors to be heard at the highest levels of white decision-making, if only temporarily. In the 1950s the civil rights movement increased dramatically, first with boycotts such as that of segregated buses in Montgomery, Alabama, then by a variety of civil rights protests across the country. The Congress of Racial Equality (CORE) asserted an aggressive black counter-frame and accelerated protest campaigns against housing and employment discrimination in the North. School boycotts, picketing at construction sites, and rent strikes spread. The growing group of organizations oriented toward greater black political and economic power included the youthful Student Nonviolent Coordinating Committee (SNCC). Actions by civil rights groups brought passage of major civil rights acts prohibiting discrimination in employment, voting, and housing. Since the 1940s, many African Americans have come together, at least for a time, and acted in unity to make the United States a freer country.[28]

Essential to these many civil rights protests was a dramatic increase in the espousal by black leaders and scholars of a strong anti-racist counter-frame. During the 1960s civil rights movements numerous African American activists and scholars publicly proclaimed and sharpened an institutional-racism framing in the tradition of W. E. B. Du Bois and Oliver Cox. Activist Stokely Carmichael (later, Kwame Ture) and historian Charles Hamilton asserted and demonstrated in their brilliant 1967 book, *Black Power*, the importance of institutional racism in the contemporary United States, of patterns of racism built into this society's major institutions today. They sharply contrasted their counter-framed view of institutional racism with the older "race relations" approach focusing on individual white prejudice and discrimination. As they showed, institutionalized racism encompassed much more than the beliefs and actions of scattered white bigots. In addition, they and others called for a dramatic increase in "black power," especially black political power, and asserted a positive framing of black people and culture under the banners such as "black is beautiful."[29] Such developments provoked a strong backlash among many whites.

Note too the continuing importance of African American Christianity and churches in the civil rights movement. Dr. Martin Luther King, Jr., and many other civil rights leaders of the contemporary era have been Protestant ministers. As in earlier times, religious leaders and organizations still play a significant role in spreading the anti-racist counter-frame and generating protests against racial oppression. From the slavery era to the present, ministers' sermons, various black celebrations (especially about black history), and church groups' activities have provided much support for the counter-frame that helps people cope with and resist the dominant racist framing of society.

In virtually all cases, African Americans who have publicly asserted the anti-racist counter-frame have used the language of equality, freedom, and "liberty and justice for all." In the supposedly post-racial contemporary era, the high level of racial hostility and discrimination still perpetrated by whites routinely contradicts key elements of the old white liberty-and-justice frame, which may be one reason that some of its idealistic language has often been used by Americans of color and dissenting whites who seek to reduce or eliminate racial discrimination. For example, Dr. Martin Luther King, Jr., often accented the ideals of liberty and justice, drawing on a centuries-old counter-frame and accenting more meaningfully the important elements of the old liberty-and-justice frame articulated by the white founders. He made much use of concepts of freedom and liberty, but linked them constantly to the related goal of social justice. Even in the middle of the civil rights movement, King looked beyond the oratory of freedom to accent major societal changes:

> Justice for black people will not flow into society merely from court decisions nor from fountains of political oratory. Nor will a few token changes quell all the tempestuous yearnings of millions of disadvantaged black people. White America must recognize that justice for black people cannot be achieved without radical changes in the structure of our society.[30]

King made it clear in a comment about the Montgomery bus boycott by local black residents there that the counter-frame includes a conception of oppression that must be overcome by assertive action bringing social justice:

There comes a time when people get tired of being trampled by oppression. There comes a time when people get tired of being plunged into the abyss of exploitation and nagging injustice. The story of Montgomery is the story of fifty thousand such Negroes who were willing to . . . walk the streets of Montgomery until the walls of segregation were finally battered by the forces of justice.[31]

Significantly, the 1950s and 1960s civil rights movements brought a meaningful emphasis on, and some implementation of, the ideals of liberty and justice back into the public sphere of the United States.

Indeed, both Democratic presidents in the 1960s, John F. Kennedy and Lyndon Baines Johnson, seemed to have learned something about the importance of actually expanding liberty and justice from the civil rights movements. A famous example of this can be seen in President Johnson's commencement address at Howard University in 1965, one titled "To Fulfill These Rights." In that address he first accented the "devastating heritage of long years of slavery; and a century of oppression, hatred, and injustice" as explanations for black poverty and inequality. Then he continued with this dramatic language:

But *freedom is not enough.* You do not wipe away the scars of centuries by saying: Now you are free to go where you want, and do as you desire, and choose the leaders you please. You do not take a person who, for years, has been hobbled by chains and liberate him, bring him up to the starting line of a race and then say, "you are free to compete with all the others," and still justly believe that you have been completely fair. . . . We seek not just freedom but opportunity. We seek not just legal equity but human ability, not just equality as a right and a theory but equality as a fact and equality as a result.[32]

Such phrasing was drawn from the bold language of the black civil rights movement and indicated that this president—and his white advisors who wrote the speech—were then willing to accent a more authentic liberty-and-justice framing of the long centuries of oppression faced by African Americans. However, President Johnson, and subsequent white presidents, soon backed off on this commitment to real justice and equality, for it was clear that major structural changes in racial inequalities and institutional racism were not supported by most whites. Still, for a brief time a few white leaders like Johnson had taken some anti-discrimination action inspired by the black liberty-and-justice framing.

Significantly, today public and private discussions of racially liberal and emancipatory views accenting equality and justice are often identified in many white minds as something distinctively "black"—probably because

African Americans have long been the most visible group carrier of a sustained liberty-and-justice tradition, one involving the most extensive civil rights organization, in U.S. history.

Black Anti-racist Counter-Framing Today

In recent years African American scholars and activists have continued to build on the extensive, often positive counter-framing of the civil rights movement era, and some have emphasized a comprehensive Afrocentric perspective, one including a strong critique of white cultural imperialism. Sociologist Molefi Kete Asante, among others, has spurred the development of this perspective, arguing for the distinctive concept of "Afrocentricity" as a counter to the dominant Eurocentric culture. Asante and other African American scholars and activists have extensively analyzed this Eurocentric culture, particularly the elements that have been substantially absorbed by African Americans. The African American anthropologist, Marimba Ani, has accented well the important parts of a contemporary Afrocentric counter-frame. On the one hand, this strong counter-frame critically problematizes the white cultural imperialism that attempts "to proselytize, encourage, and project European ideology." On the other, it underscores the need for African Americans to direct their "energies toward the recreation of cultural alternatives informed by ancestral visions of a future that celebrates Africanness."[33]

Note too that this contemporary resistance framing is quite evident in the views and actions of rank-and-file African Americans, and not just among African American intellectuals and leaders. Let us briefly summarize important elements in the contemporary black counter-frame. These encompass numerous cognitive elements, including a sometimes distinctive language of resistance, that are linked to collective understandings about black and white Americans, and about U.S. society generally. In addition, the counter-frame includes significant emotions, such as moral outrage and strong desires for social change. As we have seen frequently in this chapter, among the oldest of these counter-frame elements is a critique and naming of what has happened to African Americans, that is, the *white oppression* and *white racism*. This aspect of black counter-framing accents white discriminators as a central problem of society and incorporates some *countersystem* analysis—collectively developed understandings about how, where, and when white hostility and discrimination operate interpersonally, as well as in society generally. The counter-frame typically includes well-honed perspectives on how to deal with white discriminators, including both passive and active strategies. For example, in one field research study a veteran black police officer put it this way:

You're looking at a [racist] system that's been built up over the years with a philosophy that's been built up over the years and its taught not only in the educational system, on television, in the media. It's all around you, and you either subscribe to it because it's the easy thing to do, or actually it's the natural thing to do. Or you have to struggle with society and once that struggle, once that fever pitch struggle begins and catches on, I think you'll see some progress, but until that you deal with what you deal with.[34]

A second important element in the counter-frame is a developed sensitivity to whites' negative framing of African Americans and to commonplace stereotypes and discriminatory acts, as this black respondent made quite clear:

After so many years of overt racism and then watching the change over years from those overt acts to covert acts, . . . a lot of African Americans have developed an ability to pick up on certain things. I mean, you can pretty much meet someone [and] within two or three minutes and know if they're sincere. And it's wrong, you can say, "Well that's prejudice, and you're prejudging someone," but the truth is the truth. After you've been treated a particular way so long and heard so many things, pretty soon, they come around full circle and you know what certain phrases mean. You know what certain mannerisms mean, because you've seen it thousands of times before and you've seen what it's attached to.[35]

Operating out of a counter-frame that regularly assesses critically the surrounding racist environment, many African Americans regularly question and challenge racist stereotypes and actions when they encounter them.

A third element that is central to both older black counter-framing and the contemporary counter-frame is an assertion of the positive aspects of black humanity and achievements, such as the accent on the beauty of black women and a commitment to expanding black political or economic power. One black college student put it this way:

My parents tried to tell me one thing, they tried to instill in me that I was a beautiful person, that my blackness was a beautiful thing, that the fact that I braided my hair was fine, that I didn't have a perm was fine. But when you're like, nine, ten, eleven, you tend not to listen to your parents, and you tend to listen to everything else, which is white people, in my case white people, and all society which is white. . . .[36]

In black family and friendship circles there is often a significant affirmation of black beauty and humanity, but it is difficult to assert this counter-framing against a very strong white framing of white beauty and superiority in the larger society. Nonetheless, older generations of black Americans often pass along to youth strongly positive interpretations of black history, traditions, and beauty.

In contemporary black counter-framing, gendered racism continues to receive much attention. Since the 1970s numerous scholars and activists have shown how slavery, legal segregation, and contemporary discrimination shape the lives of black women and men in gendered-racist ways. One major analyst of the intersections of racism, classism, and sexism, Angela Davis, has underscored the point that enslaved black women had their own type of gendered oppression: They were exploited for their productive labor as workers and their reproductive labor as breeders of enslaved children. Another pioneering social scientist, Philomena Essed, interviewed black women in Holland and the United States and coined the term "gendered racism." She described how in contemporary societies black women's experiences with discrimination were gendered, how racism and sexism regularly interacted and overlapped in their lives. From years of such experiences most black women have developed distinctive systems of knowledge that are critical for fighting that everyday gendered racism. Sociologist Patricia Hill Collins has shown that a strong black-feminist counter-frame highlights and analyzes critically the negative stereotypes of black women—the white-generated stereotypes of the docile mammy, domineering matriarch, promiscuous prostitute, and irresponsible welfare mother. These severely gendered-racist framings of black women, some of which are also applied to other women of color, persist because they are fostered by the white-dominated media and undergird recurring discrimination against women of color. In research on black women, researchers like Davis, Essed, Collins, Elizabeth Higginbotham, Yanick St. Jean, and Adia Harvey Wingfield, among numerous others, have regularly emphasized the importance of liberating women of color from racial, gender, and gendered-racist stereotypes and discrimination.[37]

Today the black counter-frame, as it has for centuries, contains the ideals, language, emotions, and images of freedom, equality, and justice, which are often envisioned not only for black Americans but for all people. There is often hope of future societal fairness, of getting "what is rightfully ours"—the modern version of the old "40-acres-and-mule" promise to those freed from slavery after the 1860s Civil War. Today this positive orientation includes an insistence, as with early activist-thinkers like David Walker and Martin Delaney, on whites' accepting responsibility for racism and on full equality and social justice for African Americans. It accents as well the true American-ness of African Americans. Consider this excerpt from a 2008 National Press Club speech by Dr. Jeremiah Wright, emeritus minister at Chicago's Trinity United Church in Chicago and former pastor of President Barack Obama:

The black church's role in the fight for equality and justice from the 1700s up until 2008 has always had as its core the non-negotiable doctrine of reconciliation, children of God repenting for past sins against each other. . . . Reconciliation means we embrace our individual rich histories, all of them. We retain who we are, as persons of different cultures, while acknowledging that those of other cultures are not superior or inferior to us; they are just different from us. We root out any teaching of superiority, inferiority, hatred or prejudice. And we recognize for the first time in modern history, in the West, that the other who stands before us with a different color of skin, a different texture of hair, different music, different preaching styles and different dance moves; that other is one of God's children just as we are, no better, no worse, prone to error and in need of forgiveness just as we are.[38]

Interestingly, two of Dr. Wright's earlier sermons asserting racial justice ideas and condemning the U.S. government's long history of racist actions globally—including one that Wright ended with brief "God Damn America" language in regard to such racist governmental actions—were widely quoted out of context in the white-controlled mainstream media during the 2008 presidential campaign. The purpose seems to have been to problematize and/or derail the Obama presidential campaign. Here is a larger excerpt from Wright's strong counter-framed 2003 sermon, one indicating the context of these famous three words that the media took out of context:

The United States of America government, when it came to treating her citizens of Indian descent fairly, she failed. She put them on reservations. When it came to treating her citizens of Japanese descent fairly, she failed. She put them in internment prison camps. When it came to treating citizens of African descent fairly. . . . The government put them on slave quarters, put them on auction blocks, put them in cotton fields, put them in inferior schools, put them in substandard housing, put them in scientific experiments, put them in the lowest paying jobs, put them outside the equal protection of the law. . . . The government gives them the drugs, builds bigger prisons, passes a three-strike law, and then wants us to sing God bless America? No, no, no. Not God bless America; God damn America! That's in the Bible, for killing innocent people. God damn America for

treating her citizen as less than human. God damn America as long
as she keeps trying to act like she is God and she is supreme![39]

If Dr. Wright's prophet-like statements are placed in their larger context at
the end of a long sermon on societal injustice, one sees clearly that he is
arguing that, in contrast to the power of God, even powerful governments
such as that of the U.S., are fallible and transitory; and in his view, most
particularly, this is true of those that fail to treat all citizens equally. His
reasoning clearly makes sense and is straight out of a strong black counter-
frame directed against systemic racism.

The mass-media's repeated quoting of the "God damn America" phrasing, totally out of its analytical context in this sermon, caused such a
national political frenzy and negative reaction in much of the white population that then presidential candidate Barack Obama was forced to criti-
cize Wright sharply and, after other critical remarks by Wright out of the
black counter-frame, eventually to break fully with his former pastor and
leave the Chicago church. Moreover, in his presidential campaign Obama
preferred, with rare exceptions, not to use the strong ideas and language of
the black counter-frame. Obama and his mostly white political team
seemed to be greatly concerned about the negative white reactions to the
more forthright language and interpretations of liberty and justice in the
black counter-frame.[40]

The Jeremiah Wright sermons and Barack Obama's responses illustrate
that there are today important variations in the use of the black counter-
frame ideas and language. The use of elements from the counter-frame
runs across a broad continuum. At one end of the frame's use there is a
relatively assertive and well-developed anti-racist view that is constantly
asserted in speeches by black political officials and in sermons by black
ministers like Dr. Wright, as well as by many other members of black civil
rights organizations and organized protest movements. In these groups
and social networks there is much assertively critical analysis of the racist
dimensions of U.S. society, and the anti-racist counter-framing is mostly
conscious, overt, and assertive.

Considering the broad continuum, many black Americans seem to fall
in between this very aggressive expression of the black anti-racist counter-
frame, and the other end of the counter-frame continuum where there are
African Americans who make little or no use of its critical and anti-racist
ideas, especially in public. The latter, which include some black media
commentators (such as some on Fox News), often seem to have conformed
aggressively to white folkways; and they periodically assert publicly some
aspects of the white racial frame's negative views of African Americans. In
the past and more recently, one observes this white-framed perspective in

various commentaries on "disorganized" and "pathological" black families by a few black celebrities, scholars, and commentators. Among these more conservative African Americans, modest elements from the black counter-framing may be used, such as language about freedom and justice, but this use of the counter-frame tends to be much weaker or vaguer, as least in public, than it is for African Americans like Dr. Wright. In addition, there are many other African Americans who fall in between these two ends of the continuum and assert what might be termed a middle-strength version of the black counter-frame in their everyday lives, applying it variably as the situations demand. Thus, both the white racial frame and the black counter-frame are variable in their everyday expression and assertion depending on individual propensities, family socialization, and the pressures or requirements of particular societal settings.[41]

Throughout the three major eras of slavery, legal segregation, and contemporary discrimination we see black leaders and rank-and-file black Americans asserting and acting on the major elements of the black resistance counter-frame, elements that were already present and motivating in David Walker's courageous anti-racist appeal in the early nineteenth century.

Passing Along the Counter-Frame

Where and how do African Americans learn the anti-racist counter-frame? It is definitely not taught in the mainstream media or most public schools and colleges, with the exception of historically black colleges. Most U.S. educational institutions are in fact primary distributors and inculcators of the white racial frame. The black home-culture frame and the anti-racist frame are most centrally taught within black families, normally with the support of churches and other community organizations. The family has long been the main social institution where African Americans can get regular doses of the aspects of the counter-frame. A majority of parents teach their children significant aspects of the counter-frame, usually with lessons about how to spot and deal with white discrimination. Among parents of color in the United States, black parents seem to be the most likely to explicitly teach an anti-oppression counter-frame.[42]

Over the centuries, African Americans have done, as many often say, "what they had to do just to survive." In this way, they have developed a counter-frame with a strong dose of black pragmatism, a practical perspective toward everyday situations. Thus, in everyday encounters with whites African Americans are often cautious and may have to defer to whites and their white framing, while with black friends and relatives they can usually be freer and openly discuss negative experiences with whites and ways to counter discrimination. Family and friends remind each other of these strategies, including cautions about interactions with whites. In contrast, whites need not be aware of counter-frames held by people of color, and indeed are often unaware of their own white-racist framing.[43]

Like other important frames, the black counter-frame is variable in extent and subtlety, and versions of it include subframes that reflect the class and gender realities of black parents and their children. For example, many black working-class parents give their children nontraditional first names to provide them with something special—and not with European American first names that are commonplace. Such naming is a subtle type of resistance to whiteness, an example of everyday counter-framing. At all class levels, moreover, there is often a gendered dimension to the counter-frame and its transmission. Black parents and other socializers of black children commonly shape teachings about white discrimination to fit a child's gender. Because the white racial frame is itself gendered, with black boys and men generally seen as more frightening and dangerous than black girls and women, teaching the counter-frame is also often gendered. Given the aggressive white targeting of black boys and men for racial discrimination, including violence, in areas such as policing, black parents often provide stronger and earlier lessons about being cautious when around white police officers and police brutality for sons than for daughters. Such lessons about being wary of white officers and other government officials have long been important parts of black counter-framing. Teachings from the counter-frame also tend to be gendered in the case of black girls. Girls are frequently taught a somewhat different array of strategies, some gendered, for dealing with white racism. Thus, many black parents teach their daughters that the white frame's image of "true" beauty is racially stereotyped, and that being dark-skinned and of African descent is indeed to be beautiful. Such teaching is necessary because over their lives black daughters are likely to encounter many accented white beauty images and many negative images of and commentaries on black women.[44]

A few researchers have found that among black children and young people having significant understandings of racial hostility and discrimination, under many circumstances, can increase positive outcomes such as better grades and positive self-esteem. Yet other studies show that such awareness of discrimination sometimes links to negative effects on mental health, including higher stress and classroom conduct issues for some schoolchildren. Some analysts have viewed these research findings as contradictory, but they actually are not, for the white-racist worlds faced by black children, and adults, create stress and other negative mental health responses, at the same time that they may create a stronger will to fight—depending on the individual and level of group support.[45]

Much teaching and passing along of the home-culture frame and the anti-racist counter-frame take place in friendship and kinship groups of adults, as well as in various community organizations. Quite important venues are taverns, beauty shops, and barber shops. For example, in one recent study Adia Harvey Wingfield interviewed and observed black entrepreneurs who ran beauty salons. These women often reported going into the hair industry in order to make black women feel beautiful and supported, and they have created black-controlled spaces where women candidly discuss many important life issues, including critical aspects of a counter-framing directed at the gendered racism they daily face. Wingfield describes these safe spaces thus:

> By establishing the salon as a soothing, peaceful environment where black women could discuss anything, salon owners were able to create a place where black women and their concerns, issues, and perspectives were fundamental rather than marginalized. . . . The creation of the salon as a safe space allows black women owners to challenge systemic gendered racism by presenting their businesses as a haven from its debilitating effects. Systemic gendered racism in the larger society renders black women invisible, unimportant, and irrelevant. Owners challenge this by consciously establishing salons where black women are central, important, and necessary.[46]

Wingfield also describes the important helping ethic that the salon owners operate from and pass along, to both the black women who work for them and their clients:

> Owners' efforts to value their work, to create safe spaces for black women, and to help other women achieve the financial and social benefits of entrepreneurship are a counterframe to the systemic gendered racist ideology that black women and the work that they do are unappreciated and worthless. The helping ideology in particular is a counterframe to the systemic gendered racist ideology that black women should see one another as enemies or competitors rather than as comrades who collectively face oppressive conditions.[47]

Highly developed understandings of how gendered racial oppression works, and about the strategies that work in countering that oppression, are regularly passed along in such settings, across lines of class, age, and generation.

In addition, black beauty salons are places where black *beauty* is routinely defined, honored, and enhanced—once again in resistance to the conventional white framing of black women. While these salons are places where black hair is often straightened to conform to a certain white-framed image of good hair, since the 1960s "black is beautiful" movements, many black salons have expanded their hairstyling services to include an array of more natural hair styles with African and Caribbean origins, such as braided cornrows, other braiding, afros, and dreadlocks. Adopting these natural styles is seen by many black Americans, women and men, as rejecting the dominant white-oriented images of beauty and style. In a number of important ways, thus, black beauty salons are centers of black female resistance to the white-racist framing of black women and to the associated discriminatory practices that go with that framing.[48]

A recent ethnographic study by Reuben May of black men interacting over time in a tavern found that such settings also support the development of strong self-identities and important counter-frames that involve understandings of racial discrimination and conflict:

> By sharing their experiences with one another, African Americans bolster their confidence in their ability to deal with negative inter-racial conditions, instead of being adversely affected by them. For some patrons, a trip to the tavern is equivalent to a visit to the therapist. Patrons' knowledge that others have experienced what they are going through is key for the survival of self-identity, an identity intertwined with the understanding that racial conflict is something that happens everyday in a world that emphasizes race.[49]

In the churches, beauty salons, and taverns of their communities, black Americans develop or enhance the important home-frames and counter-frames that help them make sense out of the often difficult social worlds they find as they venture out of their communities into white-controlled institutional worlds. African Americans of various backgrounds must engage in what sociologist Elijah Anderson terms "folk ethnography," the development of important knowledge about the contours and realities of their everyday lives, including their often difficult interactions with whites and other nonblacks in schools, workplaces, government offices, and other settings, including on the street. The knowledge they develop in assessing and reflecting on their experiences, and their sharing of this knowledge with others in important community places like salons and taverns, help to build counter-frames for dealing with racial hostility, discrimination, and related issues in the everyday routines of their lives.[50]

Variations in the Counter-Frame

As we have already seen, there are some significant variations in the use of key elements of the black counter-frame, just as there are for the use of the white racial frame. Each black American or other person of color individually makes use of elements from the prevailing counter-frame of their group in dealing with a particular situation, place, and time. Those who are part of an oppressed racial group in a society, such as black Americans, are particularly likely to have to alter their orientations, statements, or actions so as to please or conform to the imagery of people in the dominant racial group. We do not have the space to deal with this matter at length, but let me illustrate this point with an example from President Barack Obama's election campaign. For almost the entire 2007–2008 campaign, as noted previously, Senator Obama mostly kept away from direct discussions of racism issues of all kinds. He engaged in a significant discussion of affirmative action only once during the campaign, and only when forced by a journalist; and he gave only one major speech, his famous March 2008 speech, dealing with racism in U.S. society—and then mostly with regard to the past and only because he was forced to do so by the media-aired comments made in a sermon by his pastor Dr. Wright.

In spite of Obama's dodging of racial issues during the campaign, and his frequent political speeches (such as one critiquing "irresponsible" black fathers) that intentionally played into the white racial frame's understandings, candidate Obama demonstrated numerous times that he understood and had regularly viewed the world from a version of the black counter-frame. For example, in his 2006 book, *The Audacity of Hope*, then Senator Obama listed numerous examples of the anti-black discrimination he had faced at the hands of white security guards, restaurant customers, and police officers. He noted having to swallow his anger at such discriminatory incidents, as well as his fears that his daughters might absorb racist story lines from the white-controlled media. He explicitly rejected then, as he likely still does, any notion that Americans have entered an era of "post-racial politics" or "already live in a colorblind society." He insisted that the country has seen significant racial change since Jim Crow segregation, but also that "better is not enough."[51] More recently in fall 2007, well before he became the Democratic Party frontrunner, Obama gave an interview to the black women's magazine, *Essence*, in which he asserted the following:

> I don't believe it is possible to transcend race in this country. . . . Race is a factor in this society. The legacy of Jim Crow and slavery has not gone away. It is not an accident that African Americans experience high crime rates, are poor, and have less wealth. It is a direct result of our racial history. . . . When you do that kind of thing [talk about black community problems] you have a corollary responsibility to take on [racial] issues that White candidates might not speak to, that it is now incumbent upon you to do.[52]

Clearly, Senator Obama was, and likely still is, well aware of the issues of white hostility and discrimination that African Americans have faced in the Jim Crow past and the still discriminatory present. In his own books and in the *Essence* interview he used some of the hard-edged language and understandings from the black counter-frame and recognized an obligation to show an understanding of white-imposed racial discrimination. In this way he signaled to black Americans, including black voters, that he did realize their discriminatory situations and inequalities.[53]

Nonetheless, Obama carefully picked the social situations in which he revealed much about his understandings of racism. As a result of this caution and much concealment, he got the necessary share, 43 percent, of the white vote. That vote, plus almost all the black vote and a significant majority of the votes of other voters of color, enabled him to become president. Most Americans of color understand well the tightrope that candidate Obama, and President Obama, have had to walk, for they too regularly walk such a tightrope in the still-racist United States.

We can now examine some of the resistance efforts and anti-racist counter-frames of other Americans of color. I do not have the space here to go into detail on these efforts, but I will trace out enough material to indicate that African Americans are not the only group to have developed significant resistance efforts and important counter-frames. Let us consider briefly the counter-frames of Native Americans, Asian Americans, and Latinos.

Native Americans and Counter-Framing

Native Americans have the longest tradition of countering white oppression, including the Eurocentric racial framing. The early European invaders and their descendants today have usually viewed Native Americans, who lived in numerous different indigenous societies, as not having had real "civilization" until it was brought by Europeans. However, at initial contact most indigenous societies had home-cultures that were at least as developed and sophisticated as those of European societies. Indeed, many indigenous societies were much more humanistic and egalitarian along class and gender lines than the societies of the European colonists.

Organized Native American protest against white subordination has been substantial over the centuries. The ever widening expansion of the European and European American invaders between the 1500s and the 1890s produced major Native American resistance movements. These movements were often armed and frequently took the form of wars with the European colonists. In North America this armed resistance was conceptualized and interpreted from within the home-cultures of the hundreds of indigenous societies that suffered from often violent white incursions. Building on the home-culture frames, various Native American groups developed counter-frames that conceptualized the white invaders as dangerous and untrustworthy in making treaties. The end of this armed resistance after the 1890s did not end significant Native American protests. By the late nineteenth century, new protest organizations had sprung up, each with some counter-framing as part of their thrust. For example, the Society of American Indians, formed in 1911 by a diverse group of Native American professionals, sought to develop national Indian leadership, counter racial stereotypes and inform the white public about Native Americans, and expand educational and employment opportunities for individual Native Americans. Later, in the 1940s, the National Congress of American Indians, a large advocacy group, was formed; it has used an anti-racist counter-frame for decades and has pressed for tribal self-determination, an end to racist anti-Indian stereotyping, and expanded education for Native Americans. These and other Native American groups have long fought vigorously for social justice and have regularly organized protests against white stereotyping and discrimination.[54]

During the 1960s a strong "red power" counter-frame was central to increased Indian activism, including picketing and civil disobedience such as sit-ins in government facilities. In 1968 an assertive American Indian Movement (AIM) was organized to address issues ranging from police brutality to housing and employment discrimination targeting Native Americans. In recent decades AIM and other Indian organizations have strongly protested the use of Indian names and sacred symbols by many white-oriented sports teams and fans. The highly stereotyped and racist use of sacred chants, face paint, headdresses, and drums for entertainment purposes have understandably outraged Native Americans and periodically generated significant anti-racist framing and protests based on this framing.[55]

For Native Americans, home-culture frames have been very important sources of anti-oppression counter-framing. Indeed, there is an unbroken line of transmission from early home-culture frames predating European invasions to home-culture frames today. Russell Means, an influential Indian activist and leader, has emphasized the central importance of spirituality and humanity in Native American home-culture frames and counter-frames, today as in the past:

Being is a spiritual proposition. Gaining is a material act. Traditionally, American Indians have always attempted to be the best people they could. Part of that spiritual process was and is to give away wealth, to discard wealth in order not to gain. Material gain is an indicator of false status among traditional people, while it is "proof that the system works" to Europeans. . . . The European materialist tradition of despiritualizing the universe is very similar to the mental process which goes into dehumanizing another person. And who seems most expert at dehumanizing other people? . . . European culture itself is responsible.[56]

Native American counter-framing often includes a strong critique of the materialistic greed, lack of spirituality, and human insensitivity of much in European American culture. In this counter-framing the white despiritual-izing is linked to whites' dehumanizing those not like them. In a 1990s speech to Dine (Navajo) students Means developed yet another impor-tant aspect of a Native American counter-frame in his critique of the untrustworthiness of U.S. government officials:

> They've admitted that they're nothing but liars, and I admit that, yes you are, and you lied about our treaty, and you lie about your Constitution. Therefore, I advocate that, under international law, constitutional law, our law, and anybody else's law, we revert back to our legal status before we signed the treaty. And guess what that legal status is? Free! We are free people. When one nation unilaterally admits they violated an international covenant, then that covenant no longer has legal force in a court of law, and you become a free people. . . . Wisdom, that's what our culture and our heritage is all about.[57]

Those operating out of this Native American counter-frame insist that the legal treaties that Native American societies made with the U.S. govern-ment over centuries were the *legal* and *moral* grounds for relationships between Native Americans and the white-run government. Because the U.S. government has broken these treaties, Native Americans no longer have obligations to the U.S. government and are "free." Not surprisingly, thus, numerous Native American leaders like Means have cited their own cultural understandings and international law, and thus called for the return of Native American lands, reparations for land theft and geno-cide, and the right to control their areas and destinies without white interference.

Alex White Plume, president of the Oglala Lakota Nation, has asserted on behalf of his people a strong version of this counter-frame in regard to the U.S. government and its treaties. He wrote a demanding letter to then President George W. Bush, asking on behalf of his Nation that the "United States fulfill its obligation to respect and protect the human rights of Indian peoples in this country." Discussing white violations of sacred Indian sites, he called on the U.S. government to honor treaty obligations. He added:

> We are also calling on the United States to fulfill its legal and moral obligations to Indian peoples by voting to approve the Declaration

on the Rights of Indigenous Peoples at the upcoming September session of the U.N. General Assembly. The United States cannot meet its existing legal and moral obligations under international law, nor its fiduciary obligations under federal Indian law, by voting against (or abstaining from voting on) the declaration.[58]

However, the U.S. government did in fact vote against the widely accepted Declaration, one of only four governments in the United Nations that did so. Significantly, Native American leaders had been part of the U.N. committee that wrote this important Declaration, one written from an indigenous counter-frame that accented the "restitution of the lands, territories and resources" and the enforcement of treaties with indigenous peoples.

In these Native American statements and actions, we see some elements of a strong Native American counter-frame that are somewhat similar to those of the African American counter-frame. We observe an insistent critique of the white theft of Native American lands and destruction of Native American societies, a forceful countering of white stereotyping, a very positive assertion of the humanity of Native Americans, and a strong accent on the importance of Native American traditions accenting freedom, justice, fairness, and respect for all human beings—doubtless the earliest liberty-and-justice framing in the Americas. Included in this too is a strong critique of Western materialism and lack of spirituality.

Asian Americans and Counter-Framing

At this stage in U.S. development, Native Americans and African Americans seem to be the groups of color that have managed, by means of collective memory and much effort now over fifteen generations of contacts with white Americans, to develop particularly strong counter-frames to the white racial frame. Research on other Americans of color, including Asian Americans and Latino Americans, suggests that most subgroups within these broad umbrella groups have at this point in time relatively less developed anti-racist counter-frames. They do, however, have strong home-culture frames, and some people in the communities have begun to move in the direction of well-developed counter-frames. One reason for the relative slowness of this development may be because today the majorities of people in most Asian American and Latino communities are immigrants and their children—that is, they are first or second generation Americans.

In one recent research study, interviews with forty-three middle-class Asian Americans found that most had an underdeveloped anti-racist counter-frame. These Asian Americans often reported trying as individuals to gain control of their lives by constructing views of Asian Americans counter to dominant white stereotypes, but most had not engaged in, or benefited from, substantial collective efforts to develop an anti-racist counter-frame. Like African Americans and other Americans of color, these respondents indicated that being critical of U.S. racism brought harsh criticism and rejection, from white teachers, coworkers, and supervisors, as well as some family members and friends. As a result, many have opted to conform more or less openly to significant elements of the white racial frame and to white folkways, and thus to stay invisible and under the white radar as much as they can. Many of these Asian American interviewees have come to view their values and needs as of necessity being close to those of whites. In this research only a minority of the respondents had so far moved beyond individual grappling with everyday discrimination to actively engage in substantial collective efforts against anti-Asian oppression.[59]

Among the larger Asian American groups, the Japanese American group appears to have the most people with a substantial anti-racist counter-framing of U.S. society, perhaps because of their longer decades of residence as families in the United States and their World War II experience with discriminatory imprisonment in U.S. concentration camps discussed previously. Japanese Americans have created the oldest Asian American civil rights organizations, organizations with significant anti-racist counter-framing. Moreover, during the 1960s–1970s era a small "yellow power" movement developed alongside the black power movement, mainly in California cities. Asian American college students constructed the term "Asian Americans" to counter racist terms like "Orientals," and they protested the lack of courses on Asian American history on college campuses and for an end to anti-Asian discrimination in the larger society. Since that era, the increase in pan-Asian organizations has helped to create a shared Asian American umbrella consciousness among college students and other Asian Americans seeking to combat the white racial framing of Asians and associated anti-Asian discrimination.[60]

In addition, numerous Asian American groups with relatively weak anti-racist counter-frames do have a strong home-culture frame on which they draw for often subtle types of everyday resistance. For example, in several cities where there are large Asian American communities one finds some organizational activity directed at asserting Asian cultural perspectives. In Houston local Vietnamese American and Chinese American organizations have been successful in putting up street signs in their home languages beneath English signs, and thereby asserting the equality and significance of their home languages. There is also action out of the home-culture frame in the area of building permits and construction. In some Asian American communities in cities like Los Angeles and Houston one finds new buildings that are built in a traditional Chinese or other Asian design. The alternative Asian cultural frames provide options for positively accenting one's cultural background and a symbolic countering of white dominance in urban space, even where there is a less developed collective anti-racist frame. Moreover, in numerous cities some Asian American groups have created organizations with a partial counter-frame, organizations supporting Asian American political candidates supportive of the political-economic interests of Asian American communities, with varying degrees of electoral success.[61]

Latino Americans and Counter-Framing

Compared to the black and Native American counter-frames, which are nearly four centuries old and have widely accepted collective ideas critical of European Americans and racial oppression, the current Latino anti-racist counter-frame seems more variable in shape, and the strong version of the counter-frame seems not so widely accepted. Some elements critical of white-run institutions are common to all versions of the Latino counter-frame, but like others this counter-frame runs across a continuum in emphasis and use. At one end there is a well-developed view deeply critical of U.S. racism that is similar to that of African Americans. Among Chicano nationalists such as veteran political activist José Angel Gutiérrez and the small groups of Chicano activists, there is much critical analysis of a white-racist society and of anti-Latino racism, as well as open resistance to imposed white pressures for one-way assimilation to the dominant culture. This anti-racist counter-framing is conscious and overtly political. At the other end of the counter-frame continuum, as with other groups of color, there are some middle class and upper class Latinos who have adapted aggressively to white norms and folkways and accepted rather uncritically important aspects of the omnipresent white racial frame. The anti-racist counter-framing of these Latinos appears to be relatively weak and apolitical.[62]

Like some other Americans of color, many Latinos have accented an "ethnic persona" strategy in trying to avoid being viewed by whites as black or near-black, and thus being recipients of societal penalties that go with the bottom rungs of the U.S. racial hierarchy. Some Mexican Americans and other Latinos have intentionally suppressed the view of themselves as part of a racial group subordinated by whites and have thus accented a Hispanic or white-Hispanic "ethnicity" in order to deal with whites and, they hope, to integrate more fully into white-run institutions.

Even relatively recent Latin American immigrants quickly learn that being identified as "not white" has seriously negative effects in U.S. society, and as a result many have tried to evade a racial classification by trying to accent their cultural and other similarities to whites. Indeed, some have joined the U.S. military to demonstrate their patriotism and "Americanness."[63]

Still, in most Latino communities some significant lessons about dealing with whites are taught. These range in degree of overtness and thoroughness depending on specific family traditions and parental choices. In discussing these issues with me, one savvy Latino professional has described well how this subtle process worked in his early years:

> I do not remember explicit advice being given as "advice," but, yes, lots of stories shared across generations (my grandfather to me, for example) with implicit advice or ideas on how to deal with whites. My father would tell stories of working a mule almost to death when his white boss criticized him for working too slowly. My uncle told stories of throwing a water drinking tin cup into the air when whites did not want Mexicans to drink out of the same water barrel at a baseball game, stories of friends who did not back down from whites, like my father's friend who shot and killed a deputy sheriff in a gun fight years after the deputy had pistol-whipped him after handcuffing him for public intoxication. The implicit advice in all of these many, many stories is you should not back down from whites because we have to defend our dignity and if you back down the whites will do even worse things to you. Many Mexican American corridos (Mexican ballads) carry a similar message.[64]

The implicit advice in these narratives is framed as not backing down in confrontations with whites if possible, although there is no explicit counter-framing of whites as racial oppressors and little explicit language for dealing with that oppression, compared to the more explicit and direct dealing with such matters in the Chicano or African American counter-frames.

In addition, home-culture frames are strong among Latino groups such as Mexican Americans, in part because many are first or second generation Americans with close ties to their home countries. Many Latinos make use of a home-culture frame, frequently choosing Latino cultural values and preferences over those of the dominant culture. These values and preferences include those having to do with daily choices in regard to language, food, music, and religion. Given the high concentrations of Latinos in certain U.S. towns and cities, such as in large areas of San Antonio, Los Angeles, New York City, and Miami, some Latinos can avoid much of the surrounding white culture and operate a great deal of time out of important home-culture frame. This reality, which one sees in numerous Mexican American, Puerto Rican, and Cuban American communities, as well as those of smaller Latino groups, underscores a major weakness in much popular and scholarly conceptualization of U.S. immigration. Contemporary discussions of Latin American and other immigration often ignore the home-culture framing that immigrants regularly operate from. Latino immigrants may be incorporated to a significant degree in the white-run economic sphere, and even accept some white racist framing of U.S. racial groups, including their own, yet actively resist incorporation on certain home-culture dimensions, such as in the areas of language, music, food, and religion. As we have seen for all groups of color, the home-cultures can provide an important base for a quiet struggle against white cultural dominance and, often but not always, for some to mount a more aggressive anti-racist counter-framing against white oppression.[65]

A Final Note: Internalizing the White Racial Frame

When it comes to racial matters faced in everyday life, Americans of color are usually multiframers, in that they have elements of the white racial frame competing in their minds with elements of the anti-racist counter-frame, if there is such a strong counter-frame in their community. Especially in the cases of African Americans and Native Americans this mental struggle between frames is often intense because members of both groups pick up elements of the imposed white racial frame and at the same time have strong anti-oppression frames that have been part of their communities for many generations.

Yet, instilling and maintaining the anti-racist counter-frame is difficult because of the constant bombardment of Americans of color, including children, with the white racial frame in most major institutional settings. The white-controlled mass media play a central role in making the dominant racial framing widespread and making it appear apparently "normal." The subtle or overt goal of many whites with influence in the media, schools, and other white-controlled institutions is to reduce the resistance to persisting racial inequalities and discrimination by Americans of color, especially by getting them to internalize important elements of the dominant white racial framing. The insidious and persisting *power* of this dominant frame can be seen in its contemporary impact on those who are generally its main targets. For example, one recent research study using the Implicit Association Test, with its white and black photos, found that just over half of African Americans who took the tests rejected the implicit negative reaction to the photos, but 48 percent actually revealed a significant, implicit, pro-white or anti-black bias.[66] Because they too are constantly bombarded with the white-framed negative images of themselves, African Americans and other Americans of color are also influenced by it, though variably and often subtly. They too are under heavy pressure from whites to adopt the dominant white framing of racial matters, and when they do that and act from that white frame, they too help to reinforce this country's systemic racism and its continuing racialized advantages for whites.

For example, when an Asian or Latino American uses the word "nigger" or other racist language or imaging of African Americans, he or she is operating out of the age-old white racial frame. Similarly, when an African or Asian American uses the anti-Latino language "spic" and similar tactics, he or she is again operating out of the white racial frame. One can think of numerous other such examples, across many U.S. groups. Given the omnipresence of the white racial frame, Americans of color often stereotype or characterize yet other Americans of color using the language, stereotyping, imaging, or emotions of that white frame. Moreover, once one thinks out of that white frame, even if a person of color, one may even discriminate against other people of color motivated by what has been learned from that white frame. In this sense, then, the dominant frame inclines all people in whose heads it is imbedded to view and treat the frame's racialized others negatively. Only when there are substantial anti-racist counterframes, generally speaking, will there be strong tendencies to resist the many racialized constructions and impulses that stem from the dominant racist frame. That frame thus plays a significant role in alienating people in numerous racial groups from yet one another in U.S. society.

In addition, the pressures to conform to the white racial frame and white folkways are intense, and the rewards of conformity can be tempting. All too often, Americans of color are bought off with, as some critics have put it, "scraps from the master's table." Although full white symbolic and socioeconomic capital is inaccessible to people of color, those who adapt vigorously to white norms and demands may be allowed certain "scraps" of social, economic, or political capital, including controlled access to white networks. Some middle class and upper class Americans of color, thus, may have enough socioeconomic resources to isolate themselves from some white discrimination and may be more likely to accept or assert certain aspects of the white frame, with counter-framing thus being less important for them. Those who internalize certain elements of the white racial frame well and often operate openly out of it are frequently rewarded by whites, sometimes dramatically so, as appears to be the case for key government figures like Clarence Thomas and Condoleezza Rice. In each historical era, some leaders from racially oppressed groups have also been bought off by whites seeking to weaken their leadership and organization in communities of color. Such co-opted leaders, including academics of color, thus become very important to the maintenance of this country's persisting white-racist system.[67]

CHAPTER 8

Toward a Truly Multiracial Democracy

Thinking and Acting Outside the White Frame

One great barrier to racial change in the United States is the pervasive and deep-seated character of the centuries-old white racial frame, with its extensive rationalizing elements and emotion-laden legitimation of white privilege and continuing racial discrimination. It is certainly possible for whites not to act out of that dominant frame, as many people periodically do. Yet, most whites, most of the time, live their daily lives unreflectively out of it. Important elements of that frame control much everyday interaction and communication, even for well-informed and otherwise savvy whites, because they are omnipresent and "normal." Most whites do not even realize they routinely operate from this dominant frame. Because of it, most whites have *never* been committed to the comprehensive racial desegregation of major U.S. institutions, to really aggressive enforcement of existing antidiscrimination laws, or to substantial reparations to Americans of color for extensive past and present discrimination. At a few points in U.S. history, a majority of whites have accepted some large-scale racial change, but this has usually come only under pressure from protest movements and with some in the white leadership moving to act to reduce aspects of racial discrimination because of the protest pressures. Most whites' view of permissible change in systemic patterns of racial discrimination and segregation has been limited by time and place. Historically, periods of dismantling aspects of the racist system have lasted a decade or two, and then been followed by significant backtracking, retrenchment, and/or the slowing down of new racial change. This was true after the brief Reconstruction following the Civil War in the nineteenth century, as well as for the contemporary period since the 1960s civil rights movements.

Today, we still live in a very hierarchical society in racial, class, and gender terms, one where white men continue to make the lion's share of major decisions about our economic development, laws, and major public policies. As a nation, we have never come close to being a real democracy where a majority of ordinary people have many representatives like themselves in Congress and have substantial input into most serious public policy issues. The U.S. Constitution was made by just fifty-five elite white men representing the upper 2 percent or so of the U.S. population in economic terms. Since that time powerful white men have ruled and run this country, for the most part in terms of their group interests and from an assertive white frame. From the founding era to the present, most whites have had great trouble giving up the notion that whites are distinctively "good" people and part of a superior European-origin civilization. One major problem with the dominant white frame is its arrogance about the great superiority of U.S. institutions compared to those of all other countries. This traditional arrogance, as we have seen previously, has often led to tragic and oppressive results in the United States and overseas.

Americans of color had no role in making the U.S. Constitution or its early amendments, nor have they had a significant role in most major judicial rulings since the Constitution's making. It is centuries past time for this to be changed. In a democracy a small elite that is mostly white, male, and wealthy should not have the power to tell the rest of the citizenry what to do, or what the laws should be. Certainly, in regard to many racial issues and numerous other societal issues the viewpoints of Americans of color should be of at least equal importance to those of the white politicians, judges, media commentators, or public. Interestingly, when African Americans and other Americans of color are "consulted" in public opinion surveys, they often make it clear they do not agree with the views of white elites and other whites on society's discriminatory structure and patterns today or, furthermore, on such matters as overseas military invasions, government health care policies, the level of federal support for education, or the weak enforcement of civil rights laws.[1]

Clearly, our dominant social, economic, and political institutions do not yet imbed anything close to the old rhetorical ideal of "liberty and justice for all," or the related ideals of fairness and equality. Indeed, the major carriers of a *vital* and progressive liberty-and-justice frame are African Americans and other Americans of color, a frame often seen in their protests against U.S. oppression. In view of the historical and contemporary evidence considered in this book, it is certainly time to completely rebuild our political and economic system so that it is indeed a true democracy that lives up to its rhetoric of liberty and justice for all. Revolutionary changes come but rarely in societies, but this country is long overdue for major changes in its *deep foundation* of racism. Even Thomas Jefferson, primary author of the Declaration of Independence, advocated a revolution periodically in a society's history so its people could overcome the dead hand of the past. That is, indeed, an ironic perspective from perhaps our leading founder.

Pressures and Possibilities for Societal Change

What can bring a significant change today in the dominant racial hierarchy and its legitimating racial frame? Public intellectuals like Thomas Kuhn and Stephen Jay Gould have written about how changes come in society and, more generally, in life on the planet. Both noted that revolutionary shifts frequently come in starts and spurts, not all at once. In discussing paradigm shifts in science, for example, Kuhn accented the important innovative role of new or younger thinkers who are less committed to prior scientific paradigms and who develop breakthrough ideas suggesting new ways of looking at the world around us. For Gould, life's long evolution has involved long periods of stability punctuated by dramatic bursts of change. Small changes accumulate to force larger changes. Choice points emerge where the system can move in two or more important directions. Gould's "punctuated equilibrium" theory of change accents a deep structure, long periods of equilibrium, and periodic revolutionary bursts. In the U.S. case racial oppression has a deep structure, long equilibrium periods, and occasional bursts of revolutionary change. Today, those concerned about significantly eradicating large-scale oppression in U.S. society need to press hard for new societal choice points and, then, to be prepared to act when those choice points actually come.[2]

Today in the United States, pressures for change are coming relatively fast. Important societal choice points have begun to appear. Even a quick look at demographic data reveals the United States is becoming less white and more racially diverse. White Americans now are less than half the populations of Hawaii, New Mexico, and the two most populous states of California and Texas. They are a minority in half the country's 100 largest metropolitan areas. Over the next few decades they will become the statistical minority in all the most populous states, as well as in all major metropolitan areas. No later than 2050, demographers estimate, Americans of color will be more than half the U.S. population. Already, in the 2008 election an American of color, the black Senator Barack Obama was elected president of the United States substantially because he got the overwhelming majority of votes of African American, Asian American,

Latino, and Native American voters. A substantial majority (55 percent) of white voters, in contrast, voted for his white Republican opponent. One significant question that these demographic changes raise is just how most whites—especially those in the powerful elites—will deal with this significant and continuing increase in racial-ethnic diversity in the near future of the United States.[3]

It is not just whites in supremacist groups like the Ku Klux Klan who worry greatly about whites losing their demographic position to those who are not white in the United States or globally. Many other whites, both national leaders and ordinary citizens, frame these demographic changes in the U.S. population as threatening. Interestingly, this concern with white population size relative to the racial others is *not* new, for the white racial frame has been concerned with such issues for centuries. Today, numerous prominent white analysts like Patrick Buchanan, a former Republican presidential candidate and media commentator, and the aforementioned Samuel Huntington, an influential Harvard social science professor, write from a strong white frame that accents the declining white percentage in the population as very negative for whites and the future of what they term "Western civilization." In their public comments they reveal the old white frame in a fiercely stated version, as well as substantial ignorance about the social realities of the world around them.[4]

Evaluating Oppression: International Perspectives

Numerous issues examined in this book raise the general question of what standard to use in evaluating the highly unjust system of racial oppression and inequality in the United States. As we have seen, the white founders, and most whites since, have periodically accented a rhetorical liberty-and-justice frame. Recall that in the first centuries of European colonialism major philosophers and religious groups sometimes articulated ideals of justice and injustice. The influential John Locke said that social justice was part of the natural law and included the right to control one's labor and property. In breaking with the British king, the U.S. founders often made use of liberty and justice language borrowed from philosophers like Locke, yet for them it was a limited or rhetorical framing, one applied in their era mainly to white men with property.[5] Since the time of the framers, however, many U.S. groups have pressed to get this idea of liberty and justice expanded to include them as individuals or groups. Some, such as white immigrant groups like the Irish Americans, have been much more successful in this process than others, such as African Americans and other Americans of color.

As it is usually expressed, the idea of "liberty and justice for all" seems rather vague, yet certain aspects of it are easy to articulate and are now widely accepted across much of the globe. For example, in the U.S. case most individuals do seek the freedom to be themselves, to speak freely, and to have healthy and supportive environments for themselves and their families without oppressive barriers. This framing of their lives is generally in line with the perspectives on civil rights in the U.S. Bill of Rights and in the Universal Declaration of Human Rights of the United Nations. Article 1 of that Universal Declaration, now a widely accepted international human rights standard, updates the U.S. Declaration of Independence with the statement that "all human beings are born free and equal in dignity and rights." The Universal Declaration's Article 7 states that "all are equal before the law and are entitled without any discrimination to equal protection of the law." The Declaration continues in Article 25 with an assertion that human rights encompass more than political rights: "Everyone has the right to a standard of living adequate for the health and well-being of himself and his family, including food, clothing, housing." This internationally sanctioned liberty-and-justice framing goes well beyond the U.S. Constitution and its limited vision of civil rights to a much broader view of full human economic, social, and political rights.[6]

Other United Nations conventions have been signed by the U.S. government and add to this larger human rights context, from which we can judge the oppressiveness of systemic racism in the United States. For example, the UN International Convention on the Elimination of All Forms of Racial Discrimination requires that all governments make illegal the dissemination of ideas of racial superiority and organizations that promote racial discrimination. The U.S. government came slowly to ratify this international convention, indeed only in 1994, even though numerous other nations had ratified long before that year. By signing the U.S. government agreed to adopt "all necessary measures for speedily eliminating racial discrimination in all its forms and manifestations."[7] As of today, top U.S. government officials in the relevant agencies have *not* undertaken to live up to this international obligation to rid the United States of all "forms and manifestations" of racial discrimination.

One reason for this lack of effective action is how a majority of white Americans view the ideals of liberty, justice, and equality. These concepts have been important for whites since at least the seventeenth century, yet a rhetorical framing and rhetorical assertion of them have long helped whites to conceal for themselves the freedom-denying reality of this country's systemic racism and other oppressions. Today, as in the past, most whites like to assert the ideals of liberty and justice, but a majority do not wish those concepts to be *aggressively* applied in their own actions every day or by their government—especially to the discrimination, difficult socioeconomic situations, and racial inequalities faced by Americans of color. A majority of whites prefer to accent these liberty concepts in rhetorical ways and often connect them to superficial signs of patriotism, such as the wearing of U.S. flag pins. As a result, whites and Americans of color often disagree over how well the country has done in regard to liberty and justice. For example, a recent national opinion poll found that most whites surveyed thought that the United States was living up to the liberty-and-justice frame of the Pledge of Allegiance, while more than half the black respondents in the poll felt the country was *not*.[8]

At a time when the federal government and most local governments still are *not* aggressively enforcing U.S. civil rights laws and are *not* enacting numerous human rights provisions of United Nations treaties and conventions signed by the U.S. government, many innovators, activists, and ordinary citizens in numerous other countries are accenting a renewed ethical language of *cosmopolitanism*—the view that all human beings are citizens of one global moral community and must be treated with dignity and fairness. To paraphrase the English poet John Donne's famous comment, "No human group can be an island to itself; every group is a piece of the global whole. Any group's oppression diminishes all of us, because we are all involved in humanity, and therefore never ask for whom the bell tolls, it tolls for thee." This cosmopolitan framing of humanity rejects the primacy of nation states and nationalism and accents instead the global citizenship of all human beings. Numerous world crises, such as human-induced global climate changes, are substantially matters of human rights and needs, yet are beyond the control of traditional nation states. In many areas of the globe there is a new language of cosmopolitanism, ethical globalization, and global democracy. Indeed, this renewed cosmopolitan emphasis builds on the broad rights perspectives expressed in the Universal Declaration and other United Nations documents—which in turn drew not only on the best in European human rights traditions but also from the human rights traditions and anti-oppression counter-frames of Native, African, Latino, and Asian Americans, as well as of other people of color across the globe.[9]

Clearly, continuing racial hostility, discrimination, and inequality directed against people of color in the United States destroy the possibility of authentic democracy for this society. To create the reality of a true democracy will ultimately require a substantial destruction of the persisting system of racial oppression, including its hierarchy and rationalizing frame.

Deframing and Reframing: Countering the White Racial Frame

The centuries-old white racial frame is a gestalt, a composite of elements and subframes fused into a whole that is more than the sum of its parts.

Countering it in white adults and children is difficult because it is fundamental to the social, material, and ideological construction of U.S. society. This white frame severely limits what most white people think, believe, feel, say, and do. Indeed, most whites, privileged by definition, have great difficulty in relating to people who are the recurring victims of great social injustice. The dominant racial frame seems to be centrally responsible for this severe lack of human empathy and cross-racial understanding. In U.S. society, moreover, we generally do not teach people to be routinely critical thinkers, but rather encourage them to mostly follow the lead of media, economic, and political leaders on racial matters. This lack of critical thinking helps to perpetuate the traditional elements of the white racial frame.

In more than four decades of college teaching experience with thousands of college students, I have found that, until whites have basic instruction in the history and contemporary reality of U.S. racial oppression, most will reject the important understandings they need to be supportive of and sympathetic to major changes in that oppression. It usually takes many hours of instruction and dialogue over several months to get white youth or adults to begin to think critically about the array of racially stereotyped images, beliefs, emotions, and interpretations of the dominant racial frame, as well as about the racial hierarchy it legitimates and structures. Substantially changing that centuries-old framing will require much human effort and innovation, and new educational strategies. Today, as in the past, very few Americans have had even a brief Stereotyping 101 course or a brief U.S. Racism 101 course in their educations, whether in elementary and secondary schools or in college and graduate schools. Clearly one step in dealing with the dominant racist framing is to create many such Stereotyping 101 and Racism 101 courses at all educational levels across the society.

Deframing and reframing education in regard to racism should be an essential part of our educational efforts. *Deframing* involves consciously taking apart and critically analyzing elements of the old racial frame, while *reframing* means accepting or creating a new frame to replace that old white racial frame. Whites, and many others, need to be made aware of the reality of the white racial frame imbedded deeply in their minds, and they need to be taught the importance of deframing it, and then reframing away from that old dominant frame to a sincere liberty-and-justice framing of society. Thus, solutions for societal racism lie in developing much more critical thinking about racial matters, and actions based on those critical understandings.[10]

As we saw in the empirical data in Chapters 5 and 6, the dominant racial frame is so deep in most white minds that people typically reject new facts that contradict or challenge it. Entrenched frames tend to trump new facts unless the latter information is presented well and as part of a clear counter-framing. Nonetheless, a savvy presentation of accurate facts about matters of racism is necessary if whites and others are to change their traditional white-washed perspective. When pressing for an anti-racist counter-frame, we need to assess what are the important facts to communicate to people about racial matters and present them so they are relevant to and contradictory of the dominant racist framing. Research suggests that even modest steps in this direction can have an impact. For example, in laboratory settings just getting white subjects with a strong racist frame to observe members of the racially targeted groups in unstereotyped settings has been shown to weaken implicit and explicit racial biases. As one review of this laboratory literature has put it, viewing a "black face with a church as a background, instead of a dilapidated street corner, considering familiar examples of admired blacks such as actor Denzel Washington and athlete Michael Jordan, and reading about Arab-Muslims' positive contributions to society all weaken people's implicit racial and ethnic biases."[11] Even simple changes in the presentation of the relevant societal information can offer racially prejudiced people some images that counter those of their traditional racist framing, and thus can have modest positive effects on their racist framing.

In addition, recent research suggests that an effective way to get people to change their framing of important social issues is to induce them to *seriously* and *carefully* review solid information about a distinctively different view from their own. In one study researchers conducted two similar experiments, one on social issues and another about personality impressions. The subjects in the experiments were persuaded to reflect on a viewpoint opposite to their own in two different ways: "through explicit instructions to do so and through stimulus materials that made opposite possibilities more salient."[12] In both experiments getting the subjects to use a consider-the-opposite-view strategy had a more substantial impact on their thinking than just the verbal instructions to be fair and unbiased in reviewing the issue at hand. Getting people to review the countering information seriously was effective in getting them to alter their judgments about important issues. The implications of this study for getting whites (and others) to reframe away from the dominant racial frame may be to get them to think seriously, even for a short time, out of a meaningful and sincere version of the liberty-and-justice frame like that often expressed by numerous U.S. civil rights organizations. That is, get them to review carefully and in detail the stated civil rights views, statements, and materials developed by these civil rights organizations.

Important Educational Strategies

Recent research on children shows that even modest educational efforts can bring a significant payoff in terms of reframing. Providing new facts set in a more accurate interpretive framing of U.S. history can have an impact on the way that children of various ages think about racial matters. One southwestern project explored the impact of teaching white and black children about the racial discrimination that had been faced by important black historical figures. The researchers studied two groups of white and black children (both were 6–11 years old) who had had six twenty-minute daily history lessons providing biographical information on important white and black Americans, all taught by the same white teacher. Each group of students was divided between those who got black biographies with some reference to the racial discrimination faced by the person under consideration and those who got the same biographies without references to the discrimination they faced. Otherwise the discussions were similar. Before and after the biography lessons the researchers gave all children a evaluative scale designed to measure positive and negative views of black and white Americans. The white children who had the brief racial discrimination lessons had significantly more positive attitudes and less negative attitudes about black Americans than the white control group that had not gotten such lessons. They also indicated a stronger preference for racial fairness and, among those over 7, indicated more racial guilt.[13]

Not surprisingly, the history presentations to the black children had less effect. Both the youngest black children (6–7) who were taught the black biographies with discrimination information and those who were taught the lessons without the discrimination information developed more positive (or less negative) views of African Americans. Children aged 8–9 became less negative toward African Americans, while the black children aged 10–11 did not change their views, probably because they were already familiar with some of these achievements. The researchers found, as with the white children, that those who had the lessons about discrimination reported a greater valuing of racial fairness than those in the control group. The black children's views of whites became both more positive on some issues and more negative on other issues as a result of the biographical lessons about white and black historical figures, probably because the teacher candidly accented the positive and the negative contributions of whites historically.[14]

This important study reveals that historical lessons about the discrimination faced by black Americans can have significant positive effects on the racial attitudes of white children. In addition, the same lessons can have positive effects on younger black children's views of their group. That changes came with only a modest number of brief history lessons suggests just how important basic courses in Stereotyping 101 or Racism 101 might be for all American youth and adults.

We might note too a typical weakness in the way that these researchers discussed their findings. In their journal article, they make it clear that they debriefed the children after the study: they offered explanations of their purpose in teaching historical biographies and told the children about contemporary white and black international figures who were "working to counter the effects of racism. Thus, all children were informed that, although some European Americans have discriminated against African Americans, other European Americans have fought against racial discrimination."[15] As in other similar research on U.S. racial matters, the central 400-year-old role of whites in creating and maintaining past and present racial oppression was not explained to the children, as "bad" whites are thus balanced with "good" whites who have fought discrimination. While it is important to stress for children the historical reality of a few whites fighting against racism, this type of rhetorical race-balancing plays down the fact that a substantial *majority* of whites, today as in the past, have perpetrated or significantly colluded in continuing racial oppression in North America. Historical and contemporary research reveals that relatively few whites have ever dissented strongly and publicly with this country's racial oppression. In my view the reality of white racial oppression in the past and present should not be downplayed in anti-racist educational strategies.[16]

In addition, there are other important educational strategies for getting whites, both students and older adults, to understand and analyze critically their imbedded racial framing. One is to have them keep diaries of racial conversations and events they engage in or encounter every day. Having them later discuss such diaries can bring racial hostility and discrimination into open and critical discussion, such as in educational settings. In one study noted previously, we had 626 white students at numerous colleges and universities keep journals of racial events for several weeks. In addition to recording about 7,500 blatantly racist episodes and events, some students reported that this diary exercise had made them more conscious of the ways they and friends or relatives regularly engaged in racist language, discussions, and actions. In one journal entry, a female college student concluded thus about her discussions with another journal writer:

> As we talked, we began discussing the contents of our journals and we both came to the conclusion that neither of us ever realized how many racial comments we hear everyday. Talking with my friend gave me a new perspective on just how much I am surrounded by racial

issues and comments, and it made me realize how often I simply ignore or don't even notice certain comments that should bother me.

A male student at another college came to even stronger conclusions about the actions he needs to take in the future:

> As my last entry in this journal, I would like to express what I have gained out of this assignment. I watched my friends and companions with open eyes. I was seeing things that I didn't realize were actually there. By having a reason to pick out of the racial comments and actions I was made aware of what is really out there. Although I noticed that I wasn't partaking in any of the racist actions or comments, I did notice that I wasn't stopping them either. I am now in a position to where I can take a stand and try to intervene in many of the situations.[17]

Using such diary exercises can lead to significant consciousness raising about white participation in everyday racism. This consciousness raising usually means bringing into the open half-conscious or unconscious racist beliefs, images, and emotions and raising them to the level of full consciousness for a thorough critical assessment.

Challenging Emotions: Listening to Americans of Color

One serious dilemma faced by those teaching deframing and anti-racist reframing is that the traditional racial frame is usually deeply imbedded in an array of significant emotions that trump overt reasoning and rational decisionmaking. When it comes to racial matters, most whites act on the basis of deeply held, emotion-laden beliefs ("values") more than they do on careful reasoning and empirical facts. Those attempting to change whites' racial framing in fundamental ways often run into problems because they view these whites as open to being convinced solely by overt and rational arguments. In such cases one possible strategy is to press people to examine critically their emotion-laden values about racial matters. We cannot change the emotional dimension of being human, but we can sometimes make good use of certain positive emotions that run counter to the negative emotions of the dominant racial frame. We can, for example, accent values that link well to a liberty-and-justice frame, such as the religion-generated belief of "love your neighbor as yourself," which is associated with the idea of fairness.

In doing anti-racist education we can also make effective use of emotional connections between individuals—for example, by relating well the personal stories of those who have suffered from oppression and fought against it. Research shows that the best human communication often makes use of personal stories. For example, political candidates who tell strong personal stories about their lives in ways voters can relate to usually do better than those who do not.[18] We have previously noted the effectiveness of personal stories in the experiment that involved teaching racial biographies to white and black children. Such biographies create personal connections. Effective transmission of anti-racist ideas can involve telling true stories about people dealing with racial hostility and discrimination, and illustrating them with strong personal images.

The reality of systemic racism is that most whites, including decision-makers in the private and public sectors, have never listened seriously and regularly to the pained voices and racism-shaped narratives of Americans of color. Creating situations where whites can encounter these narratives is very important, for equal-status interracial interaction often forces some reframing of racial matters. In pathbreaking research social scientists Tiffany Hogan and Julie Netzer examined whether white women could relate to and understand the experiences of black women with racial discrimination. Conducting in-depth interviews with white women, they found that being female did not necessarily increase understanding of anti-black discrimination, although it sometimes did. Those white women who were socially stigmatized in additional ways (for example, as lesbians) were better able than other white women to empathize with accounts of discrimination faced by black women. These researchers suggested that white women can draw on their own experiences to relate to the discrimination faced by black Americans in these ways: (1) by borrowed approximations, that is, by relying on the accounts that black friends or acquaintances give to make sense of discriminatory black experiences; (2) by global approximations, that is, by relying on general values of fairness to relate to accounts of anti-black discrimination; and (3) by overlapping approximations, that is, by relying on aspects of their own gendered oppression to make sense of black experiences with discrimination.[19]

The way in which borrowed approximations worked was illustrated in one of their interviews with a white woman who had learned about anti-black discrimination from significant interpersonal experience with a black woman with whom she worked:

> I always thought that Sally was totally accepted at work, . . . and on the surface you don't see any problems. Everyone is friendly, everyone is nice. And Sally is just about the nicest person you would ever hope to find. . . . I went to her hairdresser with her and I was the only white woman in the shop, and she was talking with her girlfriend about work and alluding to the fact that she just really had a lot of barriers there, and that some of the things that people said to her, not

intentionally but the way that they said it, were really racist. . . . It did surprise me. . . . Here's a nice person [Sally] who is at work, and I figured that most of the other people, I thought that they would just feel like I do. When I look at her, I see her as a person, . . . and I just think of her as one of my coworkers and a friend, not as a black person. And I just assumed that everybody else felt the same way. I couldn't imagine that some of the people that she was working with, that I consider to be very nice people, too, would think of her first as black. . . .

This white woman, although still in need of much more reframing, was able to understand a bit better anti-black discrimination through borrowing understandings that come from the recounted experiences and counter-framing of a fellow employee.

In the previous example some empathy was essential in this white woman's gaining understanding across the color line. One of the harsh realities of racial oppression, in the past and the present, lies in the many ways that oppression destroys human empathy across racial lines. Recall from Chapter 6 the recent journal entry from an African American student at a western college:

> This is one of those sad and angry nights for me. Tonight marks the third time since the beginning of the school year that I've been called a nigger by a bunch of white students on a . . . weekend. . . . Sometimes it seems that if I am around all white people, then I become nothing more than a token Black "exhibit" for their amusement.[20]

Here we see whites engaging in racist name-calling and other racialized practices with no thought for the impact of such actions on the young black man. This recurring breakdown of whites' empathy, what might be termed social alexithymia, is commonplace in the many such accounts of mistreatment by whites that we got from several hundred students of color who kept brief journals for us at numerous colleges and universities across the country. Recall too the national opinion survey noted in Chapter 1, in which only 5 percent of whites said that they often have sympathy and often have admiration for black Americans.

In doing antiracism education and bringing significant changes in systemic racism we need to understand better, and to activate more routinely, the deep-lying human propensity to interpersonal empathy, especially for white Americans. Without this basic emotion of empathetic understanding, such as that between infant and mother, human beings would never have survived and evolved over many millennia. Interestingly, current research on the human brain indicates that we have "mirror neuron" circuits that fire when we see someone else doing something and, thus, that enable us to sense what someone else is feeling or thinking. This underlying neurological reality assists the human mind, at least potentially, in understanding and relating to someone else's life experiences. A major difficulty, of course, lies in breaking down the major barriers that systemic racism regularly presents to generating cross-racial empathy in society.

Teaching People to Dissent Actively

In everyday situations we need many more Americans, especially white Americans, to disrupt and counter the millions of racist communications and other racist actions that take place in the United States every day. A common barrier to racial change is the reluctance of most people, including those who know racial change is morally necessary, to take significant anti-racist action. Zygmunt Bauman has made this insightful comment about the bloody Holocaust inflicted by Germans on Europe's Jews before and during World War II:

> Evil can do its dirty work, hoping that most people most of the time will refrain from doing rash, reckless things—and resisting evil is rash and reckless. Evil needs neither enthusiastic followers nor an applauding audience—the instinct of self-preservation will do, encouraged by the comforting thought that it is not my turn, thank God: by lying low, I can still escape.[21]

Today, in the United States there are too many people who know the white racist framing and the racial hierarchy with its extreme inequalities are quite immoral and need to be systematically and rapidly replaced, yet remain at a distance as passive bystanders and do not object to even the more overt aspects of racist performances and other racist actions by whites around them. Such great societal evils as the European Holocaust need not have happened if a significant number of people had acted to stop it. While most people in Europe did put self-preservation above their obvious moral duty, this was not inevitable:

> Evil is not all powerful. It can be resisted. The testimony of the few who did resist shatters the authority of the logic of self-preservation. It shows it for what it is in the end—a choice. One wonders how many people must defy that logic for evil to be incapacitated. Is there a magic threshold of defiance beyond which the technology of evil grinds to a halt?[22]

Bauman here raises a critical practical question about the number of people who need to dissent to bring significant change in difficult racial situations. Clearly, during the civil rights movement of the 1960s a very small percentage of adult Americans, considerably less than 10 percent, ever participated in any of the active civil rights protest events of that movement. In the case of contemporary racism, thus, we need to encourage many more people to defy the logic of self-preservation and disrupt racist performances that reinforce the white racist frame. With individual and collective efforts, we need to reach this threshold of everyday defiance and, hopefully, begin the process of bringing down the system of racial oppression.

To do this, we must go beyond deframing and reframing and press those who have now replaced major elements of the old white frame with significant elements of the liberty-and-justice frame to act aggressively out of the latter frame. Thus, as part of anti-racist educational strategies, we can teach whites and others how to call out and counter racist ideas and performances in both backstage and frontstage settings.

Let us consider examples of how one might dissent in specific situations. Concerned whites and others can counter racist performances by using barbed humor (for example, "Did you learn that racist joke from the Klan?"), by feigning an ignorance that highlights the racist problem (for example, "Can you please explain that racial comment?"), and, most importantly, by *reframing* racist conversations and other racist performances in terms of the important ideas of fair play, moral responsibility, justice, and inclusiveness associated with an active liberty-and-justice frame. Such reframing imbeds not only verbal-cognitive understandings but also important positive emotions.

In regard to such counter-framing, consider this example of a racist event. At a 2006 campaign rally for his reelection, Senator George Allen (R-Virginia) called out across the crowd to an Asian-Indian man (S. R. Sidarth) whom he called out as a person working for his political opponent, Jim Webb. Allen said this to Sidarth: "This fellow here, over here with the yellow shirt, macaca, or whatever his name is. He's with my opponent. He's following us around everywhere. . . . Let's give a welcome to macaca, here. Welcome to America and the real world of Virginia." Allen actually knew the young man's name, yet called him the derogatory "macaca," a racist epithet used in some places for people of color.[23]

Reviewing this event, Drew Westen, a neuroscientist and political consultant, has made useful suggestions about how someone might have responded (Jim Webb did not respond) to this racist incident with a clear and overt reframing of this particular event:

> I share with all Virginians a deep disgust for what we witnessed in our state today. Whatever your feelings about race, I do not think there's a decent, God-fearing Virginian who believes that publicly

ridiculing a young man for the color of his skin is anything short of morally repugnant. . . . In ridiculing Mr. Sidarth today, and "welcoming him to America," Mr. Allen wasn't just attacking a fellow child of God, or a fellow American. He was attacking a *fellow* Virginian. In this country, and in this state, we don't care where your ancestors come from. If you're born in Fairfax, Virginia, where this young man was born, you're just as much of an American as Senator Allen, and you don't need him to welcome you here.[24]

Westen then suggests that the assertive reframing might have continued with an accent on Allen's previous racist actions, such as his opposing the creation of the Martin Luther King, Jr., holiday in the state of Virginia.

Drawing on Westen's insightful analysis and my own research, I see three important ideas for how to dissent in social situations where whites take action that stems from stereotypes, images, or emotions of the conventional white frame. Responding to performances like this can usefully involve these strategies. (1) Remind white people in your audience of their better values, such as in this case their sense of fairness in the treatment of a young person of a different background; (2) if the audience is religious, accent the best moral ideas from their own religious tradition (such as "Love thy neighbor as thyself."); and (3) emphasize that the attacked "they" in such racist performances is actually a "we," that is, try to foster identification by the audience members with those being actively racialized and attacked.[25] One can add to this a recognition that people who regularly engage in such dissenting actions against racist performances will usually pay some price in lost friends and in other social relationships. For that reason, a fourth and major piece of advice for anti-racist dissenters should be to encourage them to build and join support groups of other dissenters of all racial backgrounds who engage in disruptive interventions in such white-racist performances. Regular dissent requires much ongoing interpersonal support in this still very racist society.

Restoration and Reparations for Centuries of Trauma

Beyond deframing and reframing toward a more meaningful liberty-and-justice framing of this society, there is a great need for significant remedial and reparative action to restore those groups that have been unjustly oppressed for centuries to their rightful place in society, with the socioeconomic and other resources they and their ancestors have rightfully earned but have lost over centuries of racial oppression. The contemporary Christian theologian Jennifer Harvey has argued that, if the creation and development of the United States is evaluated from the viewpoint of international human rights laws, the United States is today an illegitimate and immoral nation.[26] White crimes against humanity—such as the genocide inflicted on indigenous peoples and the enslavement and Jim Crow apartheid inflicted on African Americans—have *no statute of limitations*. In her view there is much need, and yet time, to deal responsibly and thoroughly with this great racialized immorality.

One deeply moral response is to provide extensive economic and other social reparations to compensate for centuries of extensive and omnipresent white oppression. For centuries, to the present day, white leaders and analysts, including physical and social scientists, have seriously ignored or downplayed the longterm costs of systemic racism—and the substantial restoration and reparations needed to address those substantial human costs. For example, recent increases in human trauma studies have generated significant discussions of the ways individual and group traumas in U.S. history, such as the slavery or legal segregation faced by African Americans, are culturally constructed and altered in individual and collective memories over time, including those of later generations of those targeted for racial oppression. Reviewing black memories of slavery and Jim Crow, for example, some scholars have argued that these black memories are mediated through the mainstream mass media and thus involve for black Americans some "selective construction and representation" and a "meaning struggle" over these painful historical memories.[27] However, one major problem with this type of human trauma analysis is the emphasis on the constructed memories of traumatic events among the targeted individuals and their descendants, rather than on the white group that created the horrific traumas and on how these damaging traumas persist not just because of meaning struggles but mainly because of the continuing structures of racial oppression.

The discerning analyst of African colonialism, Frantz Fanon, critically underscored how Western medicine, including psychoanalysis, had shifted the concept of injury and trauma from the material wounds and losses of Africans and others exploited and colonized by Europeans to an array of the exploited's own psychological difficulties. More recently, scholars Rebecca Saunders and Kamran Aghaie have similarly argued that the psychological emphasis in much contemporary analysis of human trauma neglects issues of societal responsibility and material redress:

Concomitantly—and consequentially—the meaning of recovery increasingly shifted from a material notion of reparation, indemnification, or restitution to an immaterial conception of cure or restoration. Indeed, it is worth considering how slippage between these meanings of recovery may perform considerable ideological work—

in the context, for example, of truth commissions, tort law, or national memorializations. Have truth commissions [such as in South Africa] emphasized psychological healing over material indemnification?[28]

Their argument is that there is much need for both psychological cures *and* for material reparations and restoration in response to the severely traumatic and long-lasting character of societal oppression in the United States and elsewhere.

Certainly, active and insightful psychological intervention is one important strategy for dealing with some of the traumatic impacts of the dominant racial frame and the systemic racial discrimination resulting from it. It is true that Americans of color often do absorb some of the white racist frame's negative racial stereotypes and images of people like themselves. Those internalized views, such as racial notions that their group is lacking in ability, effort, or intelligence, can have quite harmful effects on how they view themselves, indeed on a continuing basis.

Children are especially vulnerable. When influential white adults, such as schoolteachers, subtly or overtly call up racially stereotyped images of children's racial groups, that action can have significant effects on the performance of children of color under their authority. Today, there are practical solutions for this recurring discrimination by teachers in school classrooms. For example, such stereotype-threat actions by teachers need to be caught by principals and stopped, and the teachers need to be educated about the damage being done by their conventional framing. Redress and support for those children harmed by white teachers, and by whites generally, is also necessary. Researchers have found that teachers' providing even modest positive enhancements for students of color can significantly improve their school performances. One study undertook randomized experiments to see if the researchers could lessen the psychological threat for students of color by having them accent in their minds a stronger sense of their own personal abilities. They had black students do a brief in-class writing assignment asking them about their own positive values and how they applied those values to themselves. This modest exercise significantly improved the grades achieved on subsequent tests by the black students. The researchers concluded that such exercises indicate that the achievement gap between whites and students of color could be significantly lessened with "timely and targeted" instructional innovations that enhance the self-esteem of students of color.[29]

Beyond such targeted innovations, we must educate white (and some other) teachers about the white racial frame that they hold in their heads. There are numerous white narratives relevant to education that are still part of this old frame—such as the racist narrative that asserts that many children of color are constitutionally and biologically or culturally lacking in intellectual ability. In addition, the old white racial framing does not contain important and progressive narratives about children of color. For example, there is a progressive narrative in the counter-frames of black Americans and other Americans of color about how students of color are eager to learn but have been barred by whites from moving up the mobility ladder by means of an array of racial barriers—a narrative known to numerous white educators. Clearly, in regard to U.S. education, one redressive action should be to make this too often marginalized positive framing of students of color central and required for white teachers—and to press the latter to critically assess their racist framing and, thus, to reframe their views in terms of an active fairness and justice perspective.

Material Reparations: Required by a Serious Liberty-and-Justice Frame

Such psychological and instructional interventions are only a modest step forward and are far from sufficient to deal with the past and present impacts of the racial oppression inflicted on African Americans and other Americans of color. More substantial macro-level changes in the dominant racial hierarchy and its rationalizing frame require substantial material restorations and reparations. Without significant changes in the power and resources hierarchy, in the material situations of those who are white and those who are not, the societal reality of oppression will change little. The system of racial oppression has involved the great material power and great framing power of whites exercised over groups of color, now for four centuries. White "superiority" has always been much more than symbolic posturing, for it has meant having the political and economic power to restrict and reduce sharply the socioeconomic resources and life chances of African Americans and other Americans of color.

Huge inequalities in *wealth* between white Americans and black Americans or other Americans of color continue to be documented in numerous research studies by scholars such as Melvin Oliver, Thomas Shapiro, and Dalton Conley.[30] Numerous other racial inequalities, such as those of income and education, are regularly documented by social science researchers. Institute for Policy Studies researcher, Dedrick Muhammad, has recently summarized some of the more glaring racial inequalities in a report, *Forty Years Later: The Unrealized American Dream*. There he shows that the income gap between black and white Americans is closing very slowly, for at the current rate of change black Americans will gain income equality with white Americans only in about *537 years*. Moreover, at current rates of change, the wealth gap between black and white Americans will take yet another *634 years* to close.[31]

Clearly, symbolic and legal changes in U.S. racial patterns are important but are not nearly enough. Pressing just for interracial "tolerance" or "colorblindness" as many liberals do, is inadequate for a society with a strong racial hierarchy and these huge and persisting racial inequalities. Preaching tolerance may be helpful in efforts at certain types of racial change, but pursued as the central goal it tends to operate as a deflecting tactic that takes the focus off the very substantial efforts necessary to bring major changes in the highly inegalitarian racial order of the United States.

Moreover, the civil rights laws of the 1960s are thought by a majority of whites to have "solved the problem of race." In both popular and mainstream social science analyses, discriminatory acts are viewed as effectively countered by these civil rights laws. However, the civil rights laws and their enforcement patterns have been greatly shaped by our fundamentally white-framed and still-racist legal system. These 1960s laws were passed only when key members of the white elite agreed to them, to a substantial degree because such laws were then seen as in their interest. The civil rights laws did help greatly to improve the U.S. image in countries across the globe. They did bring an end to official segregation and open up some new opportunities for Americans of color, yet today these laws have only a modest impact on current patterns of racial and other discrimination in many major sectors of this society. These laws have mostly been enforced, and then often weakly, by white officials in government agencies and in courts. These agencies and courts are governed by white-generated laws and legal understandings that accent an individualistic approach to racial prejudice and discrimination. Not surprisingly, conventional white legal interpretations of prejudice and discrimination in recent decades have regularly ignored the important institutional and societal contexts that routinely create and maintain the deep structural reality of racial oppression—a societal structure that still generates and daily shapes millions of individual acts of racial discrimination rising out of the white racial frame. As a result, few of these acts perpetrated by whites each year against Americans of color are ever redressed in any significant manner by private or government remedies. Moreover, research on progress in civil rights, including the impact of civil rights laws, shows that, even when enforced well, government policies against discrimination do *not* represent significant compensation for past or present discrimination—and certainly not a meaningful atonement by whites for four centuries of extensive, often bloody racial oppression.[32]

Given the long history of economic theft from African Americans and other Americans of color by white Americans, and the trillions of dollars in costs that Americans of color have suffered over centuries as a result, the idea of major reparations is not really "radical," but rather necessarily flows from a collective moral doctrine of redressing longstanding conditions of *unjust* impoverishment and enrichment. Indeed, if the U.S. government can find more than two trillion dollars to bail out private Wall Street financial and related institutions, as it did in 2008–2009, or to invade a non-threatening country like Iraq, as it did in 2003–2009, then it likely can find the substantial amounts of money needed to meet this country's major moral obligations to oppressed Americans of color on whose ancestors' bodies, literally, this country was built. Moreover, well-planned and well-distributed reparations and other restoration programs appear to be a much better government option than the intentionally limited remedial programs of the past, such as affirmative action, which is a modest program largely created by elite whites responding to 1960s protest movements. Concrete economic reparations can be more easily seen, by all parties, as actual compensation for the great damages suffered at the hands of whites over centuries—and thus not as a white "handout." In addition, of course, whites and others need to be educated to understand this connection between major government compensation and the huge historical damages of racial oppression—which is essential if a program of reparations is ever to become an effective government policy.[33]

Especially necessary are restoration and reparations programs for the two groups that have suffered at white American hands for the longest period of time, Native Americans and African Americans. One important result of such steps would be to begin the process of accenting the black counter-frame over the ancient white racist frame, and thereby emphasizing greater black control over black lives. At a 1990s Conference on Reparations in Nigeria, the prominent Nigerian poet and journalist, Dr. Chinweizu Ibekwe, argued that

> More important than any monies to be received; more fundamental than any lands to be recovered, is the opportunity the reparations campaign offers us for the rehabilitation of Black people, by Black people, for Black people; opportunities for the rehabilitation of our minds, our material condition, our collective reputation, our cultures, our memories, our self respect, our religions, our political traditions and our family institutions; but first and foremost for the rehabilitation of our minds.... The most important part of reparation is our self repair.[34]

Societal Benefits from Racial Change

What does U.S. society as a whole have to gain from a large-scale program ending racial discrimination and generating reparations and restoration for Americans of color? A number of analysts have considered this broad question of societal gain. For example, Robert Browne has suggested that reparations for African Americans in the form of economic capital transfers would not involve a "loss of resources to the economy, but rather a redistribution away from heretofore favored classes."[35] Such transfers may boost the general economy, and there will likely be a society-wide energy gain as African Americans come out from under the shroud of racism and gain much new energy for seeking their broader group and societal goals. At the same time, white Americans could abandon their unhealthy racial obsession with African Americans and white patterns of racial discrimination and put much new energy into necessary societal goals. Just societies seem likely to work better and perhaps to last longer than those with significant social inequalities.

A century ago, the civil rights leader, W. E. B. Du Bois, made strong arguments for the general societal benefits of ending systemic racism and building a real democracy for the United States. In his view when we exclude and marginalize many people, as is routinized in our systemic racism, we leave out "vast stores" of human wisdom. When Americans of color are oppressed or marginalized in the country's major institutions not only do they suffer personally and in their families and communities, but also numerous white-controlled institutions suffer significantly—and some may eventually deteriorate and decline as a result. Excluding or marginalizing a great many people of color has meant excluding much human knowledge, creativity, and understanding that they hold in their heads and in collectively preserved memories. A society that ignores such a great store of knowledge and ability irresponsibly risks its future. Ending racial discrimination involves the kind of moral thinking and action that is in the long run good for this society's health because that frees up the knowledge and energy of millions who have long faced substantial racial barriers to knowledge-generation, achievement, and prosperity. All Americans will benefit from the inclusion of new knowledges in the public and private spheres. Only by bringing in the perspectives and experiences of formerly excluded Americans can the U.S. government and the larger society expect to meet the hard challenges of a clearly difficult national and global future. A great expansion of social and political democracy will make much essential knowledge *finally available* for the longterm development and improvement of what is still very much a democracy "under construction."[36]

There is much historical evidence supporting this argument. Consider the many benefits that have flowed to all Americans from the 1950s and 1960s black civil rights movement, and the other critical civil rights movements it helped to foster. Without these liberation struggles against the system of racial oppression, white Americans themselves would likely have fewer civil rights and liberties today. Undoubtedly, the black civil rights movement liberated southern and border states, in fact the whole country, from the extreme political and social straitjackets of legal and official racial segregation. Southern and border states developed fully modern economic and political systems only *after* the 1950s–1960s civil rights movement. Before that movement, and the important civil rights laws and presidential executive orders they helped to generate, *not one* major white-owned firm in the South had chosen to desegregate its skilled workforce. All major white employers had acted—as seen from a classical economics perspective—quite irrationally and accepted the economic costs of a worker recruitment pool severely limited by rigid racial segregation in the Jim Crow states. The 1964 Civil Rights Act, banning workplace discrimination and allowing the federal government to cut off contracts to discriminating employers, brought major changes to many southern and border state workplaces. Major manufacturing company executives finally employed significant numbers of black workers in formerly all-white jobs only as a result of the new civil rights laws, presidential executive orders, and federal court decisions. Moreover, researchers' interviews with white and black southerners have shown that most feel that legal segregation would have continued for a long time without the civil rights movement and subsequent civil rights laws. If there had been no civil rights movements against Jim Crow segregation, today the United States would likely be significantly less democratic than it currently is.[37]

Clearly too, there is a major moral gain from restoration and reparations programs for the United States, since for the first time in its history this country would make a real commitment to implementing a meaningful version of the white rhetorical liberty-and-justice frame. Today, as in the past, the system of racial oppression requires that most whites contradict their commonly expressed moral precepts of liberty and justice by living lives that maintain actively or collude in discrimination against other racial groups. By living unreflectively from the dominant racist framing of society, the majority of whites must be hypocrites and routinely misrepresent to themselves and others that they are highly moral and ethical. By regularly engaging in racial hostility and discrimination, and/or watching friends and relatives do so, a great many whites rob themselves of a strong claim to the morality they often assert. Nonetheless, some whites belatedly come to understand some aspects of this hypocritical lifestyle. For example, years after his extreme efforts in perpetuating legal segregation, former Alabama governor George Wallace came to understand better what he had done and even begged black leaders to forgive him for his actions as a rabid segregationist.

White Isolation and the Price We All Pay

Yet another benefit from large-scale racial change in the United States is that it will move many whites out of their social isolation and put them more directly in touch with more of this country's important social realities. For all their ability or education, most elite whites and most rank-and-file whites do not realize just how socially isolated they really are. Living in the mostly segregated neighborhoods of a predominantly white country, most whites do not see or understand the reality of the country's great racial segregation, nor the consequences of that for them and the larger society. Social science research has shown that most whites have no really deep and sustained contacts with Americans of color.[38]

Indeed, many Americans of color report that countless whites they encounter seem uncomfortable and even disoriented when interacting with them. One social science researcher, who is a man of color, noted recently to me that at his college he sometimes encounters intelligent whites who seem comfortable talking with other whites, even white strangers, yet have much difficulty in comfortably conversing with him. "It is like they do not know how to—as if men of color are somehow different from whites, as if we spoke a different language, or as if we are 'aliens.' "[39] Such whites pay a significant social price from years of societal segregation and isolation from people of color.

There is significant research that shows that the traditional white frame can significantly interfere with whites having successful interactions with people of color. One research study of 50 white college students found that interracial interactions were especially difficult for those with strong prejudices about racial outgroups. Interactions with people of other racial groups resulted in whites who were very prejudiced being more likely than other whites to perform poorly on a Stroop color/word matching task: Whites with high levels of prejudice "who engaged in an interracial interaction had impaired performance on the Stroop task—a task requiring executive control—compared with both high-prejudice participants who interacted with a White person and low-prejudice participants."[40] These data add more evidence on the price of contemporary racism for whites. While that price is certainly not nearly as high as for Americans of color who are targeted by most racial discrimination, there is a significant cumulative price to be paid by racism's white maintainers. The researchers here interpret their data using an energy model, what they term a "resource model of executive function." Engaging in an exercise involving significant personal self-control, such as in interacting with racial others viewed negatively, can have a temporary negative impact on one's ability to do a second important task. This is a substantial price to pay for holding strongly to the old racist framing. These research results suggest that there are some benefits for whites in abandoning the prejudices and stereotypes of their conventional racist framing.

In a few opinion surveys a substantial proportion of the white respondents have claimed that they have "black friends" or other friends of color. For example, in one NORC survey, 42 percent of whites said they had a close black friend, yet when asked for first names of their good friends, only 6 percent actually listed a black person. Most who said they had a close black friend in fact did not. A majority of whites live in very white worlds and rarely interact, especially on a sustained equal status basis, with people of color. Typically, white interactions with people of color are superficial or limited. Sustained equal status contact is not the same as co-presence in an organizational setting. The latter is often mistaken for the former. In-depth interviews with whites, from the working class to top corporate executives, indicate that they have on average few (or fleeting, such as with work acquaintances) equal status contacts with African Americans, but develop their views of African Americans mostly from their parents, peers, and the media. As a result, their views mostly reflect the old white frame's views of African Americans. If most whites who claim black friends did interact meaningfully with them and other people of color, or even if they read important writings generated by these Americans, they might come to understand that there is much important knowledge in communities of color and that the conventional white frame is a distorted and destructive way of viewing society.[41]

Some optimistic analysts have suggested that the Internet and its social networking sites will eventually break down major racial barriers and increase cross-racial interaction and networking, especially for younger Americans. However, research by Eszter Hargittai shows that racial characteristics shape Internet use in the same ways they do in the rest of society. A person's racial group, together with parents' education, enabled this researcher to predict the networking websites that a person will use. White, Latino, and Asian American students tended to segregate in their use of major networking sites on the Internet. Even dramatically new technologies do not necessarily change more fundamental patterns of racial segregation.[42]

White Isolation and International Incompetence

As the demographic worlds in which U.S. whites live become less white, the stubborn inability to look beyond the white racial frame and to really "see" and relate well to people of color will become ever more costly for both whites' everyday lives and for the political-economic decisions they, and especially white leaders, make about national and international matters.

Today, U.S. ethnocentrism and chauvinism remain strong, and are routinely asserted by U.S. politicians in their political campaigns. Elites and rank-and-file Americans, especially white Americans, share the white racial frame's accent on an assertive U.S. nationalism and (white) Americanism, a perspective that typically results in great ignorance of other countries and peoples across the globe. This narrow framing views the United States as not only the "best country," but also as not having any competition for that honor. Recall the recent Harris poll found that nearly two thirds of those polled thought that "overall the U.S. is better than other nations."[43]

Ironically but certainly, white American dominance and privilege have both personal and societal costs, which include a substantial cutting off of oneself and one's group from much of the world's population and the rich forms of knowledge that they hold. By rarely venturing out of white-controlled spaces or beyond some version of the white racial frame, most white leaders and analysts severely limit their knowledge and access to this society's, and this world's, intellectual and cultural riches. In this regard, they become rather one-dimensional human beings. By thinking only from the dominant racial frame, and excluding or marginalizing people of color and their cultures, white leaders and ordinary whites miss out on much insight and knowledge, including some that might save humanity from its likely future problems and disasters.

One major consequence and danger to all people from most powerful whites' social and cultural isolation is that they frequently make national and international political and economic decisions that shape the lives of many millions of people about whom they know little or nothing. This leads many elite whites and the powerful organizations they control to habitually justify many of their momentous decisions with rationales and conceptual models in which people are reduced to abstracted and dehumanized units, models with abstracting language like "supply and demand flows," "externalities," and "collateral damage." The most serious form of environmental destruction is, thus, that which destroys the human environments in which human beings can be fully creative, respectfully interactive, and utilizing of the full array of their knowledge and talents.

Interestingly, because of the global mass media, increasing numbers of people worldwide are becoming more aware of the huge inequalities of wealth and power across countries, and some are organizing to do something about it. They are beginning to challenge the Western accounts of their own histories, as well as of world history. They are also demanding more economic and political power globally. In 2008–2009 the U.S. financial system suddenly went into substantial decline, and with it much of the U.S. economy. This major crash in the U.S. economy led many of the world's leaders and social analysts to begin to openly discuss a possible decline in U.S. dominance and to question more openly U.S. and European control of major world institutions, such as the World Bank, which has always been headed by a white American. With the large-scale and recurring U.S. economic crises in the early twenty-first century, the world's political-economic reality began shifting to a much more multipolar world where the U.S. has increasingly been challenged by numerous other powerful countries, such as China, which has exceeded the United States in numerous economic areas and become a major "banker" that periodically bails the United States and other Western countries out of their serious economic problems.[44]

Conclusion: Taking Action for Change

Many Americans who are aware of the obligation to rebuild this society and eradicate racism are pessimistic about a significant reduction in racism's scope because racial oppression has been in place so long and is backed by much white power and privilege. Considering that we face today the results of centuries of well-buttressed racial exploitation and other oppression, major social change will not come easily. Still, it can yet be accomplished. The good news about human oppressions is that they are not inevitable or intrinsic to human societies. What has been created by human action can be dismantled by assertive human action where there is the will to bring change. We whites especially must take the responsibility for the system of racial hostility and discrimination and work with those long oppressed in developing speedy and innovative ways to bring it down. "We the people," with all the people involved this time, need to foster and elect the political and other societal leadership that will effectively coordinate efforts to change the system of racial oppression under real democratic control.

One place to start is with aggressive and effective enforcement of all U.S. civil rights laws. To this day, and in spite of common beliefs to the contrary, we have never had an aggressive enforcement of existing civil rights laws in all major areas, including housing and employment, usually because of significant white resistance. In addition, to do this enforcement, and to make other necessary changes in our racial inequalities, we need to replace the current, mostly white, leaders in our major institutional sectors with a much more diverse and representative group of leaders who do in fact support racial change, reparations, and restoration. This is especially true for the conservative, mostly white male justices on the U.S. Supreme Court, who have over the last two decades intentionally and severely limited the reach of 1960s and later civil rights laws by rejecting the legal relevance of *systemic* racism and narrowing the legal definition of discrimination to cover only those incidents in which a defendant can prove that specific (usually white) actors discriminated because of an intentional racial animus.[45]

Another critical effort should be directed at changing the structures of information presentation on racial matters for this society, so that both our mass media and our educational system regularly incorporate significant and intensive information and/or instruction on issues of racial-ethnic stereotyping and historical and contemporary racism. In this way we can significantly challenge the dominance of the white-racist framing of this society and press for its replacement with a sincere and fully implemented liberty-and-justice frame.

To get major structural changes in contemporary racial discrimination and racial inequality will likely take another large-scale movement of diverse Americans like that of the 1950s–1960s civil rights movement or the 1840s–1850s antislavery movement. This will happen only if enough Americans of all backgrounds, and especially white Americans, become much more knowledgeable about the continuing destructive impacts of systemic racism, including the deep white racial frame and the strong racial hierarchy, and then become strongly committed to major changes in these racially oppressive structures. Systemic racism can and will eventually be replaced with a more humane and just political-economic system, or U.S. society will not likely survive in the long term.

Notes

Preface

1. "President-Elect Obama: The Voters Rebuke Republicans for Economic Failure," *Wall Street Journal*, November 5, 2008, http://online.wsj.com/article/ SB122586244657800863.html (accessed December 28, 2008).
2. Ibid.
3. The CNN exit poll data were posted at *Slate's* website, "2008 Presidential Candidates Share of White Vote by State," http://www.slate.com/id/2204464/sidebar/2204528 (accessed December 12, 2008).
4. Bill Bishop, "No, We Didn't: America Hasn't Changed as Much as Tuesday's Results Would Indicate," November 10, 2008, http://www.slate.com/blogs/blogs/bigsort/ default.aspx (accessed December 17, 2008); see also Paul Taylor and Richard Morin. "Americans Claim to Like Diverse Communities but Do They Really?" Pew Research Center, December 2, 2008, http://pewresearch.org/pubs/1045/americans-claim-to-like-diverse-communities-but-do-they-really (accessed December 17, 2008).

Chapter 1

1. The first survey is in Richard Morin, "Misperceptions Cloud Whites' View of Blacks," *Washington Post*, July 11, 2001, p. A01; for countering data, see Joe R. Feagin and Clairece B. Feagin, *Racial And Ethnic Relations* (Eighth edition; Upper Saddle River, NJ: Prentice-Hall, 2008), pp. 178–189. The second survey is in Lawrence Bobo, "Inequalities that Endure?: Racial Ideology, American Politics, and the Peculiar Role of the Social Sciences," paper presented at conference on "The Changing Terrain of Race and Ethnicity," University of Illinois, Chicago, Illinois, October 26, 2001.
2. Thomas Kuhn, *The Structure of Scientific Revolutions* (Third edition; Chicago: University Of Chicago Press, 1996).
3. J. M. Blaut, *The Colonizer's Model of the World: Geographical Diffusionism and Eurocentric History* (New York: Guilford Press, 1993), p. 38.
4. Robert E. Park, *Race and Culture* (Glencoe, IL: Free Press, 1950); Milton M. Gordon, *Assimilation in American Life* (New York: Oxford University Press, 1964); Gunnar Myrdal, *An American Dilemma* (New York: McGraw-Hill, 1964). For discussions

of these mainstream scholars, see Feagin and Feagin, *Racial and Ethnic Relations,*
pp. 28–42.
5. See, for example, Geoffrey R. Stone, Louis M. Seidman, Cass R. Sunstein, and Mark
Tushnet, *Constitutional Law* (Third edition; Boston: Little, Brown, and Co., 1996).
6. Another very common social science approach is to consider individuals' racial
characteristics ("race") as they record such on a questionnaire or interview form as a
"variable" in a large-scale multivariate analysis. Such approaches often signal a serious
neglect of institutionalized discrimination and the deep structural foundation of
racial oppression. See Tukufu Zuberi and Eduardo Bonilla-Silva, eds., *White Logic,
White Methods* (Lanham, MD: Rowman & Littlefield, 2008).
7. J. M. Blaut, *The Colonizer's Model of the World: Geographical Diffusionism and
Eurocentric History* (New York: Guilford Press, 1993), p. 64, 102–103.
8. Edward W. Said, *Orientalism* (New York: Vintage Books, 1979).
9. See, for example, Talcott Parsons, "Full Citizenship for the Negro American? A
Sociological Problem," in *The Negro American*, ed. Talcott Parsons and Kenneth B.
Clark (Boston: Houghton Mifflin, 1965–1966), p. 740ff.
10. Anthony Giddens and Christopher Pierson, *Conversations with Anthony Giddens:
Making Sense of Modernity* (Palo Alto, CA: Stanford University Press, 1998), p. 94.
11. I am indebted here to scholarly discussions with Glenn Bracey.
12. Henry Wiencek, *An Imperfect God: George Washington, His Slaves, and the Creation of America* (New York: Farrar, Strauss, and Giroux, 2003), p. 7; also see
pp. 356–357.
13. Winthrop D. Jordan, *White over Black: American Attitudes Toward the Negro, 1550–1812*
(Chapel Hill: University of North Carolina Press, 1968), p. 137.
14. Drew Westen, *The Political Brain: The Role of Emotion in Deciding the Fate of the
Nation* (New York: PublicAffairs, 2007), p. 238; and Paul Krugman, *The Conscience of
a Liberal* (New York: Norton, 2007), p. 207.
15. See, for example, Patricia Hill Collins, *Black Feminist Thought: Knowledge, Conscious-
ness, and the Politics of Empowerment* (Boston: Unwin Hyman, 1990); Joe Feagin and
Hernán Vera, *White Racism: The Basics* (New York: Routledge, 1995); Eduardo
Bonilla-Silva, "Rethinking Racism: Toward a Structural Interpretation," *American
Sociological Review* 62 (June 1997): 465–480; the numerous legal scholars in Richard
Delgado and Jean Stefancic, editors, *White Studies: Looking Behind the Mirror*
(Philadelphia: Temple University Press, 1997); and Joe R. Feagin, *Systemic Racism: A
Theory of Oppression* (New York: Routledge, 2006).
16. See George Lakoff, *Don't Think of an Elephant: Know Your Values and Frame the
Debate* (White River Junction, Vermont: Chelsea Green Publishing, 2004), pp. 16–25;
David A. Snow, E. Burke Rochford, Steven K. Worden, and Robert D. Benford,
"Frame Alignment and Mobilization," *American Sociological Review* 51 (1986):
464–481; K. Fisher, "Locating Frames in the Discursive Universe," *Sociological
Research Online* 2 (1997), http://www.socresonline.org.uk/socresonline/2/3/4.ht
(retrieved October 30, 2007); and Robert M. Entman and Andrew Rojecki, *The Black
Image in the White Mind: Media and Race in America* (Chicago: University of Chicago
Press, 2001).
17. Leslie Houts Picca and Joe R. Feagin, *Two-Faced Racism: Whites in the Backstage and
Frontstage* (New York: Routledge, 2007), pp. 5–6.
18. Erving Goffman, *Frame Analysis: An Essay on the Organization of Experience* (Boston:
Northeastern University Press, 1974), pp. 1–20. I am also influenced here by G. Todd
Gitlin, *The Whole World is Watching* (Berkeley, CA: University of California Press,
1980), pp. 10–12.
19. I draw here on George Lakoff, *The Political Mind: Why You Can't Understand
21st-Century American Politics with an 18th-Century Brain* (New York: Viking, 2008),
pp. 24–33, 240, 250.
20. See Joe R. Feagin and Eileen O'Brien, *White Men on Race: Power, Privilege and the
Shaping of Cultural Consciousness* (Boston: Beacon, 2003); Feagin, *Systemic Racism;*

and Joe R. Feagin and Clairece B. Feagin, *Racial And Ethnic Relations* (Eighth edition; Upper Saddle River, NJ: Prentice-Hall, 2008).

21. Lakoff, *The Political Mind*, pp. 27–30, 42.
22. On scripts, see William H. Sewell, Jr., "A Theory of Structure: Duality, Agency, and Transformation," *American Journal of Sociology* 98 (1992): 14–22.
23. Maurice Halbwachs, *On Collective Memory*, ed. and trans. by L. Coser (Chicago, IL: University of Chicago Press, 1992), pp. 38, 52. I build here on ideas introduced in Picca and Feagin, *Two Faced Racism*, especially Chapter 1.
24. D. J. Howard, "Familiar Phrases as Peripheral Persuasion Cues," *Journal of Experimental Social Psychology* 33 (1997): 231–243; T. L. Chartrand and J. A. Bargh, "The Chameleon Effect: The Perception-Behavior Link and Social Interaction," *Journal of Personality and Social Psychology* 76 (1999): 893–910; and Henry Plotkin, *Evolution in Mind: An Introduction to Evolutionary Psychology* (Revised edition; Cambridge, MA: Harvard University Press, 2000), pp. 159, 252–253.
25. Paul Connerton, *How Societies Remember* (Cambridge: Cambridge University Press, 1989), pp. 2–3; Gary Alan Fine and Terence McDonnell, "Erasing the Brown Scare: Referential Afterlife and the Power of Memory Templates," *Social Problems* 54 (2007), p. 183.
26. Fareed Zakaria, *The Post-American World* (New York: W. W. Norton, 2008), p. 65. See also pp. 68–74.
27. Joe R. Feagin, Hernán Vera, and Nikitah Imani, *The Agony of Education: Black Students in White Colleges and Universities* (New York: Routledge, 1996), p. 18; see also Connerton, *How Societies Remember*.

Chapter 2

1. See Timothy Mitchell, "The Stage of Modernity," *Questions of Modernity*, ed. Timothy Mitchell (University of Minnesota Press, 2000), pp. 1–34.
2. Karl Marx, *Capital, Volume I*, trans. Ben Fowkes (New York: Vintage Books, 1977), pp. 915, 926; I am influenced here by Karl Kersplebedeb's review of Sylvia Federici, *Caliban and the Witch: Women the Body and Primitive Accumulation* (Autonomedia, 2004), at http://www.kersplebedeb.com/caliban/caliban_review.html#t3 (retrieved February 1, 2008).
3. Tom Keefer, "Constructs of Capitalism: Slavery and the Development of Racism," http://www.newsocialist.org/magazine/39/article03.html (retrieved December 13, 2007).
4. On racial formation theory, see Michael Omi and Howard Winant, *Racial Formation in the United States* (New York: Routledge, 1994); on the history, see Eric Williams, *Capitalism and Slavery* (Chapel Hill: University of North Carolina Press, 1994 [1944]), pp. 106–121; and Joe R. Feagin, *Racist America: Roots, Current Realities, and Future Reparations* (New York: Routledge, 2000), Chapters 1–2.
5. J. Sakai, *Settlers: Mythology of the White Proletariat* (Chicago: Morningstar Press, 1989), pp. 8–9.
6. Edmund S. Morgan, *American Slavery, American Freedom: The Ordeal of Virginia* (New York: Norton, 1975), p. 5.
7. Walter J. Ong, *Orality and Literacy: The Technologizing of the Word* (New York: Methuen, 1988), pp. 75–77. I am indebted to discussions with Shari Valentine here.
8. Charles Mills, *The Racial Contract* (Ithaca: Cornell Univ. Press, 1997), p. 93; on the men at the convention, see Feagin, *Racist America*, pp. 9–12.
9. Donald E. Lively, *The Constitution and Race* (New York: Praeger, 1992), pp. 4–5; see also Joe R. Feagin, *Systemic Racism: A Theory of Racial Oppression* (New York: Routledge, 2006), pp. 21–55.
10. Lawrence Goldstone, *Slavery, Profits, and the Struggle for the Constitution* (New York: Walker and Company, 2005), pp. 115–117.

11. Garry Wills, *"Negro President": Jefferson and the Slave Power* (Boston: Houghton Mifflin, 2003), pp. 5–9; and Irene Diggs, "The Biological and Cultural Impact of Blacks on the United States," *Phylon* 41 (1980), p. 160.
12. Robert Caro, *The Years of Lyndon Johnson: Master of The Senate* (New York: Knopf, 2002), pp. 9–11, 90–94. James Madison is quoted on p. 9.
13. Richard Kluger, *Simple Justice: The History of Brown v. Board of Education and Black America's Struggle for Equality* (New York: Knopf, 1975), Volume 1, p. 65.
14. *Dred Scott v. Sandford*, 60 U.S. 393, 408 (1856).
15. Robin Einhorn, *American Taxation, American Slavery* (Chicago: University of Chicago Press, 2006), pp. 7–8, 250.
16. Gautham Rao, "The Federal Posse Comitatus Doctrine: Slavery, Compulsion, and Statecraft in Mid-Nineteenth Century America," *Law and History Review*, http://www.press.uillinois.edu/journals/lhr/rao26_1.pdf (retrieved February 1, 2008).
17. Vincent Harding, *There is a River: The Black Struggle for Freedom in America* (New York: Harvest/HBJ Books, 1993), p. xxv. Italics added.
18. Wills, *"Negro President,"* p. 8.
19. Diggs, "The Biological and Cultural Impact of Blacks on the United States," p. 160.
20. Harriet Beecher Stowe, *A Key to Uncle Tom's Cabin* (Boston: John P. Jewett, 1853), p. 39. Most of the advertisements for enslaved runaways note they are intelligent and/or are lighter-skinned, facts that counter some of the slaveholders' racist framing of those enslaved.
21. Ibid., p. 31; on New England's racial oppression, see Joanne Pope Melish, *Disowning Slavery: Gradual Emancipation and "Race" in New England* (Ithaca, New York: Cornell University Press, 1998), pp. 165–167.
22. Quoted in Kenneth O'Reilly, *Nixon's Piano: Presidents and Racial Politics from Washington to Clinton* (New York: Free Press, 1995), p. 45.
23. I draw here on the summary of social change ideas, especially those of Michael L. Tushman and Elaine Romanelli, presented in Connie G. Gersick, "Revolutionary Change Theories: A Multilevel Exploration of the Punctuated Equilibrium Paradigm," *Academy of Management Review* 16 (1991), pp 13–19.

Chapter 3

1. Deborah L. Madsen, *American Exceptionalism* (Jackson: University Press of Mississippi, 1998), p. 1.
2. George Lakoff and Mark Turner, *More than Cool Reason* (Chicago: University of Chicago Press, 1989), pp. 210–212.
3. Arthur O. Lovejoy, *The Great Chain of Being: A Study of the History of an Idea* (Cambridge, Harvard University Press, 1973 [1936]), p. 59; see also W. Michael Byrd and Linda A. Clayton, *An American Health Dilemma* (Vol. 1; New York: Routledge, 2000), pp. 54–55.
4. I draw here on a review of Robert Bucholz and Newton Key, *Early Modern England 1485–1714: A Narrative History* (Oxford: Blackwell Publishing, 2004), at http://www.h-net.org/reviews/showrev.cgi?path=242801123091235 (retrieved December 12, 2007); on Gordon J. Schochet, *The Authoritarian Family and Political Attitudes in 17th Century England* (New Brunswick, NJ: Transaction Books, 1998), pp. xiii–xiv, 5–90; and on George Lakoff and Mark Johnson, *Philosophy in the Flesh: The Embodied Mind and Its Challenge to Western Thought* (New York: Basic Books, 1999), pp. 292–310.
5. See Helena Woodard, *African-British Writings in the Eighteenth Century* (Westport, CT: Greenwood Press, 1999), pp. xv–xviii.
6. Michael Guasco, "To 'Doe Some Good Upon Their Countrymen': The Paradox of Indian Slavery in Early Anglo-America," *Journal of Social History* 41 (Winter, 2007): 253–282; and Peter Silver, *Our Savage Neighbors: How Indian War Transformed Early America* (New York: W. W. Norton, 2008), p. xxi.

7. See Winthrop D. Jordan, *White over Black: American Attitudes Toward the Negro, 1550–1812* (Chapel Hill: University of North Carolina Press, 1968), pp. 40–43; and Richard Drinnon, *Facing West: The Metaphysics of Indian-Hating and Empire-Building* (Norman, OK: University of Oklahoma Press, 1997 [1980]), p. 51 and passim.

8. In non-English-speaking parts of Europe and in North Africa, some elements of a protoracial framing of people of African descent can be seen earlier in the writings of Jacques de Voragine (1230–1298), Ibn Khaldun (1332–1406), and Jean Bodin (1530–1596).

9. David E. Stannard, *American Holocaust: Columbus and the Conquest of the New World* (New York: Oxford University Press, 1992), p. 247.

10. Robert F. Berkhofer, Jr., *The White Man's Indian: Images of the American Indian from Columbus to the Present* (New York: Knopf, 1978), p. 4.

11. Both are quoted in Stannard, *American Holocaust*, p. 227.

12. Berkhofer, *The White Man's Indian*, p. 16.

13. All are quoted in ibid., pp. 19–22.

14. Drinnon, *Facing West*, pp. 52–53.

15. Ibid., p. 53.

16. Quoted in ibid., p. 19.

17. George Rawick, as quoted in David R. Roediger, *The Wages of Whiteness: Race and the Making of the American Working Class* (London: Verso, 1991), p. 95; see also Ronald T. Takaki, *Iron Cages: Race and Culture in 19th Century America* (New York: Oxford University Press, 1990), pp. 12–15.

18. Roy Harvey Pearce, as quoted in Drinnon, *Facing West*, p. 102.

19. Jordan, *White Over Black*, pp. 12–39.

20. Ibid., p. 80.

21. The quote and interpretation are from A. Leon Higginbotham, Jr., *Shades of Freedom: Racial Politics and the Presumptions of the American Legal Process* (New York: Oxford University Press, 1996), pp. 19–20; see also Jordan, *White Over Black*, pp. 73–74.

22. The court cases are discussed in Higginbotham, *Shades of Freedom*, pp. 21–22; see also Joe R. Feagin, *Racist America: Roots, Current Realities, and Future Reparations* (New York: Routledge, 2000), pp. 39–42.

23. Quoted in Jordan, *White Over Black*, p. 110.

24. Higginbotham, *Shades of Freedom*, p. 25.

25. Ibid., pp. 30–38; see also James Walvin, *Questioning Slavery* (New York: Routledge 1996).

26. Quoted in Jordan, *White Over Black*, p. 97.

27. Quoted in ibid., p. 275.

28. Quoted in ibid., pp. 96–97.

29. Higginbotham, *Shades of Freedom*, p. 32.

30. Roediger, *The Wages of Whiteness*, p. 21; and Manning Marable, *Black American Politics* (London: New Left Books, 1985), p. 5.

31. Quoted in A. Leon Higginbotham, Jr., *In the Matter of Color* (New York: Oxford University Press, 1978), p. 44.

32. W. E. B. Du Bois, *Darkwater* (New York: Humanity Books, 2003), p. 56; for a contemporary analyst, see Ron Eyerman, *Cultural Trauma: Slavery and the Formation of African American Identity* (Cambridge, UK: Cambridge University Press, 2001), p. 17.

33. Audrey Smedley, *Race in North America* (Boulder, CO: Westview Press, 1993), p. 38.

34. Woodard, *African-British Writings in the Eighteenth Century*, p. 28; and Bradd Shore, "Human Diversity and Human Nature," in *Being Humans: Anthropological Universality and Particularity in Transdisciplinary Perspectives*, ed. Neil Roughley (Berlin: Walter de Gruyter 2000), p. 87. I have changed the text to modern spelling.

35. Quoted in Shore, "Human Diversity and Human Nature," p. 87. I have changed the text to modern spelling.

36. Bureau d'adresse et de rencontre, *"Another Collection of Philosophical Conferences of the French Virtuosi upon Questions of All Sorts for the Improving of Natural Knowledge*

Made in the Assembly of the Beaux Esprits at Paris by the Most Ingenious Persons of That Nation," render'd into English by G. Havers and J. Davies (London: Printed for Thomas Dring and John Starkey, 1665), pp. 377–379), at http://eebo.chadwyck.com.ezproxy. tamu.edu:2048/search/fulltext?ACTION=ByID&ID=D00000127257250000 &SOURCE=var_spell.cfg&WARN=N&FILE=../session/1198083025_22267 (retrieved June 8, 2007).

37. Samuel Sewall, *The Selling of Joseph, A Memorial* (Boston: Bartholomew Green and John, 1700), as reprinted at http://www.pbs.org/wgbh/aia/part1/1h301t.html (retrieved May 11, 2008); see also, Mason I. Lowance Jr (editor), *A House Divided: The Antebellum Slavery Debates in America, 1776–1865* (Princeton University Press, 2003).

38. John Saffin, "A Brief, Candid Answer to a Late Printed Sheet, Entitled, 'The Selling of Joseph,' " in Lowance, *A House Divided*, at http://press.princeton.edu/chapters/s7553.html (retrieved May 11, 2008).

39. Cotton Mather, *The Negro Christianized An Essay to Excite and Assist the Good Work, The Instruction of Negro-Servants in Christianity* (Boston: B. Green., 1706), p. 15.

40. Ibid., p. 5. See also Anthony S. Parent, Jr., *Foul Means: The Formation of a Slave Society in Virginia, 1660–1740* (Chapel Hill, North Carolina: University of North Carolina Press, 2003), p. 200.

41. Edward Long, *The History of Jamaica* (London, 1714), Vol. 2, p. 65, 353, 371.

42. Higginbotham, *In the Matter of Color*, p. 309.

43. Quoted in Walvin, *Questioning Slavery*, p. 80.

44. See Ellis Cose, *Color-Blind: Seeing Beyond Race in a Race-Obsessed World* (New York: HarperCollins, 1997); on prototypes see George Lakoff, *Women, Fire, and Dangerous Things: What Categories Reveal about the Mind* (Chicago: University of Chicago Press, 1987), pp. 8–86.

45. Smedley, *Race in North America*, p. 27.

Chapter 4

1. A. Leon Higginbotham, Jr., *Shades of Freedom: Racial Politics and the Presumptions of the American Legal Process* (New York: Oxford University Press, 1996), p. 38.

2. Winthrop D. Jordan, *White over Black: American Attitudes Toward the Negro, 1550–1812* (Chapel Hill: University of North Carolina Press, 1968), p. 91.

3. Peter Silver, *Our Savage Neighbors: How Indian War Transformed Early America* (New York: W. W. Norton, 2008), p. 132, 282. See also pp. xx–xxv, and appendix.

4. Gregory T. Knouff, *Soldiers' Revolution: Pennsylvanians in Arms and the Forging of Early American Identity* (University Park, PA: Pennsylvania State University Press, 2003), pp. 158–174, 285–286; Silver, *Our Savage Neighbors*, p. 87ff; and Edmund S. Morgan, *American Slavery, American Freedom: The Ordeal of Colonial Virginia* (New York: Norton, 1975).

5. B. L. Rayner, *Life of Thomas Jefferson* (Boston: Lilly, Wait, Colman, & Holden, 1834), at http://etext.virginia.edu/jefferson/biog/lj08.htm (retrieved May 14, 2008).

6. Richard Drinnon, *Facing West: The Metaphysics of Indian-Hating and Empire-Building* (Norman, OK: University of Oklahoma Press, 1997 [1980]), p. 98.

7. Thomas Jefferson, *Notes on the State of Virginia*, ed. Frank Shuffelton (New York: Penguin Books, 1999 [1785]), p. 147.

8. Joseph J. Ellis, *Founding Brothers: The Revolutionary Generation* (New York: Vintage Books, 2000), p. 159.

9. "The Letters of Thomas Jefferson: 1743–1826," Arts Faculty, University of Groningen, http://www.let.rug.nl/usa/P/tj3/writings/brf/jefl224.htm (retrieved May 14, 2008).

10. Quoted in A. Leon Higginbotham, Jr., *In the Matter of Color* (New York: Oxford University Press, 1978), p. 59.

11. Ronald T. Takaki, *Iron Cages: Race and Culture in 19th Century America* (New York: Oxford University Press, 1990), p. 83.

12. Frederick Jackson Turner, *The Frontier In American History* (New York: Henry Holt and Company, 1935).
13. Drinnon, *Facing West*, pp. 355–356.
14. William H. Tucker, *The Science and Politics of Racial Research* (Urbana, IL: University of Illinois Press, 1994), p. 8; George Mosse, *Toward the Final Solution: A History of European Racism* (London: Dent & Son, 1978), p. 20.
15. See, for example, the Wikipedia article on "Enlightenment," http://en.wikipedia.org/wiki/Age_of_Enlightenment.
16. Milton Cantor, "The Image of the Negro in Colonial Literature," *The New England Quarterly 36* (December 1963), p. 468; Bernard Romans, *A Concise History of East and West Florida* (New York, 1773), p. 105.
17. Quoted in Jordan, *White Over Black*, p. 146. See also p. 158.
18. Anthony Benezet, *Short Account of that Part of Africa Inhabited by the Negroes* (Philadelphia, 1762), p. 31.
19. Quoted in Cantor, "The Image of the Negro in Colonial Literature," pp. 453, 455.
20. Benjamin Franklin, *Observations Concerning the Increase of Mankind, Peopling of Countries, Etc.* (1751), as quoted in *Benjamin Franklin: A Biography in His Own Words*, ed. Thomas Fleming (New York: Harper and Row, 1972), pp. 105–106. I have changed this to modern capitalization. See also Claude-Anne Lopez and Eugenia W. Herbert, *The Private Franklin: The Man and His Family* (New York: Norton, 1975), pp. 194–195.
21. See Joe R. Feagin, *Systemic Racism:* A Theory of Oppression (New York: Routledge, 2006), Chapter 2.
22. F. Nwabueze Okoye, "Chattel Slavery as the Nightmare of the American Revolutionaries," *William and Mary Quarterly 37* (January 1980), p. 13.
23. Quoted in "A Rhetoric of Rights: The Arguments Used in the 'American Conversation' in the Era of the Revolution," at http://assumption.edu/ahc/1770s/coreargs.html (Retrieved November 1, 2004).
24. Patrick Henry, "Liberty or Death Speech," www.historyplace.com/speeches/henry.htmhttp://www.historyplace.com/speeches/henry.hm (retrieved June 26, 2008).
25. Hume and Kant are quoted in Emmanuel C. Eze, *Race and the Enlightenment* (Cambridge, MA: Blackwell, 1997), pp. 33, 118.
26. Tucker, *The Science and Politics of Racial Research*, p. 9; Ivan Hannaford, Race: *The History of an Idea in the West* (Baltimore: Johns Hopkins University Press, 1996), pp. 205–207.
27. John C. Calhoun, "Slavery A Positive Good," http://teachingamericanhistory.org/library/index.asp?document=71 (retrieved May 5, 2007).
28. Sander L. Gilman, *Difference and Pathology: Stereotypes of Sexuality, Race, and Stereotypes* (Ithaca, New York: Cornell University Press, 1985) p. 137.
29. Alexis de Tocqueville, *Democracy in America* (New York: Random House/Vintage Books, 1945), Volume 1, pp. 344–345. The second quote is on p. 372.
30. Frederick Douglass, "The United States Cannot Remain Half-Slave and Half-Free," in *Frederick Douglass: Selected Speeches and Writings*, eds. P. S. Foner and Y. Taylor (Chicago: Lawrence Hall Books, 1999), pp. 657–658.
31. J. Gerald Kennedy and Liliane Weissberg, eds., *Romancing the Shadow: Poe and Race* (Revised edition; New York: Oxford University Press, 2001), p. 196; Elise Lemire, *"Miscegenation": Making Race in America* (Philadelphia: University of Pennsylvania Press, 2002).
32. Stetson Kennedy, *Jim Crow Guide: The Way It Was* (Boca Raton: Florida Atlantic University Press, 1990 [1959]), p. 47.
33. Martha Hodes, *White Women, Black Men: Illicit Sex in the Nineteenth-Century South* (New Haven, CT: Yale University Press, 1997), pp. 1–2; and Joel Kovel, *White Racism: A Psychohistory* (New York: Columbia University Press, 1984).
34. David R. Roediger, *The Wages of Whiteness: Race and the Making of the American Working Class* (London: Verso, 1991), pp. 106–120; and M. M. Manring, *Slave in a Box:*

The Strange Career of Aunt Jemima (Charlottesville, VA: University Press of Virginia, 1998), pp. 6–8.

35. Lerone Bennett, *Forced into Glory: Abraham Lincoln's White Dream* (Chicago: Johnson Publishing Co., 1999), pp. 90–150, 610–615; and Joe R. Feagin, "Foreword," in Sharon Rush, *Huck Finn's Hidden Lessons: Teaching and Learning Across the Color Line* (Lanham, MD: Rowman & Littlefield, 2006), pp. i–viii.

36. William G. Allen, *The American Prejudice Against Color: An Authentic Narrative, Showing How Easily the Nation Got Into an Uproar* (London: W. and F. G. Cash, 1853), preface and passim (no pagination).

37. Harriet Beecher Stowe, *A Key to Uncle Tom's Cabin* (Boston: John P. Jewett, 1853), p. 27.

38. Martin R. Delaney, *The Condition, Elevation, Emigration, and Destiny of the Colored People of the United States* (1852) (no publisher or pagination), http://www.gutenberg.org/ebooks/17154 (retrieved May 12, 2008). Italics added.

39. Arnoldo De León, "Initial Contacts: Niggers, Redskins, and Greasers," in *The Latino/a Condition: A Critical Reader*, eds. Richard Delgado and Jean Stefancic (New York: New York University Press, 1998), p. 161.

40. John C. Calhoun, "Conquest of Mexico," http://teachingamericanhistory.org/library/index.asp?document=478 (retrieved December 13, 2007). Italics added.

41. Quoted in Takaki, *Iron Cages*, p. 177.

42. Laura E. Gomez, *Manifest Destinies* (New York University), pp. 10–149.

43. Ibid., p. 149.

44. I draw here on Joe R. Feagin and Clairece B. Feagin, *Racial and Ethnic Relations* (Upper Saddle River, NJ: Prentice-Hall, 2008), pp. 279–360.

45. Ibid.

46. Rudyard Kipling, "The White Man's Burden: The United States and the Philippine Islands," *McClure's Magazine* 12 (Feb. 1899), http://www.fordham.edu/halsall/mod/Kipling.html (retrieved May 22, 2008).

47. Theodore W. Allen, *The Invention of the White Race* (New York: Verso, 1994), pp. 21–50, 184; David R. Roediger, *The Wages of Whiteness: Race and the Making of the American Working Class* (London: Verso, 1991), p. 127. I draw here on Joe R. Feagin, *Racist America: Roots, Current Realities, and Future Reparations* (New York: Routledge, 2000), pp. 14–74.

48. Gilman, *Difference and Pathology*, p. 138.

49. Ibid., pp. 87–90.

50. Audrey Smedley, *Race in North America* (Boulder, CO: Westview Press, 1993), p. 26.

51. Quoted in George Frederickson, *The Black Image in the White Mind* (Hanover, NH: Wesleyan University Press, 1971), p. 230.

52. See Frederick L. Hoffman, "Vital Statistics of the Negro," *Arena* 5 (April, 1892): 542, as cited in Frederickson, *The Black Image in the White Mind*, pp. 250–251; see also George Fitzhugh, *Sociology for the South; or, the Failure of Free Society* (Richmond, 1854); and Henry Hughes, *Treatise on Sociology, Theoretical and Practical* (Negro Universities Press, 1968 [1854]).

53. Ralph Ellison, *Shadow and Act* (New York: Random House, 1964), p. 305.

54. Tucker, *The Science and Politics of Racial Research*, p. 35.

55. Carl C. Brigham, *A Study of American Intelligence* (Princeton, NJ: Princeton University Press, 1923), pp. 124–25 and 177–210.

56. Lothrop Stoddard, *The Rising Tide of Color: Against White World-Supremacy* (New York: Scribner's, 1920), p. 3.

57. Tucker, *The Science and Politics of Racial Research*, p. 93. I draw generally on Theodore Cross, *Black Power Imperative: Racial Inequality and the Politics of Nonviolence* (New York: Faulkner, 1984), pp. 93 and 157.

58. *Plessy v. Ferguson*, 163 U.S. 537 (1896).

59. Ibid, pp. 556 and 552. Italics added.

60. *Missouri ex rel. Gaines v. Canada*, 305 U.S. 337 (1938); and *Brown et al. v. Board of*

Education of Topeka et al. 347 U.S. 491 (1954). See Robert A. Pratt, *"Brown v. Board of Education* Revisited," *Reviews in American History* 30 (2002), pp. 141–144.

61. *Brown v. Board of Education*, 349 U.S. 301 (1955). Italics added
62. *Congressional Record*, 84th Congress Second Session. Vol. 102, part 4 (March 12, 1956) (Washington, DC: Governmental Printing Office, 1956), pp. 4459–4460.
63. Ibid.
64. James J. Kilpatrick, *The Southern Case for School Segregation* (New York: Crowell-Collier Press, 1962), pp. 20–21.
65. Robert Caro, *The Years of Lyndon Johnson: Master of the Senate* (New York: Random House Vintage Books, 2002), p. 778.

Chapter 5

1. See, for example, Howard Schuman, Charlotte Steeh, and Lawrence Bobo, *Racial Attitudes in America: Trends and Interpretations* (Cambridge: Harvard University Press, 1985), pp. 71–162; Dinesh D'Souza, *The End of Racism: Principles for a Multiracial Society* (New York: Free Press, 1995).
2. Andrew Scott Baron and Mahzarin R. Banaji, "The Development of Implicit Attitudes: Evidence of Race Evaluations From Ages 6 and 10 and Adulthood," *Psychological Science* 17 (2006): 52–53; John F. Dovidio, John C. Brigham, Blair T. Johnson, and Samuel L. Gaertner, "Stereotyping, Prejudice, and Discrimination: Another Look," in *Stereotypes and Stereotyping*, eds. C. Neil Macrae, Miles Hewstone, and Charles Stangor (New York: Guilford, 1995), pp. 276–319; and Sonja M. B. Givens and Jennifer L. Monahan, "Priming Mammies, Jezebels, and Other Controlling Images: An Examination of the Influence of Mediated Stereotypes on Perceptions of an African American Woman," *Media Psychology* 7 (2005), pp. 102–103.
3. Eduardo Bonilla-Silva and Tyrone A. Forman, "'I Am Not A Racist But ...': Mapping White College Students' Racial Ideology in the U.S.A.," *Discourse and Society*, 11 (2000): 51–86.
4. Debra Van Ausdale and Joe R. Feagin, *The First R: How Children Learn Race and Racism* (Lanham, MD: Rowman & Littlefield, 2001), p. 1.
5. See D. J. Howard, "Familiar Phrases as Peripheral Persuasion Cues," *Journal of Experimental Social Psychology* 33 (1997): 231–243. T. L. Chartrand and J. A. Bargh, "The Chameleon Effect: The Perception-Behavior Link and Social Interaction," *Journal of Personality and Social Psychology* 76 (1999): 893–910. See also Henry Plotkin, *Evolution in Mind: An Introduction to Evolutionary Psychology* (Revised edition; Cambridge, MA: Harvard University Press, 2000), pp. 159, 252–253.
6. Nina Eliasoph, "'Everyday Racism' in a Culture of Political Avoidance: Civil Society, Speech, and Taboo," *Social Problems* 46 (1999), p. 484. On homogeneous networks, see Miller McPherson, Lynn Smith-Lovin, and James M. Cook, "Birds of a Feather: Homophily in Social Networks," *Annual Review of Sociology* 27 (2001): 415–444.
7. Joe R. Feagin and Hernan Vera, *White Racism: The Basics* (New York: Routledge, 1995), p. 159.
8. The quote is from a research summary by Siri Carpenter, "Buried Prejudice: The Bigot in Your Brain" *Scientific American*, May 2008, http://www.sciam.com/article.cfm?id=buried-prejudice-the-bigot-in-your-brain (retrieved June 1, 2008). See also L. S. Vygotsky, *Mind in Society: The Development of Higher Psychological Processes*, eds. M. Cole, V. John-Steiner, S. Scribner, and E. Souberman (Cambridge, MA: Harvard University Press, 1978); and Steven Shaffer, "Resurrecting the Linguistic Relativity Hypothesis," http://www.scshaffer.com/files/scsshaffer-lrh.pdf (accessed February 6, 2006), pp. 2–17.
9. Baron and Banaji, "The Development of Implicit Attitudes," pp. 52–53.
10. Thierry Devos and Mahzarin R. Banaji, "American =White?" *Journal of Personality and Social Psychology* 88 (2005): 447–466. I am also influenced here and later by

George Lakoff and Mark Turner, *More than Cool Reason* (Chicago: University of Chicago Press, 1989), p. 167, 208–210.

11. I am indebted here to comments on an earlier draft by Sean Chaplin.
12. Peter J. Richardson, Robert T. Boyd, and Joseph Henrich, "Cultural Evolution of Human Cooperation," in *Genetic and Cultural Evolution of Cooperation*, ed. P. Hammerstein (Cambridge, MIT Press, 2003), pp. 372–381.
13. Leslie Houts Picca and Joe R. Feagin, *Two-Faced Racism: Whites in the Backstage and Frontstage* (New York: Routledge, 2007).
14. Jacqueline Soteropoulos, "Skeptics Put Cops on Trial: The American Public Isn't Giving Government or Police Officers the Blind Trust It Once Did," *Tampa Tribune*, April 17, 1995, p. A1; and Nick Mrozinske, "Derivational Thinking and Racism," unpublished research paper, University of Florida, fall, 1998.
15. See the various reports on the campaign at www.racismreview.com.
16. Eduardo Bonilla-Silva, *Racism without Racists* (Second edition; Lanham, MD: Rowman and Littlefield, 2006); see also Leslie Carr, *"Color-Blind" Racism* (Thousand Oaks: Sage, 1997).
17. Brad Wilmouth, "MSNBC: Hillary the 'Al Sharpton of White People,' Obama the 'New Breeze,' " http://newsbusters.org/blogs/brad-wilmouth/2008/05/14/msnbc-hillary-al-sharpton-white-people-obama-new-breeze (retrieved June 11, 2008). I am indebted here to comments by Ben Carrington.
18. Cheryl Harris, "Whiteness as Property," in *Critical Race Theory: The Key Writings that Formed the Movement* (New York: The New Press, 1995), p. 282.
19. Irene Diggs, "The Biological and Cultural Impact of Blacks on the United States," *Phylon* 41, (1980), p. 166.
20. Toni Morrison, *Playing in the Dark: Whiteness and the Literary Imagination* (New York: Vintage Books, 1992), p. 65.
21. Ralph Ellison, *Shadow and Act* (New York: Random House, 1964), p. 304.
22. Quoted in Dan T. Carter, *The Politics of Rage: George Wallace, The Origins of the New Conservatism, and the Transformation of American Politics* (Second edition; Baton Rouge: Louisiana State University Press, 2000), p. 237.
23. See Charles Gallagher, "Miscounting Race: Explaining Whites' Misperceptions of Racial Group Size," *Sociological Perspectives* 46 (2003): 381–396.
24. Nilanjana Dasgupta, Debbie E. McGhee, and Anthony G. Greenwald, and Mahzarin R. Banaji, "Automatic Preference for White Americans: Eliminating the Familiarity Explanation," *Journal of Experimental Social Psychology* 36 (2000): 316–328; see also Shankar Vedantam, "Many Americans Believe They Are Not Prejudiced. Now a New Test Provides Powerful Evidence that a Majority of Us Really Are," *Washington Post Magazine*, January 23, 2005, p. W12.
25. The research is summarized in Vedantam, "Many Americans Believe They Are Not Prejudiced. Now a New Test Provides Powerful Evidence that a Majority of Us Really Are," p. W12; and Associated Press, "Racism Studies Find Rational Part of Brain Can Override Prejudice," http://www.beliefnet.com/story/156/story_15664_1.html (accessed November 28, 2004).
26. Ruth Frankenberg, *White Women, Race Matters* (Minneapolis: University of Minnesota Press, 1993), pp. 12–50; and Joe R. Feagin, Hernán Vera, and Pinar Batur, *White Racism: The Basics* (Second edition; New York: Routledge, 2001), pp. 186–253.
27. See "Stereotypes and Prejudice: Their Automatic and Controlled Components," pp. 5–18.
28. Thomas Jefferson, *Notes on the State of Virginia*, ed. Frank Shuffelton (New York: Penguin Books, 1999 [1785]). A simple Google search will turn up the white supremacist websites.
29. J. L Eberhardt, P. A Goff, V. J Purdie, and P. G. Davies, "Seeing Black: Race, Crime, and Visual Processing," *Journal of Personality and Social Psychology*, 87 (2004): 876–893.
30. Ibid.
31. "Bennett Under Fire for Remarks on Black Crime," CNN.com, September 30, 2005,

http://www.cnn.com/2005/POLITICS/09/30/bennett.comments/index.html (accessed January 20, 2009).

32. See, for example, P. R. Klite, R. A. Bardwell, and J. Salzman, "Local TV News: Getting Away with Murder," Press/Politics 2 (1997): 102–112; Franklin D. Gilliam, Jr., and Shanto Iyengar, "Prime Suspects: the Effects of Local News on the Viewing Public," unpublished research paper, University of California (Los Angeles), n.d; Robert M. Entman, "Violence on Television: News and Reality Programming in Chicago," Report for the Chicago Council on Urban Affairs, May 9, 1994; Daniel Romer, Kathleen H. Jamieson, and Nicole J. de Coteau, "The Treatment of Persons of Color in Local Television News," Communication Research 25 (June 1998): 286–290.

33. Givens and Monahan, "Priming Mammies, Jezebels, and Other Controlling Images," pp. 87–106.

34. "Imus Called Women's Basketball Team 'Nappy-headed Hostility'," MediaMatters, April 7, 2007, http://mediamatters.org/items/200704040011 (retrieved November 7, 2008).

35. Benjamin Franklin, Observations Concerning the Increase of Mankind, Peopling of Countries, Etc. (1751), as quoted in Benjamin Franklin: A Biography in His Own Words, ed. Thomas Fleming (New York: Harper and Row, 1972), pp. 105–106. I use modern capitalization.

36. Yanick St. Jean and Joe R. Feagin, Double Burden: Black Women and Everyday Racism (New York: M. E. Sharpe, 1998), pp. 90–91.

37. Sophie Trawalter, Andrew R. Todd, Abigail A. Baird, Jennifer A. Richeson, "Attending to Threat: Race-based Patterns of Selective Attention," Journal of Experimental Social Psychology 44 (2008): 1322–1327.

38. Sut Jhally and Justin Lewis, Enlightened Racism (Boulder: Westview Press, 1992), pp. 95–110.

39. W. E. B. Du Bois, Dusk of Dawn (New Brunswick, NJ: Transaction, 1984 [1940]), p. 6.

40. Joel Kovel, White Racism: A Psychohistory (New York: Columbia University Press, 1984), p. xl.

41. Ibid., pp. xli–xlvii. See also Feagin, Vera, and Batur, White Racism, pp. 1–33.

42. See the website www.stormfront.org.

43. Thierry Devos, Brian A. Nosek, and Mahzarin R. Banaji, "Aliens in their Own Land? Implicit and Explicit Ascriptions of National Identity to Native Americans and White Americans," research paper presented at the SPSP Groups and Intergroup Relations Pre-Conference, Memphis, Tennessee, January 2007.

44. "Bob and the Showgram," http://en.wikipedia.org/wiki/Bob_and_the_Showgram# Native_Americans (retrieved July 8, 2008). I am indebted here to Kristen Lavelle for the transcript and comments.

45. For a detailed discussion see Joe Feagin and Clairece B. Feagin, Racial and Ethnic Relations (Eighth edition; Upper Saddle River, New Jersey: Prentice Hall, 2008), pp. 141–164.

46. Laurel R. Davis, "Protest Against the Use of Native American Mascots: A Challenge to Traditional American Identity," Journal of Sport and Social Issues 17 (April 1993): 9–22; Randi Hicks Rowe, "NCAA Decides; New Policy Prohibits Usage of Racially Abusive Names By College Teams," American Indian Report 21 (2005): 8–9; C. Richard King and Charles Fruehling Springwood, "Introduction," in Team Spirits: The Native American Mascots Controversy, ed. C. Richard King and Charles Fruehling Springwood (Lincoln, NE: University of Nebraska Press, 2001). Several chapters in the King and Fruehling book detail various mascot controversies.

47. Robert G. Lee, Orientals: Asian Americans in Popular Culture (Philadelphia, PA: Temple University Press, 1999), p. 8.

48. Jacobus tenBroek, Edward N. Barnhart, and Floyd W. Matson, Prejudice, War, and the Constitution (Berkeley, CA: University of California Press, 1968), p. 31. In this section I am generally influenced by Rosalind S. Chou and Joe R. Feagin, The Myth of the Model Minority: Asian Americans Facing Racism (Boulder, CO: Paradigm

Books, 2008), pp. 3–23, and by Feagin and Feagin, *Racial and Ethnic Relations,* pp. 284–318.

49. The quote is in Dennis M. Ogawa, *From Japs to Japanese* (Berkeley: McCutchan, 1971), pp. 11–12. See also Carey McWilliams, *Brothers Under the Skin,* rev. ed. (Boston: Little, Brown, 1964), pp. 148–149; and Stanley Sue and Harry H. L. Kitano, "Stereotypes as a Measure of Success," *Journal of Social Issues* 29 (1973): 83–98.

50. "Daphne Kwok, Organization of Chinese Americans, and John O'Sullivan, *National Review,* Discuss Recent Cover Story for That Magazine That Asian Americans Are Saying Is Offensive and Racist," NBC News Transcripts, March 21, 1997; Mae M. Cheng, "Magazine Cover Ripped; Coalition Calls *National Review* Illustration Racist," *Newsday,* April 11, 1997, p. A4.

51. Doris Lin, "The Death of (Icebox.com's) Mr. Wong," USAsians.net, http://us_asians. tripod.com/articles-mrwong.html (retrieved December 14, 2006).

52. Jennifer Fang, "Team America: Racism, Idiocy, and Two Men's Pursuit to Piss Off as Many People as Possible," Asian Media Watch, October 28, 2004, http:// www.asianmediawatch.net/teamamerica/review.html (retrieved December 17, 2006).

53. Helen Zia, *Asian American Dreams: The Emergence of an American People* (New York: Farrar, Straus, and Giroux, 2000), p. 134ff.

54. Steven A. Chin, "KFRC Deejay Draws Suspension for On-Air Derogatory Remarks," *San Francisco Examiner,* December 6, 1994, p. A2; "Current Affairs," *JACL News,* http:// www.jacl.org/index.php (retrieved December 19, 2006); Media Action Network for Asian Americans, "Latest Headline News," http://www.manaa.org (retrieved December 18, 2006).

55. Rosina Lippi-Green, *English with an Accent* (New York: Routledge, 1997), pp. 238–239.

56. William Petersen, "Success Story, Japanese-American Style," *New York Times,* January 9, 1966, p. 21.

57. "Success Story of One Minority Group in the U.S.," *U.S. News & World Report,* December 26, 1966, pp. 73–76.

58. Long Le, "The Dark Side of the Asian American 'Model Student,' " August 2, 2006, http://news.newamericamedia.org/news (retrieved January 5, 2007); for examples of white mocking, see Picca and Feagin, *Two Faced Racism.*

59. Quoted in Gilberto Cardenas, "United States Immigration Policy toward Mexico," *Chicano Law Review* 2 (summer 1975), pp. 70–71; see also Ralph Guzmán, "The Function of Anglo-American Racism in the Political Development of Chicanos," in *La Causa Politica,* ed. F. Chris Garcia (South Bend, IN: University of Notre Dame Press, 1974), p. 22.

60. Quoted in Otto Santa Ana, " 'Like an Animal I was Treated': Anti-Immigrant Metaphor in U.S. Public Discourse," *Discourse & Society* 10 (1994), p. 220.

61. Samuel P. Huntington, *Who Are We? The Challenges to America's National Identity* (New York: Simon & Schuster, 2004).

62. Santa Ana, " 'Like an Animal I was Treated'," pp. 194–220; see also Otto Santa Ana, *Brown Tide Rising: Metaphors of Latinos in Contemporary American Public Discourse* (Austin, TX: University of Texas Press, 2002).

63. Carey McWilliams, *North from Mexico* (New York: Greenwood Press, 1968), p. 213; see also Feagin and Feagin, *Racial And Ethnic Relations,* pp. 213–220.

64. Quoted in George A. Martinez, "Mexican Americans and Whiteness," in *The Latino/a Condition: A Critical Reader,* ed. Richard Delgado and Jean Stefancic (New York: New York University Press, 1998), p. 178.

65. Linda A. Jackson, "Stereotypes, Emotions, Behavior, and Overall Attitudes Toward Hispanics by Anglos," Research Report 10, Julian Samora Research Institute, Michigan State University, January 1995, <http://www.jsri.msu.edu/RandS/research/irr/rr10.htm> (retrieved June 9, 2001).

66. National Conference of Christians and Jews, *Taking America's Pulse: The National Conference Survey on Inter-Group Relations* (New York: National Conference, 1994).

67. Ann V. Millard and Jorge Chapa, *Apple Pie and Enchiladas: Latino Newcomers in the Rural Midwest* (Austin: University of Texas Press, 2004).
68. Jane H. Hill, *The Everyday Language of White Racism* (New York: Wiley-Blackwell, 2008), pp. 134–157; and Jane H. Hill, "Mock Spanish: A Site for the Indexical Reproduction of Racism in American English," unpublished research paper, University of Arizona, 1995.
69. I am indebted here to scholarly discussions with Nestor Rodriguez.
70. See José Cobas and Joe R. Feagin, "Latinos/as and the White Racial Frame," *Sociological Inquiry* 78 (February 2008): 39–53.
71. Chou and Feagin, *The Myth of the Model Minority*, pp. 138–180; and Cobas and Feagin, "Latinos/as and the White Racial Frame," pp. 39–53.
72. Joan M. Herbers, "Watch Your Language! Racially Loaded Metaphors in Scientific Research," *BioScience* 57 (February 2007), p. 104.
73. Richard J. Herrnstein and Charles Murray, *The Bell Curve: Intelligence and Class Structure in American Life* (New York: Free Press, 1994), pp. 295–316.
74. "Nobel Winner in 'Racist' Claim Row," CNN.com, October 18, 2007, http://edition.cnn.com/2007/TECH/science/10/18/science.race/index.html?iref=mpstoryview (accessed January 20, 2009).
75. "James D. Watson," Wikipedia, http://en.wikipedia.org/wiki/James_D._Watson#Political_activism (accessed January 20, 2009); and "Nobel Winner in 'Racist' Claim Row."
76. Winthrop D. Jordan, *White over Black: American Attitudes Toward the Negro, 1550–1812* (Chapel Hill: University of North Carolina Press, 1968), p. 264.

Chapter 6

1. R. H. Fazio, J. R. Jackson, B. C. Dunton and C. J. Williams, "Variability in Automatic Activation as an Unobtrusive Measure of Racial Attitudes: A Bona Fide Pipeline?" *Journal of Personality and Social Psychology* 69 (1995): 1013–1027; and, generally, Debra Van Ausdale and Joe R. Feagin, *The First R: How Children Learn Race and Racism* (Lanham, MD: Rowman and Littlefield, 2001).
2. Laurie A. Rudman and Richard D. Ashmore, "Discrimination and the Implicit Association Test," *Group Processes and Intergroup Relations* 10 (2007): 359–372.
3. Leslie Houts Picca and Joe R. Feagin, *Two Faced Racism: Whites in the Backstage and Frontstage* (New York: Routledge, 2007), p. 101. I have reworked my ideas here, but draw generally in this section on our joint analysis of the diary excerpts.
4. Ibid., pp. 17–18.
5. Nina Eliasoph, " 'Everyday Racism' in a Culture of Political Avoidance: Civil Society, Speech, and Taboo," *Social Problems* 46 (1999): 479–95.
6. Picca and Feagin, *Two Faced Racism*, p. 124.
7. See Joe R. Feagin and Melvin P. Sikes, *Living with Racism: The Black Middle Class Experience* (Boston: Beacon, 1995); and Joe R. Feagin, *Racist America: Roots, Current Realities, and Future Reparations* (New York: Routledge, 2000).
8. Pew Research Center, "Blacks See Growing Values Gap Between Poor and Middle Class: Optimism about Black Progress Declines," November 13, 2007, http://pewsocialtrends.org/pubs/700/black-public-opinion (retrieved May 5, 2008). The survey was done with National Public Radio.
9. Thomas Jefferson, *Notes on the State of Virginia*, ed. Frank Shuffelton (New York: Penguin Books, 1999 [1785]), p. 146.
10. Leslie Houts Picca and Joe R. Feagin, "Experiences of Students of Color," University of Dayton, unpublished research, 2008.
11. Quoted in Roxanna Harlow, "Teaching as Emotional Labor: The Effects of Professors' Race and Gender on the Emotional Demands of the Undergraduate College Classroom," Ph.D. dissertation, Indiana University, Bloomington, Indiana, 2002.

12. Jefferson, *Notes on the State of Virginia*, p. 146.
13. James F. Bonilla, " 'Are You Here to Move the Piano?': A Latino Reflects on Twenty Years in the Academy," in *Faculty of Color: Teaching in Predominantly White Colleges and Universities*, ed. Christine A. Stanley (Bolton, MA: Anker Publishing Company, 2007), p. 70.
14. See Rosalind S. Chou and Joe R. Feagin, *The Myth of the Model Minority: Asian Americans Facing Racism* (Boulder, CO: Paradigm Books, 2008); and José Cobas and Joe R. Feagin, "Latinos/as and the White Racial Frame," *Sociological Inquiry* 78 (February 2008): 39–53.
15. African American professional, email communication, May 27, 2008. Used by permission.
16. W. E. B. Du Bois, *Dusk of Dawn: An Essay Toward an Autobiography of a Race Concept* (New Brunswick, NJ: Transaction Books, 1984 [1940]), p. 131.
17. "Documenting the Costs Of Slavery, Segregation, And Contemporary Discrimination: Are Reparations In Order For African Americans?" *Harvard BlackLetter Law Journal*, 20 (2004): 49–80.
18. I am indebted here to scholarly discussions with Nestor Rodriguez.
19. Joe R. Feagin and Eileen O'Brien, *White Men on Race* (Boston: Beacon, 2003); Wendy Moore, *Reproducing Racism* (Lanham, MD: Rowman & Littlefield, 2008).
20. Gilles Fauconnier and Mark Turner, *The Way We Think* (New York: Basic Books, 2003), pp. 17–73; and Gilles Fauconnier "Tip of Iceberg," http://www.cogsci.ucsd.edu/~faucon/151/Tip%20of%20iceberg.pdf (retrieved November 7, 2007).
21. See, for example, Tiffany Chaparro, "America Celebrates Constitution Day," http://teacher.scholastic.com/scholasticnews/indepth/constitution_day/constitution_day/index.asp?article=constitutionday (retrieved December 21, 2007); and Weldon Havins, "Overview of the Legal System," http://whavins.com/nnlh1.htm (retrieved December 21, 2007).
22. Derrick Bell, "Brown and the Interest-Convergence Dilemma," in *Shades of Brown: New Perspectives on School Desegregation*, ed. Derrick Bell (New York: Columbia University Press, 1980), p. 97.
23. See Herbert Aptheker, *Early Years of the Republic and the Constitution: 1783–1793* (New York: International Publishers, 1976).
24. Robert Caro, *The Years of Lyndon Johnson: Master of the Senate* (New York: Random House Vintage Books, 2002), p. 104.
25. Paul Krugman, *The Conscience of a Liberal* (New York: Norton, 2007), p. 181.
26. Paul Jenkins, "The GOP's White Supremacy," Huffington Post, December 28, 2008 http://www.huffingtonpost.com/paul-jenkins/the-gops-white-supremacy_b_153823.html (accessed December 29, 2008); and James Wright, "Black Republicans Ponder Their Future," Afro Newspapers November 24, 2008 http://news.newamericamedia.org/news/view_article.html?article_id= (accessed December 18, 2008).
27. See Joe R. Feagin, "Smearing Dr. Wright," http://www.racismreview.com/blog/2008/11/02/smearing-dr-wright-white-fear-and-republican-leaders-again (retrieved November 3, 2008).
28. *Matthew* 25: 29. See Robert K. Merton, *The Sociology of Science* (Chicago: University of Chicago Press, 1973), pp. 439–458.
29. Virginia Valian, *Why So Slow? The Advancement of Women* (Cambridge, MA: MIT Press, 1998), p. 4. See also pp. 3–5, 144.
30. R. F. Martell, D. Lane and C. Emrich, "Male-Female Differences: A Computer Simulation," *American Psychologist* 51 (1996): 157–158. I draw on the summary in Valian, *Why So Slow*, p. 3.
31. See Feagin and O'Brien, *White Men on Race*; Ken Bolton and Joe Feagin, *Black in Blue: Black Police Officers in White Departments* (New York: Routledge, 2004); and Feagin and Sikes, *Living with Racism*.
32. W. E. B. Du Bois, *The World and Africa* (New York: International Publishers, 1965 [1946]), p. 23.

33. Ibid., pp. 23–99; Robert J. C. Young, *Post-Colonialism* (Oxford: Oxford University Press, 2003); and John Willinsky, *Learning to Divide the World: Education at Empire's End* (Minneapolis: University of Minnesota Press, 1998).
34. Young, *Post-Colonialism*; and Willinsky, *Learning to Divide the World*.
35. See James Fulcher, *Capitalism: A Very Short Introduction* (Oxford: Oxford University Press, 2004), pp. 82–115; and Fareed Zakaria, *The Post-American World* (New York: W. W. Norton, 2008).
36. See Zakaria, *The Post-American World*.
37. Irene Diggs, "The Biological and Cultural Impact of Blacks on the United States," *Phylon* 41 (1980), p. 161.
38. William Henry III, *In Defense of Elitism* (New York: Doubleday, 1994). On the military-industrial complex and issues of colonialism, see Joe R. Feagin, Clairece B. Feagin, and David V. Baker, *Social Problems: A Critical Power-Conflict Perspective* (Sixth edition: Upper Saddle River, NJ: Prentice-Hall, 2005), pp. 440–446 and passim.
39. See, for example, "World Conference Against Racism," http://en.wikipedia.org (retrieved June 11, 2008).
40. Harris Interactive and the Bradley Project, "E Pluribus Unum: A Study of Americans' Views on National Identity," May 13, 2008, http://www.bradleyproject.org/EPUReportFinal.pdf (retrieved November 3, 2008).
41. Zakaria, *The Post-American World*, p. 46. The data on the survey and on Western historians are on p. 34.
42. Feagin, Feagin, and Baker, *Social Problems*, pp. 459–499; Richard J. Barnet and John Cavanagh, *Global Dreams: Imperial Corporations and the New World Order* (New York: Touchstone, 1994), p. 138; Joe R. Feagin and Pinar Batur-Vanderlippe, "The Globalization of Racism and Antiracism: France, South Africa and the United States," University of Florida, unpublished manuscript, 1996; and Robert W. McChesney, "The New Global Media: It's a Small World of Big Conglomerates," *The Nation*, November 29, 1999, http://www.hartfordwp.com/archives/29/053.html (retrieved July 3, 2008).
43. Hsia-Chuan Hsia, "Imported Racism and Indigenous Biases: the Impacts of the U.S. Media on Taiwanese Images of African Americans," presented at Annual Meeting of American Sociological Association, August 1994, Los Angeles, California; and Nestor Rodriguez, personal communication, March 1996.
44. McChesney, "The New Global Media," n.p.

Chapter 7

1. John Locke, *Two Treatises of Government*, ed. Peter Laslett (Cambridge: Cambridge University Press, 1988), p. 170. Some scholars have argued with substantial evidence that some ideas on equality and justice of certain framers, especially Thomas Jefferson and Ben Franklin, were shaped by the thought of Native American societies.
2. See Scott L. Pratt, *Native Pragmatism: Rethinking the Roots of American Philosophy* (Bloomington: Indiana University Press, 2002); and "Pragmatism," http://en.wikipedia. org/wiki/Pragmatism#Central_pragmatist_tenets (retrieved June 20, 2008).
3. Quoted in Winthrop D. Jordan, *White over Black: American Attitudes Toward the Negro, 1550–1812* (Chapel Hill: University of North Carolina Press, 1968), pp. 273–274. I use modern capitalization here.
4. "PBS Interview with James O. Horton," http://www.pbs.org/race/000_About/002_04-background-02-04.htm (ret: December 19, 2003).
5. John Woolman, as quoted in *A House Divided: The Antebellum Slavery Debates in America, 1776–1865*, ed. Mason I. Lowance, Jr. (Princeton: Princeton University Press, 2003), at http://press.princeton.edu/chapters/s7553.html (November 3, 2008).
6. Sterling Stuckey, *Slave Culture* (New York: Oxford University Press, 1987), pp. 25–45; and Bonnie L. Mitchell and Joe R. Feagin, "America's Racial-Ethnic Cultures: Opposition within a Mythical Melting Pot," in *Toward the Multicultural University*, ed.

Benjamin Bowser, Terry Jones, and Gale Auletta-Young (Westport, CT: Praeger, 1995), pp. 65–86. I am indebted here to the scholarly comments of Louwanda Evans.

7. Nat Turner, http://en.wikipedia.org/wiki/Nat_Turner (retrieved June 6, 2008); Stuckey, *Slave Culture*, pp. 27–43; and Joe R. Feagin and Clairece B. Feagin, *Racial and Ethnic Relations* (Upper Saddle River, NJ: Prentice-Hall, 2008), pp. 197–198.

8. Feagin and Feagin, *Racial and Ethnic Relations*, pp. 197–199.

9. Quoted in Jordan, *White over Black*, p. 111.

10. See Jessica McElrath, "David Walker," About.com, http://afroamhistory.about.com/od/davidwalker/a/bio_walker_d.htm (accessed January 11, 2009).

11. David Walker, *Appeal to the Coloured Citizens of the World*, ed. Charles M. Wiltse (New York: Hill and Wang, 1965), pp. 7, 16, and 56.

12. Ibid., p. 75. His italics and punctuation.

13. Thomas Tryon, *Advice to the Gentlemen Planters of the East and West Indies* (London, 1684), p. 115.

14. Henry Highland Garnet, "An Address to the Slaves of the United States of America," Buffalo, New York, Electronic Texts in American Studies, University of Nebraska, 2007 [1848]), Lincoln Nebraska, pp. 2, 4, 7, 9.

15. Martin R. Delany, *The Condition, Elevation, Emigration, and Destiny of the Colored People of the United States* (1852), no pagination (ebook).

16. Ibid.

17. W. E. B. Du Bois, *John Brown* (New York: International Publishers, 1962), pp. 263–264.

18. *John Washington's Civil War*, ed. Crandall Shifflett (Baton Rouge: Louisiana State University Press, 2008), p. 49. His emphasis. Some capitalization has been removed, and two words have been clarified.

19. Quoted in David W. Blight, *A Slave No More: Two Men Who Escaped to Freedom* (Orlando: Harcourt, Inc, 2007), p. 257.

20. Quoted in *Bartlett's Familiar Quotations*, 15th ed., ed. Emily M. Beck (Boston, MA: Little, Brown, 1980), p. 556.

21. Frederick Douglass, "The United States Cannot Remain Half-Slave and Half-Free," in *Frederick Douglass: Selected Speeches and Writings*, ed. P. S. Foner and Y. Taylor (Chicago: Lawrence Hall Books, 1999), pp. 657–658.

22. Anna Julia Cooper, *The Voice of Anna Julia Cooper*, eds. Charles Lemert and Esme Bhan (Lanham, MD: Rowman and Littlefield, 1998); and Ida B. Wells-Barnett, *A Red Record* (Chicago, IL: Donohue and Henneberry, 1895).

23. William E. B. Du Bois, *The Souls of Black Folk* (New York: Bantam Books, 1989 [1903]), p. 3.

24. W. E. B. Du Bois, "The Future of Africa," *Advocate of Peace* 81 (January 1919), p. 12; Manning Marable, *W. E. B. Du Bois: Black Radical Democrat* (Boston: Twayne, 1986).

25. Oliver C. Cox, *Caste, Class, and Race* (Garden City, NY: Doubleday, 1948), p. 332–333.

26. *Brown et al. v. Board of Education of Topeka et al.* 347 U.S. 491 (1954); and Nathan Newman, "Remembering the Popular Will for Civil Rights: Robert Caro's Master of the Senate," *Progressive Populist*, June 15, 2002, http://nathannewman.org/populist/06.15.02pop.html (retrieved September 9, 2003).

27. Richard Kluger, *Simple Justice: The History of Brown v. Board of Education and Black America's Struggle for Equality* (New York: Knopf, 1975), Volume 2, p. 945.

28. Joe R. Feagin, "School Desegregation: A Political-Economic Perspective," in *School Desegregation: Past, Present, and Future*, eds. Walter Stephan and Joe R. Feagin (New York: Plenum Press, 1980), pp. 25, 29–35; W. E. B. Du Bois, "What is the Meaning of 'All Deliberate Speed'," in *W. E. B. Du Bois: A Reader*, ed. David L. Lewis (New York: Henry Holt, 1995), pp. 419, 422; and Philip A. Klinkner and Rogers M. Smith, *The Unsteady March: The Rise and Decline of Racial Equality in America* (Chicago: University of Chicago Press, 1999), pp. 3–4.

29. Stokely Carmichael (Kwame Ture) and Charles V. Hamilton, *Black Power* (New York: Vintage, 1967).

30. James M. Washington, ed., *A Testament of Hope: The Essential Writings and Speeches of Martin Luther King* (New York: HarperCollins, 1991), p. 314.
31. Coretta Scott King, ed., *The Words of Martin Luther King, Jr.* (New York: Newmarket press, 1996), p. 52.
32. Lyndon B. Johnson, "To Fulfill These Rights" June 4, 1965, http://www.lbjlib.utexas.edu/johnson/archives.hom/speeches.hom/650604.asp (retrieved July 9, 2008). See also George Lakoff, *Thinking Points: Communicating Our American Values and Vision* (New York: Farrar, Straus and Giroux, 2006), pp. 92–94.
33. Marimba Ani, *Yurugu: An African-Centered Critique of European Cultural Thought and Behavior* (Trenton, NJ: Africa World Press, 1994), pp 567, 570. See Molefi Kete Asante, *Afrocentricity* (Trenton, NJ: Africa World Press, 1988).
34. Ken Bolton and Joe Feagin, *Black in Blue: Black Police Officers in White Departments* (New York: Routledge, 2004), p. 94.
35. Ibid., p. 64.
36. Yanick St. Jean and Joe R. Feagin, *Double Burden: Black Women and Everyday Racism* (Armonk, NY: M.E. Sharpe, 1998), pp. 83–84.
37. Angela Davis, "Reflections on the Black Woman's Role in the Community of Slaves," *Black Scholar* 3 (December 1971): 2–15; Philomena Essed, *Understanding Everyday Racism* (Newbury Park, CA: Sage, 1991); Patricia Hill Collins, *Black Feminist Thought: Knowledge, Consciousness, and the Politics of Empowerment* (Boston, MA: Unwin Hyman, 1990); Elizabeth Higginbotham, *Too Much to Ask: Black Women in the Era of Integration* (University of North Carolina Press, 2001); and Yanick St. Jean and Joe R. Feagin, *Double Burden: Black Women and Everyday Racism* (New York: M. E. Sharpe, 1998).
38. Jeremiah Wright, "National Press Club Address," April 28, 2008, http://www.americanrhetoric.com/speeches/jeremiahwrightntlpressclub.htm (retrieved November 7, 2008).
39. Jeremiah Wright, "Confusing God and Government," http://en.wikipedia.org/wiki/Jeremiah_Wright_controversy#cite_note-22 (accessed January 29, 2009).
40. For more detailed discussions, see Joe R. Feagin, "Dr. Wright is Still Right on Racism: Check the Research Data," http://www.racismreview.com/blog/2008/04/28/dr-wright-is-still-right-on-racism-check-the-research-data (retrieved November 9, 2008); and Adia Harvey Wingfield and Joe R. Feagin, *Yes We Can* (New York: Routledge, 2009).
41. On black commentators using white framing, see Joe R. Feagin, "Senator Obama's Critique of Black Fathers: Playing to the White Frame?" http://www.racismreview.com/blog/2008/06/15/senator-obamas-critique-of-black-fathers-playing-to-the-white-frame (retrieved November 9, 2008).
42. See Robert B. Hill, et al., *Research on the African American Family: A Holistic Perspective* (Westport, CT: Auburn House, 1993); and Yanick St. Jean and Joe R. Feagin, *Double Burden: Black Women and Everyday Racism* (New York: M. E. Sharpe, 1998).
43. Feagin and Sikes, *Living with Racism*, pp. 311–318; and St. Jean and Feagin, *Double Burden: Black Women and Everyday Racism*, pp. 2–100. I am indebted to Sean Chaplin, Yanick St. Jean, and Adia Harvey Wingfield for scholarly comments here.
44. Debra Van Ausdale and Joe R. Feagin, *The First R: How Children Learn Race and Racism* (Lanham, MD: Rowman & Littlefield), pp. 190–196; Feagin and Sikes, *Living with Racism*, pp. 311–314; and St. Jean and Feagin, *Double Burden: Black Women and Everyday Racism*, passim. I am indebted here to scholarly comments by Brittany Slatton, Louwanda Evans, and Adia Harvey Wingfield.
45. William E. Sedlacek, *Beyond the Big Test* (San Francisco, California: Jossey-Bass, 2004), pp. 43–44; and Julie M. Hughes, Rebecca S. Bigler, Sheri R. Levy, "Consequences of Learning About Historical Racism Among European American and African American Children," *Child Development* 78 (November/December 2007); 1689–1705.
46. Adia Harvey Wingfield, *Doing Business With Beauty: Black Women, Hair Salons, and the Racial Enclave Economy* (Lanham, MD: Rowman and Littlefield, 2008), pp. 83–84.

47. Ibid., p. 92.
48. Ibid., pp. 2–92. See also my preface to this book.
49. Reuben A. B. May, *Talking at Trena's: Everyday Conversations at an African American Tavern* (New York: NYU Press, 2001), pp. 164.
50. Elijah Anderson, "The Cosmopolitan Canopy" *Annals of the American Academy of Political and Social Science* 595 (2004): 14–31.
51. Barack Obama, *The Audacity of Hope* (New York: Three Rivers Press, 2006), pp. 232–233.
52. Gwen Ifill, "The Candidate," *Essence*, October 2007, pp. 226, 230.
53. I draw here on Adia Harvey Wingfield and Joe R. Feagin, *Yes We Can* (Routledge, 2009), Chapter 8.
54. Feagin and Feagin, *Racial and Ethnic Relations*, pp. 143–152, 158–164.
55. Ibid.
56. Russell Means, "For America to Live, Europe Must Die!" Black Hills International Survival Gathering, Black Hills, South Dakota, July 1980, http://www.russellmeans.com (retrieved September 19, 2008).
57. Russell Means, "Free to be Responsible," Navajo Community College, Fall, 1995, http://www.russellmeans.com (retrieved September 19, 2008).
58. White Plume, "An Open letter to President George W. Bush," *Indian Country Today*, August 31, 2006, http://www.indiancountry.com/content.cfm?id=1096413572 (accessed September 12, 2006).
59. Rosalind Chou and Joe R. Feagin, *The Myth of the Model Minority: Asian Americans Facing Racism* (Boulder, CO: Paradigm Books, 2008).
60. Roger Daniels, *Asian America: Chinese and Japanese in the United States Since 1850* (Seattle: University of Washington Press, 1988), p. 113; Min Zhou and James V. Gatewood, "Introduction: Revisiting Contemporary Asian America," in *Contemporary Asian America: A Multidisciplinary Reader*, ed. Min Zhou and James V. Gatewood (New York: New York University Press, 2000), pp. 27–35.
61. Helpful insights on Houston were provided by Nestor Rodriguez.
62. I am indebted in this section to scholarly comments from Hernán Vera, Nestor Rodriguez, and José Cobas. See José Cobas and Joe R. Feagin, "Latinos/as and the White Racial Frame," *Sociological Inquiry* 78 (February 2008): 39–53.
63. Brenda Gayle, editor, *Window on Freedom: Race, Civil Rights, and Foreign Affairs, 1945–1988* (Chapel Hill, North Carolina: University of North Carolina Press, 2007).
64. Anonymous Latino professional, communication spring 2008. Used by permission.
65. Marcelo M. Suárez-Orozco and Mariela M. Páez, editors, *Latinos: Remaking America* (Berkeley: University of California Press, 2002).
66. Nilanjana Dasgupta, Debbie E. McGhee, and Anthony G. Greenwald, and Mahzarin R. Banaji, "Automatic Preference for White Americans: Eliminating the Familiarity Explanation," *Journal of Experimental Social Psychology* 36 (2000): 316–328; and Shankar Vedantam, "Many Americans believe they are not prejudiced; now a new test provides powerful evidence that a majority of us really are," *Washington Post Magazine*, January 23, 2005, p. W12.
67. I am indebted here to scholarly discussions with Sean Chaplin and Adia Harvey Wingfield.

Chapter 8

1. See, for example, Richard Morin, "Misperceptions Cloud Whites' View of Blacks," *Washington Post*, July 11, 2001, p. A01; and Jon Cohen and Jennifer Agiesta, "3 in 10 Americans Admit to Race Bias," *Washington Post*, June 22, 2008, p. A01.
2. Thomas Kuhn, *The Structure of Scientific Revolutions* (Chicago: University of Chicago Press, 1962); Niles Eldredge and Stephen. J. Gould, "Punctuated Equilibria: An Alternative to Phyletic Gradualism," in T. J. M. Schopf, ed., *Models in Paleobiology*

(San Francisco: Freeman, Cooper and Company, 1972), pp. 82–115. I draw in part on summaries in Connie G. Gersick, "Revolutionary Change Theories: A Multilevel Exploration of the Punctuated Equilibrium Paradigm," *Academy of Management Review*, 16 (1991), p. 13.

3. See Joe R. Feagin and Clairece B. Feagin, *Racial and Ethnic Relations* (Upper Saddle River, NJ: Prentice-Hall, 2008), pp. 363–365.

4. Patrick Buchanan, *State of Emergency: The Third World Invasion and Conquest of America* (New York: St. Martin's Griffin, 2007); and Samuel P. Huntington, "The Erosion of American National Interests," *Foreign Affairs* (September, 1997/October, 1997), p. 28ff.

5. See John Locke, *Two Treatises of Government*, ed. Peter Laslett (Cambridge: Cambridge University Press, 1988), p. 170. (First Treatise, Chap. 4, sec. 42).

6. United Nations, "Universal Declaration of Human Rights," in *The United Nations and Human Rights, 1945–1995* (New York: United Nations, 1995), pp. 153–155.

7. United Nations, "International Convention on the Elimination of All Forms of Racial discrimination," in *The United Nations and Human Rights, 1945–1995* (New York: UN Department of Public Information, 1995), pp. 219–225.

8. Rasmussen Reports, "What They Told Us: Reviewing Last Week's Key Polls," http://www.rasmussenreports.com/public_content/lifestyle/general_lifestyle/82_say_u_s_is_best_place_to_live_41_say_u_s_lacks_liberty_and_justice_for_all (retrieved July 6, 2008).

9. See John Donne, http://en.wikipedia.org/wiki/Devotions_upon_Emergent_Occasions (retrieved October 2, 2008); and "Cosmopolitanism," http://en.wikipedia.org/wiki/Cosmopolitanism (November 4, 2008).

10. For a useful discussion of deframing see, M. L. J. Karskens et alia, "Framing Conflict in Society," http://72.14.205.104/search?q=cache:WG1ZQ1LkLsUJ:www.nwo.nl/files.nsf/pages/NWOA_7GJHQ3/%24file/NWO%2520Framing%2520Conflict%2520in%2520Society.pdf+deframing+lakoff+reframing&hl=en&ct=clnk&cd=2&gl=us&client=firefox-a (retrieved October 2, 2008).

11. Siri Carpenter, "Buried Prejudice: The Bigot in Your Brain" *Scientific American*, May 2008, http://www.sciam.com/article.cfm?id=buried-prejudice-the-bigot-in-your-brain (retrieved June 1, 2008).

12. Charles G. Lord, Mark R. Lepper, and Elizabeth Preston, Considering the Opposite: A Corrective Strategy for Social Judgment," *Journal of Personality and Social Psychology* 47 (1984): 1231–1243.

13. Julie M. Hughes, Rebecca S. Bigler, Sheri R. Levy, "Consequences of Learning About Historical Racism Among European American and African American Children," *Child Development*, 78 (November/December 2007): 1689–1705. The quote is on p. 1695.

14. Ibid., pp. 1700–1701.

15. Ibid., p. 1693.

16. See Joe R. Feagin, *Systemic Racism: A Theory of Oppression* (New York: Routledge, 2006); and Leslie Houts Picca and Joe R. Feagin, *Two Faced Racism: Whites in the Backstage and Frontstage* (New York: Routledge, 2007).

17. Picca and Feagin, *Two Faced Racism*, p. 275.

18. See Drew Westen, *The Political Brain: The Role of Emotion in Deciding the Fate of the Nation* (New York: PublicAffairs, 2007).

19. Tiffany Hogan and Julie Netzer, "Knowing the Other," unpublished research paper, American Sociological Association, Miami Beach, Florida, 1993, as summarized in Joe R. Feagin, Hernan Vera, and Pinar Batur, *White Racism: The Basics* (Second edition; New York: Routledge, 2001), pp. 231–233.

20. Leslie Houts Picca and Joe R. Feagin, "Experiences of Students of Color," University of Dayton, unpublished research, 2008.

21. Zygmunt Bauman, *Modernity and the Holocaust* (Ithaca, NY: Cornell University Press, 1989), p. 206.

22. Ibid., p. 207.
23. Tim Craig and Michael D. Shear, "Allen Quip Provokes Outrage, Apology Name Insults Webb Volunteer," http://www.washingtonpost.com/wp-dyn/content/article/2006/08/14/AR2006081400589.html (retrieved October 6, 2008).
24. Drew Westen, *The Political Brain: The Role of Emotion in Deciding the Fate of the Nation* (New York: PublicAffairs, 2007), pp. 222–223.
25. Ibid., pp. 222–223.
26. Jennifer Harvey, *Whiteness and Morality* (New York: Palgrave Macmillan, 2007), pp. 148–160.
27. See the summary in Rebecca Saunders and Kamran Aghaie, "Introduction: Mourning and Memory," *Comparative Studies of South Asia, Africa and the Middle East* 25 (2005), p. 18. See also Christopher Lane, editor, *The Psychoanalysis of Race* (New York: Columbia University Press, 1998).
28. Saunders and Aghaie, "Introduction," p. 19. See also Frantz Fanon, *Black Skin, White Masks*, trans. Charles Markmann (New York, Grove Press, 1967 [1952]).
29. Geoffrey L. Cohen, Julio Garcia, Nancy Apfel, Allison Master, "Reducing the Racial Achievement Gap: A Social-Psychological Intervention," *Science* 313 (September 2006), pp. 1307–1310.
30. Melvin L. Oliver, and Thomas M. Shapiro, *Black Wealth/White Wealth: A New Perspective on Racial Inequality* (New York: Routledge, 1995); and Dalton Conley, *Being Black, Living in the Red: Race, Wealth and Social Policy in America* (Berkeley, CA: University of California Press, 1999).
31. Dedrick Muhammad, *Forty Years Later: The Unrealized American Dream* (Washington, DC: Institute for Policy Studies, 2008), pp. 5–6.
32. On discrimination patterns, see Joe R. Feagin, *Racist America: Roots, Current Realities, and Future Reparations* (New York: Routledge, 2000); and Feagin, *Systemic Racism*. On redress issues, see Joe R. Feagin, "Documenting The Costs of Slavery, Segregation, and Contemporary Discrimination: Are Reparations In Order For African Americans?" *Harvard BlackLetter Law Journal*, 20 (2004): 49–80. On the failure of the legal system to deal with systemic racism, see Wendy Moore, *Reproducing Racism* (Lanham, Md.: Rowman & Littlefield, 2008).
33. Feagin, "Documenting The Costs of Slavery, Segregation, and Contemporary Discrimination," pp. 50–79.
34. Chinweizu Ibekwe, "Reparations and A New Global Order: A Comparative Overview," speech given to Second Plenary Session, Pan-African Conference on Reparations, Abuja, Nigeria, April 27, 1993.
35. Robert S. Browne, "Achieving Parity through Reparations," in *The Wealth of Races: The Present Value of Benefits from Past Injustices*, ed. Richard F. America (New York: Greenwood Press, 1990), p. 205.
36. W. E. B. Du Bois, "On the Ruling of Men," in *The Oxford W. E. B. Du Bois Reader*, ed. Eric J. Sundquist (New York: Oxford University Press, 1996), pp. 555–557.
37. See James J. Heckman and Bruce Payner, "The Impact of the Economy and the State on the Economies Status of Blacks: A Study of South Carolina," *American Economic Review* 79 (1989): 138–177; Stanley Greenberg, *Race and State in Capitalist Development* (New Haven: Yale University Press, 1980), pp. 231–233; and Gavin Wright, "The Economics of Civil rights," unpublished paper prepared for the Citadel Conference on the Civil Rights Movement in South Carolina, March 5–8, 2003, p. 5.
38. See Joe R. Feagin and Eileen O'Brien, *White Men on Race* (Boston: Beacon, 2003); and Leslie Houts Picca and Joe R. Feagin, *Two Faced Racism: Whites in the Backstage and Frontstage* (New York: Routledge, 2007).
39. From a scholarly discussion with a professional of color, spring 2008. Used by permission.
40. Jennifer A. Richeson and J. Nicole Shelton, "When Prejudice Does Not Pay: Effects of Interracial Contact on Executive Function," *Psychological Science* 14 (May 2003): 287–290. The measure of racial bias was relatively unconscious, the Implicit

Association Test (IAT). Subjects associate stereotypically white and black names with either pleasant or unpleasant words by pressing marked response keys. Differences in response times were used to measure implicit favoring of one racial category over another. The researchers point out that the negative impact on these whites' cognitive functioning might have been reduced if they had regularly interacted with the same people of color.

41. The survey is discussed in Tom W. Smith, "Measuring Inter-Racial Friendships: Experimental Comparisons," GSS Methodological Report, National Opinion Research Center, University of Chicago, no. 91 (1999). On weak white contacts, see Feagin and O'Brien, *White Men on Race*; and Picca and Feagin, *Two Faced Racism*.

42. Eszter Hargittai, "Whose Space: Differences Among Users and Non-Users of Social Network Sites," *Journal of Computer-Mediated Communication* 13 (2007), http://jcmc.indiana.edu/vol13/issue1/hargittai.html (retrieved November 6, 2008).

43. Harris Interactive and the Bradley Project, "E Pluribus Unum: A Study of Americans' Views on National Identity," research report, May 13, 2008.

44. Fareed Zakaria, *The Post-American World* (New York: W. W. Norton, 2008), p. 46.

45. See Barbara J. Flagg, "'Was Blind But Now I See': White Race Consciousness and the Requirement of Discriminatory Intent," *Michigan Law Review* 91 (1993): 953; and Moore, *Reproducing Racism*.

Index